LOCKED OUT

CRITICAL CULTURAL COMMUNICATION

General Editors: Jonathan Gray, Aswin Punathambekar, Adrienne Shaw
Founding Editors: Sarah Banet-Weiser and Kent A. Ono

Locked Out

Regional Restrictions in Digital Entertainment Culture

Evan Elkins

NEW YORK UNIVERSITY PRESS
New York

NEW YORK UNIVERSITY PRESS
New York
www.nyupress.org

References to Internet websites (URLs) were accurate at the time of writing. Neither the author nor New York University Press is responsible for URLs that may have expired or changed since the manuscript was prepared.

Library of Congress Cataloging-in-Publication Data
Names: Elkins, Evan, author.
Title: Locked out : regional restrictions in digital entertainment culture / Evan Elkins.
Description: New York : New York University Press, [2019] | Series: Critical cultural communication | Includes bibliographical references and index.
Identifiers: LCCN 2018044166| ISBN 9781479830572 (cl : alk. paper) | ISBN 9781479873876 (pb : alk. paper)
Subjects: LCSH: Multimedia systems | Interactive multimedia. | Digital media. | Entertainment computing. | Trade regulation.
Classification: LCC QA76.575 .E534 2019 | DDC 006.7—dc23
LC record available at https://lccn.loc.gov/2018044166

New York University Press books are printed on acid-free paper, and their binding materials are chosen for strength and durability. We strive to use environmentally responsible suppliers and materials to the greatest extent possible in publishing our books.

Manufactured in the United States of America

10 9 8 7 6 5 4 3 2 1

Also available as an ebook

For my parents

CONTENTS

Introduction

Regional Lockout as Technology, Distribution, and Culture

"Imagine this happening to you when shopping." So reads the opening title of a hidden-camera video produced by the European Consumer Organization (BEUC) and set in an English bakery. As unsuspecting customers enter the establishment and place their orders, the cashier asks to see identification. The confused patrons hand over ID cards and passports to the cashier, who tells one woman that pain aux raisins and bread are unavailable to German and Bulgarian customers and charges Belgian and French customers different prices for the same product. He explains, "We've been doing this for a while. It's an industry standard practice." Titles onscreen ask, "You wouldn't accept this in the physical world, so why should you accept it when shopping or watching content online?" Then we see a hashtag: #endgeoblocking.[1]

A second video, released by the European Commission, begins with narration by Commission president Jean-Claude Juncker, who laments digital fragmentation in the continent: "You can drive from Tallinn to Turin without once showing your passport, but you can't stream your favorite TV shows from home once you get there." During this, we see other members of the Commission experience the frustrations of a regionally restricted internet. Commission vice president Andrus Ansip tries to watch a Dutch documentary on YouTube, but he encounters the platform's "This video is not available in your country" screen. Another commissioner attempts to buy a book online (*Investment for Dummies*) and looks comically aghast when he realizes that the shipping charges will nearly double the total purchase price. Acting ability of the Commission members notwithstanding, the video puts forward a rather convincing representation of the hassles that come with a geographically segmented digital landscape. In response, Juncker says in the video that Europe should represent a "digital single market" rather than a series of fragmented spaces.[2]

This choice of words is not an accident. Both videos were created and distributed online to promote a European Commission initiative called the Digital Single Market (DSM). Introduced in 2015 with the goal of knocking down digital trade borders among EU countries, the DSM in part proposed an EU-wide ban against the topic of this book: regional lockout. Regional lockout refers to technological mechanisms in digital media hardware and software that control entertainment media's geographic distribution: region codes in DVDs and video game consoles and geoblocking in on-demand services, for instance. Regional lockout functions through a logic of prohibition, blocking people in certain regions from accessing media platforms as a way of ensuring that digital distribution remains consistent with region-based licensing agreements and release schedules. As media consumers, we encounter it whenever we see that familiar "This content is not available in your country" message. With the DSM in place, no longer would a streaming video platform remain available only to certain European viewers.

Both videos speak to dimensions of regional lockout that this book will explore: the logics of market segmentation that make it a natural part of global digital entertainment; the perception that it unfairly and arbitrarily limits access to and from certain parts of the world; a perceived distinction between the "online" and "physical" worlds; the tensions it produces among sovereign nations, media corporations, multinational governing bodies, and consumers; and the ways consumers and institutions alike invoke cultural difference as an important component of it. The first video joins the pain of cultural discrimination to the frustration felt when one is blocked from enjoying a morning coffee and croissant. The second video blends the everyday irritations of regional lockout with its broader implications. Through its humanizing, "European Commissioners: they're just like us!" perspective, the EC's video articulates complex geopolitical battles through the all-too-real personal experiences of bumping into "content not available" messages. *Locked Out*'s analysis of regional lockout likewise focuses on large-scale institutional decisions about media distribution and regional lockout, local effects on consumers and media access, and the various intermediaries that ensure unequal access to global digital entertainment culture.

Figure 1.1. "This video is not available," not even to European Commissioners.
Screenshot: European Commission, "Digital Single Market," YouTube.

Understanding Regional Lockout

This book argues that regional lockout has shaped global media culture
in three interconnecting ways: as a form of technological regulation that
limits digital media's affordances, as a mechanism of distribution that
sets the paths that media follow around the world, and as a fulcrum of
geocultural discrimination that divvies up media access along lines of
privilege and power. I stress *interconnecting* to emphasize the ways digital regulation systems, distribution practices, and notions of geographic
and cultural difference and inequality all work together to shape global
media culture.

1. *Regional lockout is a technology of digital regulation.* As a form of
   technological regulation, regional lockout limits the affordances of
   digital software and hardware. Region codes and IP address detection software are methods of digital rights management (DRM)
   that shape how we can and cannot use digital technologies. Over
   the past couple of decades, the entertainment industries' use of
   digital technologies for distribution and exhibition has intensified

a problem of control. Although controlling how people buy and consume media has been a long-standing concern of media industries, the ease of copying digital information and sharing it across vast spaces through networked technologies has made it especially difficult to keep tabs on who consumes products and whether these users pay for them. In response, regional lockout is part of a broader push by entertainment industries (with the assistance of legislative bodies and the tech field) to limit unauthorized or illegal forms of trade and consumption.

2. *Regional lockout is a technology of media distribution.* As DRM, regional lockout shapes the geography of global entertainment by seeking to ensure that digital technologies accommodate the traditional ways media industries have exploited intellectual properties in geographically segmented markets. Historically, media industries have divided global content markets geographically for a combination of logistical, cultural-linguistic, and economic reasons. Namely, by splitting the world into territories corresponding with national and regional borders and treating each territory as a market, they can alter prices, stagger release dates, and distribute different versions of a product to different places. Regional lockout exists to preserve these release windows in an environment where digital media threaten to erode them. It shows us that global media distribution functions through intentional exclusion, delay, and failure as much as accessibility and availability. At the same time, I am careful to note that regional lockout *shapes* rather than *determines* media distribution because it is a by-product of media-industrial economic imperatives rather than their driver. It does not in itself define global media distribution's geographic contours but instead manages preexisting circulation practices. Additionally, regional lockout quite simply does not always work, and users have long found ways to circumvent it. Rather than a top-down form of distributional control that operates exactly as the media industries expect, regional lockout is a process involving tugs-of-war among industries, regulators, and users.

3. *Regional lockout is a technology of geographic and cultural difference and discrimination.* Media distribution has historically corresponded with social status and discrimination.[3] Thus, as a means

of divvying up access to media throughout the world, regional lockout works along existing lines of difference and power. At macro levels, industry stakeholders and regulators make decisions about regional lockout based on culturally informed market research and ingrained assumptions about particular nations and regions. At the everyday level of media use, the onscreen "not available in your country" notification plants would-be consumers within established geographic hierarchies of cultural status. Regional lockout affects global media access on a functional level, but it also provides a landscape on which users, industries, and regulators debate and make decisions about access. It thus shapes global media *culture* at many levels: it facilitates the Othering of users living in certain regions of the world, reminds diasporic communities and individuals of their cultural positions, shapes the cultural and geographic contours of participatory culture and networked publics, and both reflects and defines transnational taste cultures. It also enables unexpected user practices and the development of informal media economies as consumers seek the means to bypass territorial blockades.

DRM, Distribution, and Difference

Corresponding with these three strands of my argument, *Locked Out*'s investigation into regional lockout draws together several traditions in the study of media technologies, institutions, and cultures: first, a school of thought that views digital media regulation and governance as processes that shape digital infrastructures, technological affordances, and individual and communal user practices; second, a range of political-economic and critical-cultural approaches to evaluating and critiquing media institutions' operations and motives; and third, a cultural studies–inspired approach that investigates the many ways media structure cultural-geographic difference, discrimination, and inequality.

Regional lockout is what happens when media industries incorporate digital delivery technologies into their established business models— and in particular, the market-segmentation logics of global media distribution.[4] Digital technologies' potential for allowing industries to ease distribution and expand their reach also posed a threat to *controlling* that distribution and therefore protecting intellectual property rights. To combat this threat, entertainment industries worked with tech industries to place tight constraints on the technologies themselves. As Siva Vaidhyanathan puts it, media industries and regulators "have found that it has been easier to regulate machines than people."[5] In order to ensure that films, video games, and television programs stayed put, media industries developed DRM systems like region codes and IP address detection and filtering software to prohibit people in certain places from using the technologies. Lawrence Lessig captured this dynamic in his well-known work on code and regulation, which understood that digital media are regulated not merely through legal means but through their technological characteristics as well.[6] DRM operates by limiting digital media's affordances (i.e., what we can and cannot do with them), which as Tarleton Gillespie has shown, affects our own sense of agency and power in relation to media technologies. As he puts it, through DRM, users' "perception that they have the capacity and the right to operate and manipulate their own technology must be actively frustrated."[7] The perceived affordances of region-locked technologies thus reflect the industry-favored range of possible uses. Indeed, Sonia Livingstone and Ranjana Das adapt Stuart Hall's encoding/decoding model to new media use, suggesting that a technology's built-in affordances present something analogous to a "preferred reading."[8] The capabilities that dominant industries want us to perceive have been quite literally "encoded" onto the device. Because code cannot do the job by itself, however, regional lockout is buttressed through an interlocking series of legal, contractual, political, and cultural efforts to ensure not only that people abide by the system but that it seems like a natural and reasonable part of a technology—a mechanism that Gillespie calls a "regime of alignment."[9] The fear of digital piracy in particular has given major media companies a pretext to work with regulators and convince technology manufacturers to build devices in ways that restrict unacceptable uses.[10]

Indicating the interlocked nature of my argument's three strands, it is virtually impossible to talk about regional lockout as a regulatory mechanism without also considering media distribution. After all, this particular form of regulation is less about regulating copyright per se and more about the preservation of geographic market segments. Thus, *Locked Out* combines a look at digital regulation with a political-

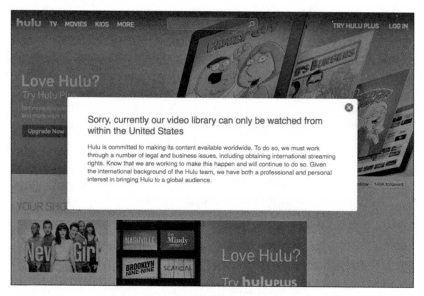

Figure I.2. This content is not available in your country. Screenshot: Hulu.

economic critique that evaluates industry decisions and organizational structures. Given distribution's importance to media corporations' bottom lines, political economists steeped in Marxist traditions have long pointed to it as a means by which such institutions allocate resources and accumulate power.[11] One only needs to look at the long-standing debates over cultural imperialism to see how various parties have been concerned about the relationship between distribution and corporate hegemony in the global media landscape. However, regional lockout allows us to consider connections between distribution and power from different angles, in part by reframing the usual anxieties related to cultural imperialism. On the one hand, regional lockout is clearly a form of power and control over distribution often put in place by major media corporations. On the other hand, this form of power operates ironically by keeping media *out* of particular places. This indicates that traditional concerns over transnational corporate media's global expansion and ubiquity do not fully explain why regional lockout exists. What regional lockout *does* tell us is that media corporations' distribution routes are just as often about carefully routed and carved-out paths as they are about blunt-force expansion. Contrary to concerns about the invasion and proliferation of dominant culture at the level of *content* (e.g., super-hero movies in every theater, American programs on every television set), regional lockout's methods of control via software and databases are more structural and invisible in nature.[12] By choosing which territories should and should not receive media texts and platforms at particular times, media companies can more precisely manage economies of scale, pricing, and release strategies in certain markets. This is at once a more insidious and banal form of control than that envisioned by critics of cultural imperialism.

After all, regional lockout is not only a form of DRM meant to control individual users' activities and consumption habits or a way to make more money. It also intends to shape global media geography at large scales. The DVD region code, for example, was developed to limit what people could do with DVDs and DVD players, but it had a broader goal of shaping the spatial and temporal relations of global home video release schedules. The preferred uses of the media industries become the default uses, as region codes are baked into the DVD's technical standards—standards built to maximize profits at the expense of a more open digital media environment. As a result, regional lockout punctures some of the more celebratory assumptions about what new media would mean for global media distribution and access. Such accounts continue to find purchase, as in one volume arguing that the migration of films onto online video-on-demand (VOD) platforms represents "a democratizing process" and that, through such platforms, film becomes liberated from the "tyranny of geography."[13] There is some measure of truth here, as digital media have undoubtedly made it easier for certain people to access particular films in specific places. But even allowing for the rhetorical power of hyperbole, to suggest that VOD platforms have made geography irrelevant ignores how DRM implants geographic borders into the functions of digital technologies. In contrast to popular visions of digital media erasing or minimizing global inequalities, then, regional lockout suggests that global flows are built on disconnection and discrimination. It suggests that we should be skeptical of the concept of "flow" and instead follow Anna Tsing in adopting "friction" as way of explaining global cultural interaction.[14] This enables us to view digital distribution as a process that intentionally builds in frustrations, incompatibilities, and inefficiencies so media companies can more easily control content circulation.

At the same time, political economic and "digital freedom" approaches that take regional lockout as wholly, unequivocally *bad* are on their own overly simplistic. This is not to say that regional lockout is often or even usually *good*. To be clear, it is restrictive and discriminatory in ways that place the harshest limitations on the least privileged. But beyond the more regularly occurring binaries of good/bad and just/unjust, we might consider the complex ways regional lockout creates certain conditions of media access and use. In other words, regional lockout has *produced* the contours of global media distribution over the last few decades as much as it has *restricted* them. Indeed, it makes little sense to see these two dynamics as separate or oppositional to each other. This view of digital-industrial power is indebted to Timothy Havens's Foucauldian analysis of global television distribution, where he argues that corporate power "produces both social realities and available forms of resistance."[15] As standard industrial practice and dogma, regional lockout sets guidelines for how industrial players make distribution decisions and how manufacturers design and produce their products. Global media industries' creation and representation of knowledge about a territory—knowledge used to control the flow of resources through it via regional lockout mechanisms—is part of a power/knowledge regime. This regime produces imagined understandings of geography that thus shape the very real, material conditions of global media circulation. Regional lockout has also shaped the ways global consumers have used and understood digital entertainment over the past few decades. As I discuss in chapter 2, for instance, region codes in video games did not simply reduce the number and kinds of games that people could play. They also helped create a vibrant subculture of transnational, informal video game traders looking for region-locked games and consoles from across borders, which in turn helped shape the contours of gamer culture.

To comprehend regional lockout as a meeting point of technology, industry, and cultural practice, *Locked Out* blends cyberlaw-inflected studies of digital regulation and critical political economy of media industries with a cultural-studies approach to media globalization attuned to power and difference. The point is not to reproduce that hoary, cliché, and faulty binary between political economy and cultural studies, but to highlight how the concerns of all these areas can be mutually constitutive. As a regulatory practice that draws on media-distribution logics to encode lines of geocultural difference into technologies, re-gional lockout shows how media's "objective" and "subjective" elements blend together. Drawing on a distinction developed by Nick Couldry, the objective dimensions are media institutions and regulation while subjective elements refer to culture and social experience.[16] In regional lockout, the two work together to reveal ways geocultural *difference* can be inscribed onto seemingly straightforward economic and regulatory decisions.[17] Region-locked technologies remind us where and who we are and confront us with the reality of a global media landscape divided along familiar lines of privilege. Like Jonathan Sterne's reading of the MP3 as a "cultural artifact" saturated with social meanings associated with the circumstances of its production and use, *Locked Out* explores how region-locked technologies carry meanings related to geographic and cultural difference.[18] Because the DVD region code map groups par-ticular countries together in an ordered, numbered system, this *means* something about which countries belong together and how highly those territories rank on Hollywood's hierarchies of value (more on this in the next chapter). Furthermore, when immigrants and diasporic communi-ties have trouble accessing digital platforms or buying DVDs from their home territories, this is much more than a matter of failed commercial exchange. It marks one's geocultural situation and place in the world.

Because regional lockout is made meaningful beyond technological code and industry charts, it lends itself well to cultural studies' "circuit of culture" models of understanding cultural artifacts. Such models trace an artifact's articulations of social meaning and power across several are-nas of cultural production, regulation, identification, and use. As global, corporate-manufactured, public- and private-sector-regulated mecha-nisms of media distribution and use, consumer electronics are ripe for this kind of analysis—something made evident by the fact that the best-known work advancing the circuit model is an extended analysis of the Sony Walkman.[19] A technology of unequal distribution, regional lock-out shows how media can articulate cultural difference even before they reach end users. This emphasizes the importance of distribution to the relationship between media and culture, in contrast to critical-cultural media studies' long-standing production/consumption bias that Denise D. Bielby and C. Lee Harrington have pointed to in their own critique of the circuit model.[20] In response, *Locked Out* is about how a technology of media distribution in fact gets taken up as a mechanism of geocultural difference at multiple points in the circuit of culture—by media companies, regulators, audiences, commentators, and various intermediaries.[21] Regional lockout is thus not so much a form of restrictive control as it is an assemblage of technological mechanisms, regulations, distribution practices, industry lore, and audience frustrations. When media industry executives consider a particular nation or region more or less valuable—a kind of institutional logic based not just on economic matters but also on cultural issues like language, demographics, and taste—this translates into technological regulations that are buttressed by national and global forms of media governance.[22] Outside the media industries, trade sources and media users also interpret and occasionally reject regional lockout's assertion of industrial/technological power and geocultural difference. This is all to say that understanding regional lockout requires developing a vocabulary for how to think about global media distribution and regulation as systems that articulate geocultural difference and discrimination across multiple realms of social action.

Geocultural Capital: A Way to Talk about Media Access, Geography, and Status

The promotional push for the Digital Single Market understood something fundamental about regional lockout: for many users, the inaccessibility of the entertainment they want is about more than simply what to do on a Tuesday night. It is about where they sit within global hierarchies of media access and cultural status. This is why the aforementioned bakery video promoting the DSM emphasized the pain of national discrimination. Commission members also made sure to speak to personal frustrations and the affective dimensions of geoblocking as much as they did to the policy implications. In public comments about the DSM strategy, Commission vice president Andrus Ansip underscored how closely tied the issue is to media consumption's emotional and experiential dimensions: "Deep in my heart, I hate geoblocking. It is old-fashioned, and it is not fair. We do not have to use these instruments in the 21st century."[23] *Hate. Old-fashioned. Not fair.* These words speak volumes about how decisions made in boardrooms and parliament halls come to bear on the pleasures and frustrations that attend day-to-day media experience.

Indeed, *frustration* tends to be a common theme in anti-geoblocking rhetoric. Consider the bakery video, where media metamorphose into pastries and coffee, or this statement, from a Kenyan man quoted in an NPR story about his response to Netflix's announced arrival to the country: "Think of it as a child who tries to get sugar from the sugar bowl. And they're doing it illegally when Mom's not looking. And one day Mom says, 'Hey, you can have all the sugar you want.'"[24] Comparisons to food are not accidental. Like food, entertainment media is consumable, embodied, and a road to fulfillment and self-actualization. Both examples compare media to a special treat—a pain aux raisins, sugar, or a piping hot cup of coffee. Media and popular culture are resources— not ones that keep us alive like clean air or water, but cultural resources that, in their capacity to help us build communities, understand and express our identities, arm ourselves with knowledge, and provide pleasures, fulfill essential functions in our lives. Statements that compare the frustrations of geoblocking to hunger or a caffeine headache offer a reminder that media access and inaccessibility weigh on our worldly, embodied experiences.

Regional lockout ties these personal frustrations to larger-scale forms of national and regional discrimination. To understand regional lockout's relationship to hierarchies of global territories—and, by proxy, the people who live within them—this book proposes and employs the concept of geocultural capital. Geocultural capital refers to a kind of capital that geographic territories (nations, regions, cities) accumulate and exchange in order to attain cultural status. Cultural status is related but not reducible to "hard" forms of power like economic, military, or political strength. Nor is it merely "soft power" via cultural influence. Rather, it is a form of status based in part on the quantity and quality of media resources in a particular territory as well as that territory's ability to shape what kinds of media are made available within its borders and around the world. Thus, regional lockout both reflects and shapes relations of geocultural capital.

While capital refers traditionally to the financial assets that people and institutions trade and accumulate, sociologist Pierre Bourdieu has described other kinds of capital that structure social divisions. One of these is cultural capital, or the knowledge and competencies—good taste, manners, and so forth—that shape one's standing within social

hierarchies. For Bourdieu, people within a particular field of social action accumulate cultural capital through their access to, and knowledge
of, cultural resources and assets (art, film, fashion, food, etc.). Cultural
capital is thus a means by which people achieve social mobility, esteem,
and status.[25] Geocultural capital adapts Bourdieu's idea to describe a
comparable process at the level of geography. Put simply, it is a kind of
cultural capital or achievement of status embodied by *places* rather than
people. Just as cultural capital is about social status and mobility, *geocultural* capital affords nations, regions, and cities opportunities to shape
and participate in various global cultural economies of media, fashion,
art, and so on. It illustrates how various stakeholders make Bourdieuian
"distinctions" among territories within and across many different sites
of discourse and action.[26] Global media distribution offers a useful case
study of the accumulation and use of geocultural capital, as it is a major
way that territories attain and circulate cultural resources around the
world. In fact, Bourdieu points to the importance of distribution to relations of capital in a more general sense, writing that capital "depends for
its real efficacy on the form of the distribution of the means of appropri-
ating the accumulated and objectively available resources."[27]

Nations and regions gain geocultural capital through both the accessibility of media within their borders as well as their ability to shape
what kinds of media resources are made available within their borders
and around the world. For example, audiences, industries, and regulators may consider the United States as having a lot of geocultural capital
in the global media economy because it has access to a great deal of
mediated art and entertainment and because American institutions have
significant power in shaping what kind of media get circulated around
the world. Alternately, many of the same stakeholders would likely consider a nation like Kenya as embodying a lower amount of geocultural
capital. This is both because of a relative scarcity of "valued" cultural
resources in the country (given mainstream media industries' general
apathy toward sub-Saharan Africa, as evidenced by the above-discussed
NPR story on Netflix) as well as its lack of influence on global media
distribution policy and practice. These perceptions exist in part due
to the former's status as a rich, powerful nation and the latter's status
as a poorer, less powerful one, but geocultural capital allows us to talk
about each country's status in global media culture without reducing

the discussion to economic power. Indeed, many oft-repeated markers of status—GDP, military might, political influence—are on their own insufficient to help comprehend the kinds of cultural hierarchies discussed here.[28]

Rather than a term synonymous with power, geocultural capital is better thought of as the amount of cultural wealth, measured in access to cultural resources or Bourdieu's "rare assets," that a particular place has in a particular situation. Geocultural capital points to a softer form of inequality—an inequality of cultural, artistic, and entertainment experiences between broadly scaled geographic places. No wonder, then, that in the context of regional lockout we can most often see people invoking geocultural capital in moments of frustration or envy regarding their inability to access media. When people say "we don't have access to this" or "we should have access to this" (with "we" referring to people living within a nation or region), these complaints amount to laments over unequal relations of geocultural capital. Bourdieu points to capital's seemingly zero-sum nature when he argues that people are always in competition with one another for the scarce resources that allow one to accumulate different kinds of capital.[29] With geocultural capital, we can extrapolate this process onto understanding the competition between geographic territories to acquire resources. A nation's endowment of geocultural capital, for example, becomes most apparent when compared and contrasted against that of another nation.

Geocultural capital synthesizes existing work on cultural capital's spatial dimensions in order to advance a theory of differential cultural status that centralizes geography. After all, Bourdieu himself points out that the resources necessary to gain cultural capital are distributed unequally among "socially ranked geographic space."[30] What are distribution charts and maps of geoblocked territories if not such geographic rankings? Geocultural capital diverges from Bourdieu and other accounts of the geographic nature of cultural capital in that it takes these "socially ranked" spaces as embodying capital in and of themselves. In developing the concept, I draw inspiration from scholars who have likewise linked notions of status, taste, and capital to cultural geography. Aíhwa Ong and Victoria Johnson, for instance, have each pointed out how geographic locations embody a kind of capital in and of themselves.[31] Immigrants looking for neighborhoods in which to live and TV viewers engaging with the American Midwest on television (to draw on two of Ong and Johnson's respective examples) make *distinctions* between different places based on perceived status. The idea that places both *are* and *accumulate* capital is likewise central to Michael Curtin's theory of media capital, which shows how particular cities at certain points in history represent nodes in the flow of money, media, and creative labor throughout the global media industries.[32] In part, then, the concept of media capital is about status—about how locales become more and less important to cultural industry operations. In his analysis of the American video store, Daniel Herbert adapts Curtin's concept while amplifying Bourdieuian implications of capital and status. Arguing that particular video stores in the United States embody a great deal of "video capital" in the size and scope of their offerings, Herbert illustrates how home entertainment structures relations of taste and distributions of cultural capital within and across social space.[33] Collectively, these authors offer models for comprehending how places themselves can embody kinds of capital that include but are not limited to financial wealth. Herbert's concept of video capital shows how capital can be accumulated through the process of media availability and accessibility. Geocultural capital captures this dynamic at larger scales, illustrating how various stakeholders perceive nations' and regions' cultural status based on their possibilities of media engagement.

Thus, while others have talked about the relationships that bind media, geography, and capital, *Locked Out* draws this material together in order to develop a sustained analysis of how one particular mechanism of digital distribution/regulation shapes global understandings of geocultural difference and distinction. The concept of geocultural capital intends to lend a term to a phenomenon that many media scholars and commentators have discussed in some way, but which requires further exploration—that industry lore and established popular knowledge about geographic territories' value in the global mediascape is as much about *cultural* status as it is about *economic* status. Geocultural capital is not solely shaped through regional lockout—indeed, the idea that geographic spaces embody status and capital in the global media economy is one that extends well beyond (and before) the phenomenon explored in this book. Rather, regional restrictions in digital media offer a useful space to observe geocultural capital because they bring about moments when industries, governing bodies, and users employ the language of cultural discrimination and inequality as they structure and talk about media's geographic availability. For entertainment industries, the perceived status of a territory—again, as an economic market but also as a space worth engaging in practices of cultural distribution—shapes territorial distribution licenses and prices. Meanwhile, a VOD platform like Netflix invokes notions of fair and equal access among all nations as a way of publicly lobbying against media industries' territorial licensing agreements. In the minds and rhetoric of national politicians upset at the lack of streaming platforms in their country, regional lockout exemplifies unfair discrimination against their nation (and represents a way to push free trade regulation). All these responses to regional lockout circulate around a fundamental premise of both geocultural capital and this book: that there is a relationship between the availability of media texts and platforms in a certain territory and the perceived cultural value of that territory.

Method and Map: Regional Lockout across Time, Space, and Technology

Because *Locked Out* traces regional lockout's articulations of geocultural capital across the realms of technology, governance, economics, distribution, geography, culture, and difference, the book employs a variety of methods. To understand how industries and regulators develop and make use of regional lockout, I use critical discourse analysis of many primary and secondary sources: news stories and books about regional lockout, legal documents, media technology guides and FAQs, industry trade routes and economic data, popular media criticism invoking regional lockout and its circumvention, and other sources where we can observe alignments among regulation, media distribution, and geocultural difference. I also attend to audience and user responses to regional lockout, but because it is often a structurally invisible form of control, it is not suited well to traditional ethnography. Rather, I seek out moments when users confront regional lockout and express public frustrations about it. These usually take place in online spaces like message boards, comment sections, websites, and YouTube videos where users from around the world summarize regional lockout systems and offer tips on how to hack them. To emphasize regional lockout's effects on localized circuits of distribution and consumption, I also draw from interviews conducted with employees and owners of diasporic video stores that specialize in region-free media. As spaces where media retailers and customers alike negotiate regional lockout, such stores serve as rich sites of activity related to regional lockout within informal and semiformal media trade networks. Looking at both broad institutional processes and local adoption and resistance, *Locked Out* shows how regional lockout functionally closes off certain territories from media access but discursively opens up a space for popular, industrial, and regulatory discussions about cultural distribution and territorial discrimination.

Regional lockout's assemblage of technology, distribution, regulation, and culture is apparent in the DVD region code. As the first widespread, globally successful digital home video platform, the DVD offered both opportunities and potential problems for film and television distribution. On the one hand, the optical disc format was a relatively inexpensive, portable, and high-definition product that would appeal to consumers, manufacturers, and distributors alike. Viewers could enjoy a crisper image via a medium that was less bulky and more interactive than VHS, while manufacturers and media corporations saw an opportunity to boost home video rentals and sales and usher global media industries into a long-promised digital age. At the same time, the format's portability and its easily copied digital contents threatened to destroy film and television industries' geographically segmented release schedules. Because a film could be released on DVD in one territory while still in its theatrical release in another, the film industry needed a system to prevent parallel imports (i.e., the unauthorized import of a product meant for another territory) that might undermine the theatrical release's profit potential. So, as the DVD and its technical standards were developed, Hollywood film studios pressured consumer electronics manufacturers to implement a DRM system called Regional Playback Control, wherein each DVD and DVD player are assigned a numerical "region code" based on the geographic market in which they are sold. The respective codes in the software and hardware must match before the DVD will play. Chapter 1 details the DVD region code's history, showing how the system was put in place and governed through complex negotiations and alignments among content creators, consumer electronics manufacturers, and public- and private-sector governing bodies. I argue in this chapter that the system is not only a hard-nosed form of technological and distributional control but also a system of symbolic global representation. Region codes represent the world and its places through maps, public explanations of the system, DVD player instruction manuals, industry lore, and news stories. In doing so, they perpetuate a certain imagination of the world that clusters territories together and ranks those clusters within economic and cultural hierarchies. Exemplifying the divisional logic that Roger Silverstone refers to as media's "boundary work," region codes therefore functionally shape the geography of digital video distribution and symbolically perpetuate the idea that this geography should be based on hierarchical logics of segmentation that privilege traditionally powerful nations and regions.[34]

While DVD region codes brought regional lockout into a more mainstream global conversation about digital entertainment in the late 1990s and early 2000s, it had long been a nuisance for video game aficionados. Chapter 2 jumps back in time a bit to explore the long history of regional lockout in console games, which was more complex than the DVD region code given its many manifestations in a variety of different systems. As console video games became popular throughout both Japan and North America with Nintendo's Famicom (Nintendo Entertainment System in the United States) in the 1980s, the industry's hybrid Japanese-American orientation forged a system of carefully managed adaptation and distribution of games to each market.[35] As a result, video game companies introduced region chips and differently shaped cartridges to ensure that consumers were playing games on approved devices. As video games became bigger and bigger business around the world, similar regional lockout systems were implemented into newer consoles. Companies adopted a region code format similar to the DVD when they moved to disc-based software, and they began geoblocking online content when internet delivery became central to the game industry's operations. The industry's longtime use of regional lockout helped set the contours of global distribution, but it also fomented a robust network of piracy, game and console hacking, and informal trade among consumers who typify what Nick Dyer-Witheford and Greig de Peuter have called the "hardcore" gamer.[36] Knowing how to navigate and circumvent regional lockout became a marker of the particular form of subcultural capital—what Mia Consalvo refers to as "gaming capital"— that signaled participation in hardcore gamer communities.[37] As a result, I argue in chapter 2 that regional lockout did more than simply control global video game distribution paths. It also helped shape the contours of hardcore gamer culture: its structures of subcultural capital, its informal circulation and production practices, and the ways the video game industry targeted this group.

Chapter 2 thus illustrates two of this book's central premises about regional lockout: first, that it is as much *productive* of global media culture as it is restrictive; and second, that it represents a space where people make sense of and debate issues of geocultural difference. The next chapter continues to emphasize this by thinking about how people engage the ideas of geography and belonging within geoblocked online video-on-demand platforms. A form of regional lockout for the internet age, geoblocking is the practice of barring a user from an online platform (say, Hulu or BBC's iPlayer) based on that user's geographic location. Exploring a few illustrative case studies—geoblocking in Australia and New Zealand, the debates over the geoblocked iPlayer platform, and the EU's recent attempt to ban geoblocking among its countries' borders—I argue in this chapter that geoblocking represents an arena where consumers, industries, and regulators negotiate the realities of national and regional control over digital entertainment platforms versus fantasies of a globally open internet. In doing so, I draw on the concept of geocultural capital to clarify the occasionally hard-to-articulate stakes of regional lockout: that is, what it means for particular consumers and territories beyond notions of economic equality. Consumers' vocalized frustrations about lack of access as well as industry and regulatory decisions about distribution and technology are based in ideas regarding the economic and cultural value of certain territories. This chapter illustrates that geoblocking, which enables certain geographic markets to have access to more texts, better technologies, and higher-quality software than others (not to mention access to all of them *first*), can help us better articulate inequalities in access to cultural resources.

Chapter 4 continues to explore the relationships between unequal media access, geography, and status by analyzing how regional lockout in digital music platforms regulates a problem long familiar to radio and music industries: controlling the spatial circulation of sound. Part of what makes regional lockout in music somewhat distinct from other media is the commonly held myth that sound and music are more ethereal and mobile than visual media. Throughout the 2000s and 2010s, this perceived immateriality was often expressed in popular discourses about cloud-based platforms and the "celestial jukebox," which as legend had it would make music ubiquitous and universally available.[38] Exploring these issues in the context of broader debates over DRM and digital music, this chapter shows that regional lockout in music is a relatively recent phenomenon, having grown out of the record industry's increasing reliance on digital download stores and streaming platforms at the expense of the region-free compact disc format. My analysis of streaming music focuses on a case study of the popular Swedish streaming music service Spotify. Built around a brand promoting music "everywhere" and "for everyone," the platform has instead been central to debates over regional lockout. Spotify and other similar streaming music platforms belie their geoblocked condition by presenting themselves as services offering global, omnipresent, and individually customizable listening experiences. Chapter 4 argues that streaming music platforms' promises of easily accessible music, mobility, and cosmopolitan interconnection in part mask their inconsistent global availability and mechanisms of geolocative back-end control. In doing so, they conflate mobility in an individualized, experiential sense with a broader, global erasure of borders. Furthermore, these platforms point to how geoblocking can contribute to homogeneous echo chambers in online listening spaces, as their algorithmic recommendation systems pull and make use of listener data from a geographically limited user base.

Chapter 5 builds on but diverges from the industry-specific analyses of the previous four chapters, taking a closer look at some of the informal distribution economies that have built up as a result of regional lockout. In particular, I focus on region-free DVD, a format that became widespread globally as consumers encountered and reacted to DVD region codes. Region-free DVD is prevalent within two broad, occasionally overlapping perspectives that embody different sets of power relations: diasporic video cultures and cinephile DVD collectors. Chapter 5 investigates the different articulations of power and privilege in region-free DVD cultures, beginning with an analysis of region code circumvention and region-free DVD use by diasporic video retailers in the United States. Interviews with video store owners and employees reveal how region-free DVD can represent both a bottom-up challenge to dominant media industries' distribution routes as well as a more everyday practice of making cultural resources available to localized diasporic communities. If this shows how less powerful groups get around regional lockout, the use of region-free DVD by self-identified cinephiles and film cultists shows that region-free DVD cultures also reflect a seemingly contradictory blend of cosmopolitanism and cultural dominance. The practice of seeking out region-free DVDs in order to access global cinema often blends an admirable engagement with the wealth and diversity of global cultural production with a commodifying approach to cultural tourism. Chapter 5 explores these tensions, pointing to moments when region-free DVD culture carries overtones of masculinized cosmopolitanism and a collector's mind-set that commodifies and flattens global creative cultures. Ultimately, this chapter argues that while region-free DVD at times reflects an oppositional and transgressive orientation toward oppressive global cultural industries, region-free media's cultural politics are more ambivalent than many of its celebrators might suggest.

By pointing to the contradictory cultural politics of circumvention, chapter 5 characterizes Locked Out's broader argument that regional lockout reflects different vectors of politics and privilege. Spanning three decades of regional lockout, this book shows that utopian visions of infinite media access have not come to pass. Critically interrogating media industries' utopian promotional rhetoric as well as the expressed frustrations of consumers and digital rights activists, the following pages explore regional lockout and its consequences in all their complexity.

1

DVD Region Codes

Technical Standards and Geocultural Status

In 2009, British prime minister Gordon Brown paid a state visit to US president Barack Obama. As the story goes, the two administrations traded gifts, with Brown offering Obama a penholder carved from an antislavery ship and Obama giving Brown a collection of twenty-five "classic" American films on DVD. However, when Brown finally returned to 10 Downing Street, he discovered that the DVDs were unplayable in his British DVD player. Purchased in the United States, they were encoded Region One. Brown's player, manufactured in the UK, was designated Region Two, and thus would not play the American DVDs. The leaders of two of the most powerful states in the world (or at least the staffers put in charge of finding gifts) had been stymied by the DVD region code system, which maintains established film-distribution routes by ensuring that discs from one part of the world do not work on players from another.[1]

Silly and inconsequential as it may seem, this story illustrates a few things about DVD region codes. For one, it characterizes a certain style of reporting that portrays region codes as a mechanism that frustrates and irritates non-US users primarily, even those who hold high status.[2] Even if the story is indeed suspicious (after all, it does seem unlikely that 10 Downing Street would not have access to a region-free DVD player), its presence in the tabloids indicates that the British government would not find it politically savory to admit that it surreptitiously accessed intellectual property not meant for British viewers. Additionally, it hints at the power of private, multinational corporations, more than the state, in controlling the global flow of entertainment culture. A number of media companies and industrial consortia developed the region code system, with the state taking a back seat during this process of technological regulation. In other words, Brown's PR machine would not likely

23

plant a story about how he was frustrated by a form of national or trans-national regulation; rather, Hollywood (and, by extension, the United States) could remain the culprit. This speaks to a final point: that DVD region codes have, for nearly two decades now, represented a landscape on which cultural difference, and the disagreements and inequalities in geocultural capital that can attend that difference, have been articulated. As the British tabloids were quick to point out, Obama's dysfunctional gift paled in comparison to Brown's more thoughtful present. Here, Brown figures as an avatar of British viewers frustrated by region codes: a relatable victim of a Hollywood-driven form of economic and cultural discrimination.[3]

How did an entertainment platform become a battleground for even mild public tussles between closely allied nations? To begin to answer this question, this chapter outlines a cultural history and analysis of the DVD region code. It shows that region codes perpetuated and up-dated for the digital age a dominant logic in the cultural industries: that world regions are differentiated spatial markets to be placed on hierar-chies of economic and cultural power. By carving up the world into six geographic regions, with DVDs from one region unable to play on the DVD players of another, the region code scheme retained the disjunc-tive, market-driven relationships that were already familiar to global home video distribution.[4] This all occurred during a historical moment marked by intertwining forces of media globalization, digitization, and privatized technological standard setting and (de)regulation. While dominant stories about these forces suggested they would all work mu-tually to expand the distribution of filmed entertainment, region codes show that powerful actors tried to ensure that media distribution fol-lowed controlled paths directed by digital blockades.

This chapter argues that region codes' hierarchy of segmentation worked both technologically as digital regulation and discursively as a system of representation. In its technological function, the region code system limited the affordances of the DVD in a way that retained tra-ditionally segmented entertainment markets. Region codes' represen-tational dimensions appear in industry memos, instruction manuals, maps, and news stories, all of which employ shared understandings of geocultural difference and discrimination in order to make sense of region codes. Industry players draw on dominant ideas about certain countries' and regions' levels of geocultural capital when discussing region codes with one another, trade reporters deploy cultural shorthand and even stereotypes to help explain region codes, and users invoke charges of cultural discrimination as a way of protesting region codes. Thus, this chapter deepens our understanding of digital media regulation by emphasizing how regulation can reveal and produce discrimination and difference in global media economies. Most broadly, DVD region codes provide a series of stories about the cultural implications of global entertainment distribution during a time when cultural industries were transitioning to digital delivery technologies. Tracing involvement by global film and television studios, private and state regulatory bodies, media industry consortia, the computing and IT industries, consumer electronics manufacturers, trade presses, and consumer rights groups, this chapter shows media convergence at work in all its messiness.[5]

But why bother writing about the DVD at all? After all, many inside and outside the media industries are quick to point out its obsolescence. Part of my motivation is to outline how region codes institutionalized a particular approach to maintaining the globe's divisibility in an era of digital entertainment. While certain forms of lockout and regionally specific technological standards have always existed, media technologies such as the DVD and early video game consoles like the Nintendo Entertainment System were among the first to include components that *intentionally* locked out users from other regions. Thus, the DVD region code was a key origin point of the last two decades' debates over regional lockout and digital media technology. It is also worth pointing out that despite pronouncements of the DVD's death at the hands of Blu-ray and online streaming, the technology is still very much alive, even if sales have dipped.[6] The suggestion that the DVD will be (or has already been) replaced by Blu-ray and streaming video carries classist and Western-centric assumptions. Namely, taking the habits of users who gravitate toward emergent, top-of-the-line technologies as the norm privileges those who are not only upper or middle class, but are often constructed in trade discourse as young, white men from the Global North.[7] Taking for granted the erroneous assumption that the world's media practices resemble those of a privileged minority risks reproducing accounts that ignore the continued existence of supposedly "residual" cultural forms.

That DVDs have enjoyed longer life spans in various parts of the world highlights another crucial point: the DVD region code system did not wholly shape the flow of home video around the globe. Indeed, methods of circumventing these forms of regulation always immediately follow their development, and a dominant narrative produced by media industries, technology manufacturers, and users throughout the history of the DVD is that region codes simply did not work. Informal or semiformal economies of media distribution, which exist outside and at times in direct violation of the state-recognized and -sanctioned media economies that adopt such forms of regulation, are quite widespread (or even, as Ramon Lobato argues, the dominant norm) around the world.[8] Many gray markets throughout parts of Asia and Africa, for instance, sustain distribution economies built in part around the DVD.[9] So, to argue that the DVD region code completely and utterly served its function to direct global media flows would be to adopt a view that is both technologically determinist and Hollywood-centric.

Still, even if region codes did not function as ideally as Hollywood had hoped, they worked well enough to irritate many users and help studios maintain some semblance of market segmentation. Furthermore, region codes' cultural effects are apparent in their promotion of division and discrimination in the global media ecosystem. Region codes characterize what Roger Silverstone called media's "boundary work," or the multitude of ways media systems generate and sustain lines of geographic, political, and cultural difference.[10] At the macro level, media's boundary work reinforces borders of nation and community by providing infrastructural and formal means through which we construct communities and include and exclude people from those communities.[11] However, region codes do not merely inscribe difference at this broader level of spatial relations. At the micro level, or the level attuned to media consumers' everyday experiences with texts, boundary work inscribes difference within media texts and discourse. Region codes assert geocultural difference at the macro level by building digital walls between territories and at the micro level through their textual and visual representations in forms like maps, industry talk, and user discourse. Region codes shape the material geographic flows of media around the world, and they offer a discursive landscape on which various players discuss and contest the relationships among home video, digital media, and geo-cultural difference.

The Region Code System

Before going too much further, it is worth explaining what region codes actually *are* and how they work. In order to ensure that DVD players from one part of the world cannot play DVDs from another, most discs include a flag on their software that a player from the same region must read before it will play the DVD.[12] Region codes are officially called Regional Playback Control (RPC), and they are part of the DVD's anti-copying technological architecture called the Content Scrambling System (CSS). CSS (not to be confused with the identically abbreviated web-design language) was developed and standardized by the DVD Forum, a consortium of studios and electronics manufacturers. Currently, a California-based nonprofit corporation called the DVD Copy Control Association (DVD CCA) controls and licenses the technology.[13]

The system requires a DVD to be encoded as one of eight possible regions, with six of these corresponding to different geographic territories around the world. There is also a technological reason motivating the use of eight regions. Since eight bits fit on a byte, and each region flag takes up one bit, the regional playback mechanism as a whole fits on one byte.[14] The regions are as follows:

1: Canada, United States, Puerto Rico, Bermuda, the Virgin Islands, and some islands in the Pacific
2: Japan, Europe (including Poland, Romania, Bulgaria, and the Balkans), South Africa, Turkey, and the Middle East (including Iran and Egypt)
3: Southeast and East Asia (including Indonesia, South Korea, Hong Kong, and Macau)
4: Australia, New Zealand, South America, most of Central America, Western New Guinea, and most of the South Pacific
5: Most of Africa, Russia (and former Russian states), Mongolia, Afghanistan, Pakistan, India, Bangladesh, Nepal, Bhutan, and North Korea
6: China and Tibet

7: Reserved

8: Special nontheatrical venues (airplanes, cruise ships, hotels)

DVD region codes came about at a moment when global audiences were increasingly important to Hollywood, which needed to figure out how to exploit these markets while maintaining control over distribution. A major part of this global expansion was the development of the overseas home video market, which by 1989 had become the top source of international revenue for the Hollywood studios.[15] The mid-1990s saw a slowdown in global video sales, but the introduction of the DVD in 1996 led to a second boom—this time in DVD hardware and software.[16] For Hollywood, this growing global market was both a boon and a potential new crisis of unchecked distribution.

In this context, the studios encouraged the development of some form of regional control in order to preserve their theatrical and home video release schedules. Each territory, placement on a network, or release period represents a window for the studios to exploit, and Hollywood's theatrical distribution strategies had long operated by dividing markets by space and time.[17] While the specific parameters of this separation have shifted over time due to post–studio era industrial changes and the rise of home video, the general philosophy of geographic discrimination remained. At the time of DVD's development, Hollywood operated almost exclusively under a "tiered" or "staggered" form of windowing, where theaters in certain markets would run a film before studios released it in other markets (e.g., second-run theaters, theaters in different regions of the world, home video).[18] Because Hollywood often put a film out on video in the United States before giving it a theatrical debut overseas, there was a danger of parallel imports, or products meant for one geographic market introduced into another, usually illegally. In theory, DVD region codes would allow the studios to maintain these staggered windows by ensuring that DVDs of a film would not appear in a market while that film was still in theaters. Region codes could also maintain price discrimination practices, where DVDs varied in cost significantly among different markets. If a Region Four DVD from Mexico will not play in a Region One player from the United States, this would prevent a northward flood of comparatively less expensive discs.[19]

With these motives on the part of studios, region codes help maintain conditions for an industry orthodoxy that former Hollywood executive Jeff Ulin refers to as, naturally enough, Ulin's Rule. According to Ulin's Rule, "content value is optimized by exploiting the factors of time, repeat consumption (platforms), exclusivity, and differential pricing."[20] By helping Hollywood maintain temporal lags and spatial borders between different windows, region codes ideally would ensure that distributors and retailers could keep markets isolated enough to control prices within them.[21] Furthermore, since different companies own home video distribution rights to a film in different territories, region codes help these companies keep control over distribution to their respective markets.[22] Whether space, time, or price, region codes were meant to shore up corporate control over variables in distribution that threatened to become less predictable in a digital era. The result is that some parts of the world (usually North America) have access to the most content in the best quality, thus enjoying the geocultural capital that comes with existing as a premier market. In addition to the more apparent spatial/geographic disjuncture (i.e., that only certain privileged territories can have Region One DVDs), there is a temporal dimension to this. Because DVD releases of Hollywood films are generally hyped first and most intensely in Region One, other territories are left behind in a media environment where value is placed on early access. If there is a certain cultural cachet that comes with owning a product *first*, or even at all, then the staggered release dates that region codes attempt to preserve represent a hierarchy of global difference inscribed in the technical standards of the DVD. As this might suggest, region codes have been received with different degrees of irritation, apathy, and ignorance in various parts of the world. While the privileged position of the United States as Region One means that region codes have gone largely unnoticed in America, except by cinephiles or cultists who seek out differently coded DVDs, region codes proved to be more of a nuisance in much of the rest of the world. As we will see below, region codes (for both DVDs and console games) proved quite controversial in Australia and New Zealand. Throughout much of Asia, however, the significant presence of the (non-region-coded) Video CD (VCD) format meant that DVD region codes were not as central to discourses involving home or portable video entertainment—though that is not to say they were nonexistent.[23]

People also dislike region codes for reasons beyond an inability to access a particular film. Differently coded DVDs for the same film are not identical across regions. They differ textually and paratextually, as a DVD from one region may contain different bonus features and commentaries, available languages, and audiovisual quality. Indeed, DVDs are not simply ancillary products or functional delivery systems for messages or content, but commodities that, in their promises of high-fidelity sound and image, bonus features, and collectible packaging, offer a holistic aesthetic experience to the consumer. They are constitutive of film and television's textuality in a variety of ways.[24] The quality of the audiovisual transfer, menus, and bonus features add value to the DVD— something that becomes apparent when comparing high-quality Region One releases with bare-bones Region Five products. One trade report characteristically refers to Region One DVDs as the most "desirable" in the world, and a later *Billboard* piece quoted European DVD Lab CEO Michael Tucker explaining why: "Region One imports are the source of all our troubles. . . . The consumer is going to prefer them. I've never seen anything in Europe today that can stand up against the average American title. It's not just the extra features or the menus; it's also the transfer quality, the audio quality. . . . The quality generally is of a different standard. We're getting transfers [in Europe] that would be completely unacceptable even to any independent American distributor."[25] In the eyes of those who value audiovisual quality and bonus features, viewers outside Region One—that is, any territory that is not the United States or Canada—officially receive an often-inferior product, which in turn communicates to those territories that they do not rank as highly on the hierarchy of global audiovisual media markets.

A Brief History of Region Codes

The history of the DVD region code is the story of a cluster of industries attempting to outline the geographical contours of media markets through a contested process of regionalization from above. Region codes emerged during the DVD format's creation and standardization—a long process built out of debates and discussions among the three industrial sectors that were collectively responsible for developing DVD technology: global entertainment industries (and the Hollywood film studios in particular), the computing industries, and consumer electronics manufacturers.[26] All this occurred at a time when media corporations consolidated and globalized their operations in order to tighten control and achieve greater economies of scale.[27] The development of the DVD region code system was also global in scope, created through a number of collaborations and discussions taking place in conferences and meetings around the world. While use of region codes is technically voluntary for DVD hardware and software manufacturers, studios will not license their properties to manufacturers that do not use it.[28] Because manufacturers had an understandable desire to sell boatloads of popular films on DVD, they were required to abide by a system that had Hollywood's backing.[29] Hollywood used its stubbornness concerning international distribution as a way of gaining leverage over the electronics manufacturing industry. As a Hitachi Canada executive noted in 2002, "We'd have a hard time getting studios to release product if it could be viewed anywhere in the world at any time."[30] By threatening to hold back content, the studios heavily influenced the DVD Forum's technical specs.

In the fall of 1994, entertainment companies Columbia Pictures, Disney, MCA/Universal, MGM / United Artists, Paramount, Viacom, and Warner Bros. jointly formed the Hollywood Digital Video Disc Advisory Group in order to call for a new optical digital video format. Ideally, this new format would supplant videotape as the industry's preferred home entertainment delivery medium.[31] Two months later, electronics manufacturers Sony and Philips responded by announcing plans for the Multimedia CD (MMCD), a video disc that would provide what the advisory group was seeking. Soon thereafter, a competing camp comprising Hitachi, JVC, Matsushita, Mitsubishi, Pioneer, Thomson, and Toshiba announced their own competing standard, the Super Density Disc (SD). Because the Advisory Group called for a single global standard, the MMCD and SD camps would either have to compromise or one would have to cede its ground—paths neither seemed willing to take. Although both sides filed patents for their respective technologies, neither would be able to offer Hollywood films without studio-approved copy protection and region code systems.[32] Eventually, several computing companies including Apple, Compaq, Hewlett-Packard, IBM, and

Microsoft intervened, trying to persuade each group to agree to a single standard. This took several months, but in December 1995 the DVD Consortium (the original name of the aforementioned DVD Forum) formed out of a consensus between the MMCD and SD alliances.[33] The Consortium/Forum would be responsible for developing, standardizing, and promoting the DVD technology.

The development and standardization process included a long tug of war between studios and manufacturers over region codes. A March 1996 trade report indicated that the idea for region codes had been "floating around for months" and that a group of Hollywood studios had met the previous year to include region codes on their "wish list" for the DVD.[34] At the same time, manufacturers and the home video industry trade press expressed their doubts. One news report from 1996 noted, in what would become a trend, that consumer electronics manufacturers "hate" region codes.[35] *Video Business* magazine suggested that while DVD was "meant to be the first truly global playback device . . . the studios' insistence on regional coding will make a DVD player no more universal than a conventional VCR."[36] Whereas the studios wanted a globally differentiated system in order to maintain staggered release schedules, hardware and software manufacturers preferred to make and distribute their products as easily and efficiently as possible—something they could not do if they needed to make a different product for each region. Complicating all this was that the computing industry also wanted to include DVD-ROM drives in home computers because of the format's significant storage capacity.[37] While region codes would ultimately not apply to PC software discs and only to DVD-Video discs played in a computer's disc drive, the need to satisfy the home computing industry along with the studios and consumer electronics manufacturers meant that any region code system would inevitably arise out of a compromise that would work against the least powerful players.

Disagreements over region codes and other IP protection measures kept the DVD off shelves even after the stakeholders involved agreed on many of the format's other specifications. By July 1996, MGM / United Artists Home Entertainment president Richard Cohen predicted accurately that if copy protection issues and region codes were not hammered out soon, a fall launch for the format would be unlikely.[38] Agreements on regional coding were still not in place at the September

1996 DVD Forum conference in Brussels, as DVD manufacturers continued to object to the studios' attempts to force their hand in installing region codes.[39] Manufacturers also indicated during the conference that consumers in territories like Russia, China, and South America tended to buy their VCRs from other countries; they wondered how these consumers would cope in a more disjunctive digital media environment.[40] However, the region code's technological specifications and geographic contours were finalized soon thereafter. In late September, manufacturers agreed in principle on a system that would divide the world into six geographic regions (Hollywood had initially wanted eight).[41] In January 1997, Sony and Warner Bros. announced that DVDs—complete with region codes—would be available in the United States by April.[42]

Even after the technology hit shelves, however, region codes were not making many people happy. Non-US distributors and retailers felt that region codes were hindering their business, consumer electronics companies protested that they made DVD manufacturing inefficient, and Hollywood was confronted with a system that did not work as well as the studios had hoped. For different reasons, manufacturers were also upset by the DVD's globally segmented configuration. Not only did it add extra steps in the design and manufacturing processes, it meant they could not reroute products meant for one market to another in order to satisfy demand.[43] At the same time, studios began to notice that region codes proved somewhat ineffective in stalling parallel imports. Even during the technology's earliest years, the complaint that DVD region codes were not fulfilling their goals grew louder.[44] A 2000 *Billboard* article's headline states, bluntly, "DVD Regional Coding Not Working."[45] In response, the major studios pushed for the development of a stronger region code called Region Code Enhancement (RCE), with the major change being that Region One DVDs equipped with RCE would be unplayable in region-free players. The results were mixed, with RCE likewise failing to operate as stringently as the studios would have liked.[46] Adding insult to injury, Blockbuster Video argued in 2003 that not only did region codes fail to stall international gray markets, but DVD pirates were in fact exploiting the time between international runs (which, of course, was shored up by region codes) in order to put out their own product ahead of official releases.[47] Still, even if region codes remained porous, they protected the bottom line well enough that Hollywood and other global cultural industries have been in no rush to get rid of them. Despite critiques that region codes were ineffectual and predictions that they would be short-lived, the mechanism still operates in DVDs and Blu-ray—even if the latter has loosened its guidelines somewhat in an age of increased simultaneous release (i.e., releasing a film to theaters, home video, and streaming in multiple markets all at once).[48] That the region code system remains in place, but with a few concessions, indicates an ongoing tension between global fluidity and intellectual property control.

As this history shows, region codes were consciously, intentionally, and artificially installed in the DVD standard. In other words, nothing about the DVD *as a video compression and transmission technology* required the use of region codes. This may seem obvious, but Jonathan Sterne reminds us that because technological specifications are often hidden to users, we think of them as natural components of a technology rather than intentionally crafted mechanisms.[49] If indeed we often take technical specs for granted, it is worth shedding light on the practices and unquestioned ideologies that guide their implementation. The DVD's technical standard—including its region code system—has no innate qualities that exist outside or before human intervention. People working for a cluster of major media corporations with specific, profit-driven motives built the entire technology. Thus, region codes exemplify a now-commonplace critical interpretation of media technologies: as manufacturers and cultural industries manipulate the technology's code, user practices can be shaped and delimited in ways that reflect cultural industries' preferred uses.[50] Regional lockout systems like DVD region codes characterize what Julian Kilker refers to as "meta-control," or the ways technology designers shape and define a technology's interactive elements—essentially, what the user can and cannot control.[51] For example, when we pop in a DVD, we can control whether we watch the film itself or one of the special features, or we can turn on audio commentary by interacting with the DVD menu. However, we cannot change the region code on a Region Three disc to ensure that it plays in a Region One player.

Region codes are thus a form of technological regulation, but not primarily a legislative or state-based one. Rather, they were created and have been maintained in the private sector through processes of global governance.[52] In the case of DVD region codes (and DVD technology more broadly), governance manifests as not only the continued control and regulation of the DVD standard, but also the development of that technology in the first place. The standard creators and regulators are not impartial actors but a consortium of companies—the DVD Forum—who would eventually profit from DVD hardware and software. Thus, although the governance of digital media with little state interference might seem like a tech-libertarian panacea, in reality it tends to serve the most powerful corporate players involved. While audiovisual standards are often presented through the rhetoric of a free and open market, more often than not they affirm traditional media industry oligopolies.[53] Developing *international* standards in particular helps the cultural industries maintain their bottom lines while expanding their economies of scale, and audiovisual digital standards in general have contributed greatly to media globalization in a number of forms.[54] Region codes are nothing if not an oligopolistic attempt to control lucrative international distribution routes through digital code.

While private-sector institutions shaped region codes, legal mechanisms shored them up. In the studios' view, laws would be necessary to keep industries and users alike compliant with region codes and other DRM systems. As one Twentieth Century Fox executive asked, "Without legislation, what do you have?"[55] International treaties and national laws affirmed the legality of region codes as well as the illegality of hacking or circumventing them. In 1996, the United Nations World Intellectual Property Organization (WIPO) developed an international treaty on copyright, the guidelines of which have been implemented by national and transnational laws and regulations around the world. To comply with the WIPO treaty, the Unites States passed the Digital Millennium Copyright Act (DMCA) in 1998, which among other things broadly restricted the sale and use of technologies meant to break or bypass DRM. This included provisions outlawing the circumvention of CSS, region codes, and other digital IP protection systems. Many users did not take kindly to this set of conditions. In the early 2000s, the US Copyright Office prepared a report on possible exemptions to the DMCA that included more public complaints on the region code system than any other issue. Despite this, the Office rejected a proposal to legalize hacking and circumvention, and region codes remain protected by the DMCA to this day.[56]

Lest this sound like the dealings of a shadowy cartel meeting in a secret, Strangelovian war room, all available evidence suggests that the day-to-day practice of this oligopolistic form of governance reflected the more banal enterprise of conference calls, meetings, and other trappings of contemporary global business culture. Region codes were created by executives flitting across the world to meetings and conferences in Los Angeles, Tokyo, Dublin, and a host of other cities. Much like the television program salespeople Timothy Havens describes in his book on the global television marketplace, this international business culture of consumer electronics, computing, and entertainment industry executives and middle managers helped shape the last twenty years of global home video distribution.[57] As the history described above indicates, this long process of networking could be contentious, with various parties using the trade press to snipe at one another and force the hands of the other stakeholders involved. One 1996 report quotes a Toshiba spokesman saying, "We expected that these matters, copy protection and regional coding, would be solved earlier."[58] MGM/UA exec Richard Cohen (quoted above) took his fellow studio heads to task more bluntly: "We have the opportunity to have one of the biggest, most successful launches of a product ever, or we can blow it . . . I think there are a bunch of people being short-sighted and narrow-minded and self-serving who should get off their ass."[59] DVD region codes illustrate the forces of contemporary media globalization not just in their attempts to maintain distribution paths, but also in their emergence out of an often conflictual, and personal, transnational business project.

Representing and Coding Regions

These tales set in corporate boardrooms and legislative chambers might lead one to think that region codes operate only through legal, economic, and technological forms of power. Beyond this, however, they are also a system of media discourse and representation. They offer a way of talking about, defining, and making sense of the world and its territories. Patrick Vonderau has called for a greater degree of attention to the "ontology work" that goes into the creation of digital markets—how markets are made *real* in the minds of industrial players.[60] According to Vonderau, cultural industries conjure digital video markets in part through "representational practices," or "activities that contribute to the depiction of markets and/or how they work."[61] These transform markets from abstract entities into realizable, representable things with their own geographies, cultures, and economies. The cultural industries' definition and mapping of geographic markets, as well as the ensuing business practices based on these maps and definitions, are not merely decisions based on externally defined, preexisting geographies. Industrial players arrange and create those geographies in their own interests. Scholars of media and culture tend to think of representation in terms of mediated sounds and images of people, places, and cultures. We talk about representations of race, gender, sexuality, and other forms of identity. Because region codes are functionally invisible to users—as digital code in hardware and software—it may seem an odd place to invoke the issue of representation. However, consider the fact that the region code system operates through a series of numbers that correspond with certain nations and regions. These numbers represent particular places by virtue of standing in for them, just as all representations tell us something about the actual person, group, or thing represented. The numbers are therefore more than just instrumental. Designating the United States as Region One and Mexico as Region Four, for example, is meaningful in its implied hierarchy: region code logic reinforces American privilege.[62] This is one simple, clear example, but traditional lines of privilege are present throughout many representations of region codes as well as in how region codes *themselves* represent the world. Maps, trade reportage, and industry lore are all forms of discourse that represent nations and regions in particular ways, all filtered through the dominant logics of global media industries.

The region code map is the most apparent example of region codes as a form of representation. The map shows up in DVD player instruction manuals, onscreen interfaces, online retail sites, and other sources users might consult to try to figure out why their DVD player is not working (or, more accurately, why it is working exactly the way it is supposed to by disabling playback). A seemingly banal, functional way for people to visualize which DVDs and DVD players they need to buy, the map is actually a jarring travesty of accepted global geography. Upon first glance it looks familiar, but look at it long enough and you begin to discover color-coding, borders, and territorial alignments that do not reflect traditional understandings of how the world is mapped out. South Africa and Japan are apparently part of Europe, while the rest of Africa is aligned with Russia, Mongolia, and South Asia. Latin America and Australia are together. China exists on its own, often colored in red in a perhaps unintentional—but nevertheless telling—reminder of Cold War geopolitics. Indeed, the map brings to mind heavily gerrymandered congressional districts, where the wills of powerful institutions over-come coherent renderings of established geography and culture.

The map asserts industry-driven logics of macro-scale geography, making them seem natural and objective rather than arbitrary and con-structed. But while cartography is nominally a science, maps represent the world in ways that reflect mapmakers' (literal) worldviews. Seem-ingly innate borders are in fact representations of the world, with all the implications of subjectivity, synecdoche, and social construction that "representation" implies. John Krygier and Denis Wood remind us that "mapmakers proposition you with different realities," and the re-gion code map is a proposition about the world's hierarchical shape put forward by media executives.[63] It exemplifies what Edward Said would call an "imaginative geography" developed by the media industries.[64] Because imaginative geography helps structure power and knowledge about places and people in the world, the DVD region code map is more than just a mechanism to make sure consumers do not accidentally buy the wrong DVDs. The map is a form of power enacted on the globe by a number of media institutions and a text that people inside and outside the media industries interpret in order to make sense of the world.[65] The arrangement of global spaces within this hierarchically organized map perpetuates powerful discrimination within and beyond the media in-dustries. It reflects and shapes relations of geocultural capital—both as-serting which territories are more privileged in circuits of global media access and visualizing a system meant to keep these lines of privilege in place.

By making a claim on the "regional" as a useful category for the media industries, region codes and their attending maps helped define what regions were and what they meant to Hollywood at the beginning of a digital era. The DVD's geographic scope and scale were at the front of executives' minds during the format's long gestation. Much of a 1998 professional conference organized by the editor of *Inside Multimedia* was taken up by debates over whether the DVD as a medium would be fundamentally global, regional, or national.[66] The region code map and nomenclature suggest that the answer would be regional, but "region" in this particular DRM system masks more than it reveals. The region code map is constructed out of negotiated industry decisions regarding which nations belonged together. It draws on an established understanding of region as a geographic category—namely, a cluster of culturally and geographically proximate countries—in order to legitimize and make sense of the unusual groupings of countries that make up the region code map. Indeed, while DVD region codes partially follow the contours of markets defined through traditional geocultural and geolinguistic lines, they do not follow them exactly. Rather, they indicate that industrial trade routes' regional divisions are determined by regions' perceived similarities and differences as *economic* markets primarily—hence sub-Saharan Africa, South Asia, the Middle East, and Eastern Europe being lumped together as one "region." The framing of the system as *regional* is what Anna Tsing calls a "scale-making project," which makes claims on what the size and scale of the world and its divisible spatial territories mean to institutions and their interests. In the region code system's scale-making project, the region is not an empirical category that exists between the national and global, but rather an idea that the media industries constitute and use toward a particular economic goal.[67]

Industry lore and "trade storytelling" about region codes likewise reflect this understanding of the region as a useful, industry-constructed mechanism rather than a stable, objective geographic entity.[68] A 2001 *Consumer Electronics* piece quotes extensively from a memo by the Hollywood studios that detailed the rationale behind each region, which each reflect a combination of cultural, regulatory, and economic logics. It indicates that Mexico was split from Region One (the United States and Canada) and included in Region Four in part to "harmonize" the country as a distribution window with the rest of Latin America.[69] The split reflects a certain logic in the media industries that builds markets out of different territories that Hollywood's international distributors and marketers perceive as having some commonalities—perhaps commonalities of language, culture, and geography, but even more important, commonalities of potential as markets to exploit. To the industrial entities that built region codes, Canada and the United States have certain similarities, and Mexico's similarities lie more readily with the rest of Latin America. Given the ways differently coded DVDs have been used to distribute DVDs with different languages to a variety of locations around the world, the inclusion of Mexico with the rest of Latin America indicates the role language has in shaping the world's home video markets. Aside from this regional "harmonization," however, there was a functional reason to place Mexico in a separate region from the United States and Canada: fears of parallel imports. Since Mexican DVD prices would be lower than those in the United States, the studios added Mexico to Region Four to forestall the sale in the United States of DVDs meant for Mexico.[70] Often, this attempt to close off parallel imports aligned with linguistic commonalities to shape the regional placement of certain nations. The memo also indicates that Japan and South Korea were placed in Region Two and Australia in Region Four in order to minimize parallel imports of Region One DVDs in those territories—a potential problem due to these nations' high number of English-speaking consumers. Because language differences could not act as a natural barrier against parallel imports, the territories were placed in their own region code. Similarly, due to studio fears of piracy in China, that country (though not Hong Kong, which is included in Region Three) was placed into its own region (Six). Regions came out of the pragmatics of media distribution as much as through actual geocultural proximity.

Some places did not apparently rank highly enough as markets to be considered at even this level. In an indication of how region codes both reflect and structure relations of geocultural capital, a broad swath of what the memo refers to as "underdeveloped theatrical markets" such as South Asia, most of Africa (except for South Africa and Egypt—both Region Two), and Russia were all placed together in Region Five.[71] Referring to these places as underdeveloped brings to mind theories of media modernization and development that began to circulate in the mid-twentieth century and have shaped both American cultural policy and Hollywood's view of the world's media markets. Here, modernity as a set of social, psychological, governmental, and economic conditions, and development and modernization as processes leading to that condition, usually refer to archetypically

Western ideals of scientific rationality, control of advanced technologies, and flourishing capitalism. Territories that are less developed or modern, according to these views, tend to lie in the Middle East, Latin America, sub-Saharan Africa, and other postcolonial regions of the Global South. As a driver of global capitalism, Hollywood measures the development of a market in terms of sufficiency in economic and technological infrastructure. It also articulates modernity in the terms of geocultural capital by suggesting that less modernized territories do not enjoy the wealth of cultural resources available in the Global North. As is always the case, referring to a territory as developed or not is not just a rational economic decision, and it aligns with well-established forms of cultural discrimination and oppression against people living throughout the Global South based on the idea that they are behind the times or otherwise backward.

As this suggests, region codes came to have cultural meanings and significance beyond their functional and technical capabilities. Within industry discourse and trade reportage, tropes and stereotypes associated with global cultures and otherness became a kind of shorthand for talking about region codes.[72] A DVD player review in *Popular Electronics* warns, "If someone from Region Two (Europe and Japan) tries to play a DVD obtained from Region One, it's not supposed to run in his or her *indigenous* player. The same principle applies if you pick up some DVDs while on vacation in Mexico (Region Four) that seem to be a steal at the currency exchange rate. They're not supposed to play in your U.S. Region One deck."[73] Similarly, a 1996 *Variety* report on the interindustry disputes over the implementation of the region code system includes an illustration where individuals representing cultural stereotypes— Japanese geisha; Bavarian man in lederhosen; and British man with mustache, bowler hat, and umbrella—plant flags on a globe marked "DVD" in order to claim their territory on the global home video landscape.[74] In 1999, Disney released a number of animated films in the Mexican market on discs encoded in both Region One and Region Four. A trade report noted that such releases would "boast dual citizenship of sorts."[75] In such examples, the DVD stands in metonymically for people and cultures, indicating that media's connection to cultural difference and identity reaches even further beyond onscreen images, reception, or labor. Its presence can be felt in the technology itself.

Region Four

The question of which countries belonged to which regions animated much of the controversy around region codes. A territory's placement within one of the hierarchically ordered regions was a statement about geocultural capital in the global DVD market—which countries owned a great deal, which did not, and how they might be lumped together based on their wealth and poverty of media resources. Perhaps no part of the world better exemplifies region codes' functional and representational dynamics of inclusion and exclusion than Australia and (to a somewhat lesser extent) New Zealand, where the technology was highly contested among consumers, consumer rights groups, media industries, and politicians alike. Functionally, region codes meant that consumers in these countries could not play Region One or Two DVDs without a region-free player and were stuck with Region Four DVDs, which tended toward later release dates and lower audiovisual quality. Beyond that, because region codes are also a site of media representation and discourse, the placement of Australia and New Zealand in Region Four resulted in much talk about how these nations could be defined through the strength and status of their media economies. After the DVD Forum settled on the region code system in 1997, Australian consumer electronics and software distributors expressed dismay about the nation's placement in Region Four. A report from that year on the widespread use in the country of region-free DVD players imported from Asia touches on this disappointment, highlighting DVD distributors' laments about Hollywood's attitude that Australia was "too small, too poor and too linguistically diverse to make it viable for studios to release any DVD movies in Region Four other than those which have already proved to be box-office hits." In response, distributors hoped to be included in Region One or Two, with the United States or Europe, respectively.[76] Such debates touch on Australia's complicated relationship to the geocultural construction of "the West" and its Anglo-American contingent in particular. The country's English colonial and linguistic heritage and hegemonic whiteness align it with the United States / UK / Canada axis while its geographic location, Aboriginal and diasporic cultures, and economic status mark it as not quite *of* the West as traditionally defined. Given this, the suggestion that Australia should be included in Region

One expresses a desire to operate at a similar level of privilege in the global cultural economy as the United States and the UK. For this reason, Australian protests against region codes do not always call for the elimination of the system full stop; occasionally, they simply want to be considered part of the same privileged market.

Discussions about Australia's geocultural capital in global DVD markets were apparent in discourse surrounding intellectual property and parallel import, which have long been central to debates within Australian media industries.[77] Throughout the late 1990s and 2000s, consumer groups, journalists, and politicians in Australia and New Zealand lambasted region codes as a measure of North American dominance that unfairly closed off the region and its denizens from full integration into the global media economy. In 2001, Australian economists argued that that DVD price discrimination sustained by region codes "may benefit the seller but it will often lead to a social loss" due to the negative impact on the Australian consumer.[78] Focusing on one of these social losses, a 2004 piece in the *New Zealand Herald* states bluntly, "Film studios want to control what we can and cannot watch, and have devised region-encoded DVDs to ensure this."[79] Here, rather than taking them as a measure of market segmentation and staggered releases, the author interprets region codes as a detriment to personal freedoms caused by Hollywood's global dominance. Indeed, a common theme of Australian and New Zealander discourse about region codes held that as the countries strengthened their IP laws in order to comply with the desires of American corporations, local consumers got the raw end of the deal.[80]

Soon enough, anger at region codes led to legal challenges that loosened domestic restrictions on region-free media. The Australian Competition and Consumer Commission (ACCC), Australia's chief consumer watchdog group, expressed its disapproval of region codes and by the end of 2000 began an investigation into whether the price discrimination practices propped up by the technology violated fair trade agreements.[81] In 2002, the ACCC began an investigation as to whether the studios illegally colluded when forming the region code system and announced it would intervene in a court case filed by Sony against an Australian who sold PlayStation mod chips that would allow users to bypass region-coded discs. Here, the ACCC acted as a friend of the court in order to "challenge Sony's claim that anti-circumvention provisions of copyright law made region code modifications illegal."[82] As the chairman of the ACCC argued, "This is a private agreement to divide up the world market, and we believe it is probably unlawful and one we are investigating."[83] After several years of battles, the High Court of Australia legalized the circumvention of DVD region codes in 2006. Specifically, the court ruled that while hacking the DVD's broader CSS copy protection remained illegal, this did not apply to the region code technology specifically.[84]

More recently, these issues flared up again with New Zealand and Australia's participation in an international trade agreement among Pacific Rim nations known as the Trans-Pacific Partnership (TPP). Initially, and at the behest of the United States, the TPP included strict limits on copying audiovisual material, including prohibitions against hacking and circumventing region codes similar to those put in place by the DMCA. Tech reporters pointed out that these rules could outlaw the use of region-free DVD players.[85] This would also make it easier for states to take legal action against people using proxies or virtual private networks to get around online geoblocks, since doing so would violate a company's distribution rights within a certain window. The United States would thus be imposing its own intellectual property rules and restrictions on the citizens of other countries. Activists and legal experts in New Zealand and Australia reacted strongly against these proposed limits, which led one district court judge in New Zealand to quip, "We have met the enemy and he is [the] U.S."[86] A purported final draft of the TPP, released by WikiLeaks in 2015, indicated that despite such protests, the agreement would indeed implement regulations enabling the prosecution of users who try to bypass geoblocking.[87] A version of the TPP that included these anti-circumvention provisions was ratified in 2016 but then jeopardized by the Trump administration pulling the United States from the agreement. A new version called the Comprehensive and Progressive Agreement for Trans-Pacific Partnership (CPTPP) was approved by the remaining nations in 2018. After the United States left the agreement, most of the provisions regarding intellectual property were suspended, making the CPTPP much less concerned with digital technology circumvention than the TPP was.[88]

Nevertheless, that regional lockout can elicit such animosity between allied states indicates its power to spur international tensions and feelings of discrimination related to geocultural capital. In Australia, this intensified at a moment when policy makers and cultural industries were increasingly attuned to the idea that art, media, and culture were "something of national economic and social significance, a public good."[89] Here, the articulation of DVD distribution to broader forces of national identity and global belonging animated an opposing set of arguments. On the one hand, the perceived injustice of region codes brings about feelings of geographic and cultural discrimination. Consider how one might respond to the "too small, too poor" quotation cited above, which touches on both economic and geocultural forms of capital. On the other hand, some in favor of DVD region codes take a protectionist stance, arguing that the system minimizes American dominance by enabling a healthier *local* DVD market. Australia in the early 2000s was marked with anxieties over the definition of its national popular culture audience in the face of globalization and internationalization.[90] These anxieties reflected conversations about whether the Australian media industries should be closed off from encroaching global processes or part of a media economy based in free trade. While some saw region codes as unfairly forestalling access to global culture, these same debates also brought out a contingent that saw region codes as protecting local media industries. As Dunt, Gans, and King summarize this line of argument, if region codes and a ban on parallel imports enable higher prices for Australian consumers, the Australian cultural industries (and in particular local DVD distributors and film producers) would benefit through higher profits.[91] On both ends of this debate, we can see the invocation of national or regional identity and even pride—whether in the suggestion that Australians and New Zealanders do not deserve the shabby treatment that comes with placement in Region Four or in the argument that region codes would in fact strengthen local media sectors. The early to mid-2000s arguments regarding Oceania's inclusion in Region Four function as a desire for the region to exist in a more elevated position in global media hierarchies, emphasizing the relationship between the region code system and the global distribution of cultural status via home video markets.

More than simply a technological curio, then, DVD region codes involve complex relationships among international trade agreements, nation-based intellectual property regulation, cultural difference and representation, and media access. While DVD did much to center these concerns within global conversations about media distribution, more niche communities of video game fans had been dealing with these issues for well over a decade before the DVD's release. The history of regional lockout in game consoles begins earlier than the DVD, and over time the use of regional lockout within these two industries would run parallel to and occasionally intersect each other. Just as DVD region codes reflected the cultural and economic circumstances leading to the DVD's emergence and global presence, regional lockout in console games reflects the particular transnational dynamics of a largely (though not exclusively) Japanese and American industry. Beyond questions of geography, console video game regional lockout raised questions about user empowerment and agency touched on briefly in this chapter. Indeed, the game industry often found itself at loggerheads with various factions of a gaming community that had long since developed an interest in hacking and "modding" hardware and software in order to use the technology in ways unintended and unforeseen by the industries that created them. Ironically, though, regional lockout also helped *produce* game culture by inspiring a demand and market for difficult-to-find overseas games. The next chapter shows how, in its own way, regional lockout could be simultaneously restrictive and productive for users.

2

Console Games

How Regional Lockout Shaped the Video Game Industry

In 2013, Twitter user @lite_agent tweeted at Dan Adelman, then head of Nintendo's indie development initiative, asking him to help make the company's handheld 3DS console region-free. Up to that point, the company's previous handhelds (Game Boy, Game Boy Advance, DS) lacked region codes, but the 3DS bucked that trend and ensured that games purchased in Japan would not play on US consoles—and vice versa. In response, Adelman tweeted, "I too used to live in Japan. Had 2 SNESs—one Japanese, one US. I feel your pain."[1] Although a seemingly innocuous commiseration over a common annoyance among gamers, Adelman's tweet also served as a complaint about his employer's distribution policy. As a result, it put him in a bit of hot water. The next year, video game publication *Gamasutra* posted an article suggesting that Nintendo banned Adelman from tweeting and conducting an interview with the publication due to his comments about regional lockout.[2] A few months later, he offered an update on Twitter: "Happy to announce I reached an arrangement w/ @NintendoAmerica whereby I can tweet again. Arrangement includes my not working there anymore."[3] That Nintendo would protect its DRM policy so tightly as to stonewall and ultimately drive out one of its own executives suggests that, in the eyes of the company, regional lockout's legitimacy cannot be questioned.

Locked Out began with the DVD region code because of how well the technology crystalizes the relationship between digital regulation and global cultural hierarchies. However, regional lockout in video games predates the DVD by a number of years. Regional incompatibility has been an issue since the early days of home gaming on platforms like the Commodore 64 and the Atari 2600, and regional lockout as a way of *intentionally* controlling distribution dates back to the Nintendo Entertainment System / Famicom in the mid-1980s.[4] While the specific technological mechanisms have shifted—from physical impediments on cartridges and consoles to complex arrangements of software and firmware—regional lockout has sustained the console game industry's particular "Japan-West" geographic dynamic for several decades. It has done so by controlling the flow of games and consoles among the industry's largest regional markets—North America, Japan, and Western Europe—and enabling the industry to treat each market as a distinct entity.[5] Like other forms of regional lockout, this draws lines and sketches hierarchies of geocultural capital in global video game culture, prohibiting or allowing certain types of play in different parts of the world. In the context of a game industry highly concerned with localization, region codes and chips are as much about adapting games to particular markets as they are about intellectual property control and price discrimination. By ensuring that Japanese software could not play on American hardware (and vice versa), regional lockout in the Japan-West nexus allowed game developers to create different versions of games for American and Japanese consumers.[6]

The existence of these local adaptations resulted in consumers and collectors seeking out different international versions of games. Within transnational gaming cultures, regional lockout provided conditions for the cultivation of "hardcore" gamers, who invest a great deal of time, money, and knowledge on video games.[7] That effort results in the accumulation of what Mia Consalvo calls "gaming capital," or the (sub)cultural capital that comes with insider knowledge of video games, game culture, and the game industry.[8] An understanding of regional lockout, and how to bypass it, is one component of gaming capital and a way of demonstrating fluency in video game technology, culture, and institutions. Hardcore gamer identity involves knowledge about the Japan–United States–Europe geographical shape of the game industry: where particular companies and publishers are based, how they divide their markets, which games they make available to which territories, and how to access consoles and games meant for other nations. Regional lockout helps *produce* global gaming cultures and gamer identity since it shapes people's gaming experiences and functions as a site where users from around the world gain and share knowledge about games.

Thus, I argue in this chapter that regional lockout was a central force in shaping the geographic parameters and political economies of formal and informal console video game industries as well as the participatory consumer cultures that formed around them. After providing a cultural history of regional lockout in the big-budget, high-profile consoles produced by companies like Atari, Nintendo, Sega, Sony, and Microsoft, I show how regional lockout helped build and sustain subcultures of hardcore gamers by giving them a common annoyance, creating a canon of sought-after rare and imported games, and encouraging hacking and modding activities that became central to the hardcore gamer identity.[9] Ironically, then, the ability to circumvent regional lockout and violate preferred distribution paths is part of a constructed (and gendered) "gamer" identity that has been quite beneficial to the game industry. This is in part what makes regional lockout in video games different from DVD region codes and other examples explored throughout the book. While DVD region codes and geoblocked streaming platforms have been important components of global media distribution and exhibition, neither have been quite as central to the consumer culture built around their respective platforms.

Distribution, Regional Lockout, and Console Video Games

The console sits at the center of the game industry and the gaming experience. The major console manufacturers, who operate as an oligopoly, drive the industry by producing the hardware for which most video games are produced.[10] On one level, these consoles are simple pieces of technology: collections of wires, circuits, and chips encased within a plastic shell. However, Ben Aslinger argues that the console is also an "[artifact] of modern industrial design" that becomes fetishized through both its technological characteristics and its aesthetic qualities.[11] While game development studios and publishers are undoubtedly crucial to building the games we play, players are more likely to identify (and identify with) a particular console than a particular studio.[12] However, the console is but one facet of the gaming experience, and the console manufacturer but one player in the game industry. Games still need to attract to users, and the routes they take set the terms for the shape of regional lockout in video games.

In the path from production to consumption, games move through a supply chain run by a number of intermediaries, the different parts of which are summarized by Peter Zackariasson and Timothy Wilson:

Developer => Publisher => Distributor => Retailer => Customer => Consumer[13]

Distribution—as the process by which a game moves from the zone of production (the developer) to the zone of consumption (the customer and consumer)—can be located within the publisher, distributor, and retailer zones. Publishers handle the release of games on consoles, marketing and promoting these titles to distributors. The top game publishers are mostly multinational companies based in North America and Japan. Distributors then operate as intermediaries or wholesalers that sell these games to retailers. Developers, publishers, and distributors are not always separate entities. Particularly for larger companies, development, publication, and distribution might represent arms or extensions of one corporation. For example, the same conglomerate handled the development, publication, and distribution of the massively popular *Grand Theft Auto V*. Development studio Rockstar North, an Edinburgh-based subsidiary of Rockstar Games, developed the game initially for PlayStation 3 and Xbox 360. Rockstar Games served as publisher, and Rockstar's parent company, Take-Two Interactive, distributed the game to retailers often using distribution subsidiaries like the UK-based Exertis Gem.

The importance of software sales to the console game industry puts a premium on controlling distribution. Because games do not have secondary windows such as home video or syndication in the film and television industries, initial sales of a game are crucial to the bottom lines of console manufacturers, game developers, and publishers.[14] Console manufacturers make little money from the units themselves, which are usually loss leaders.[15] Rather, profit comes from money they receive from game sales as well as the license fees paid by publishers.[16] In order to release a game on a console, publishers and developers must pay this license fee to the console company and sign contracts agreeing to manufacturers' quality and technological standards, which usually include lockout and DRM systems. Not all of these are region-based. Many are designed to keep independent game developers and publishers from releasing games without the consent of the console manufacturer. Other agreements, however, required developers and publishers to region-lock games according to the desires of the console manufacturer, though this has changed somewhat over time. While console manufacturers still maintain the greatest amount of control over the games that get played on their systems, including decisions about whether they are region-locked, game developers and publishers have more recently had a say in such matters.

The game industry's economic rationale for regional lockout extends beyond abstract notions of control and power. Rather, Barry Ip and Gabrielle Jacobs point to two justifications for regional lockout in games: protecting against piracy / parallel imports and maintaining the quality of games and software.[17] As Consalvo reminds us, the industry employs regional lockout to ensure that games flow "only along well-marked paths, designed to ensure careful tracking and control."[18] Because the game industry has always been transnational, it has long had to deal with the issues that come with controlling and guiding commodities at a rather vast scale. Given the ever-increasing importance of global markets, console manufacturers and game publishers and distributors have an obvious interest in controlling distribution, particularly among the industry's three largest regional markets: the United States, Japan, and Europe.[19] As with DVDs, part of the reasoning is price discrimination—a strategy that became even more important as the industry globalized. There are other reasons for regional lockout, such as ensuring the ability to control games' content based on different regions' ratings systems. When asked why its handheld DSi console was region-locked, Nintendo's UK general manager David Yarnton argued that because Nintendo UK subscribed to the Pan European Game Information ratings system, it made sense to lock out other territories that have different content restriction guidelines.[20] This way, users from regions with stricter restrictions would be barred from importing mature-rated games from the UK. The game industry also often suggests that regional lockout helps it localize games for certain markets and ensures that it can distribute certain versions of games to different territories. However, this is not merely a benign process of giving the people what they want. The ability to control localization helps the major companies like Nintendo, Sony, and Microsoft consolidate their power over the localization process by using it to shape content, release dates, and prices according to their desires.

Reterritorializing Games: Regional Lockout's Origins

In the early days of home console gaming, international restrictions were not intentional forms of DRM as much as they resulted from the same incompatibilities that hampered the international videotape trade. Because consoles like the Atari 2600 connected to analog televisions, they were beholden to the three different analog color standards: PAL, NTSC, and SECAM. Because PAL and NTSC televisions operate using different numbers of scan lines and frames per second, the Atari could not automatically adjust to the television. As a result, different consoles and games had to be developed for each system.[21] Systems built for one standard were incompatible with another, which led to an early form of regional disconnect driven not by the profit motives of media companies but by the contingencies of divergent technical standards. Even if the Atari 2600 did not contain any intentional regional lockouts, its technical makeup meant that games and consoles intended for one region were effectively contained to that region.[22]

DRM systems that would set a template for regional lockout arrived in the next generations of game consoles. In 1983, Japanese toy company Nintendo released an eight-bit home video game console in Japan known as the Famicom, short for Family Computer. Three years later, the company introduced the North American version, called the Nintendo Entertainment System (NES). The NES (though not the Famicom) included a Checking Integrated Circuit (CIC) lockout chip that ran a program called 10NES wherein the console and the cartridge needed to handshake before a game would run on the system. Although it does not contain regional controls, this form of lockout is functionally comparable to the DVD region codes described in the previous chapter for a few reasons. For one, it relies on an agreement between hardware and software in order to let the software play. In addition, it ensures that certain parties in the game industry maintain control over the production, distribution, and use of the technologies. In this case, the CIC and 10NES were early forms of DRM that placed the console manufacturer (i.e., Nintendo) in the driver's seat.[23] While the chip was installed nominally to prevent the production of counterfeit games, it effectively meant that any company had to get Nintendo's approval before developing a title. This strict control over games produced for the system was key to Nintendo's domination of the market in the late 1980s and early 1990s.[24]

While Nintendo was concerned about controlling game production and development, it also recognized the need to keep distinct its two dominant markets, Japan and the United States. Because both nations use the NTSC system, the company could not rely on disagreeing television standards to keep games from moving between the two. As a result, the Famicom and the NES were region-locked through more overtly physical, material means: the number of pins on the cartridge board and the shape of the cartridge. Whereas the board in a Famicom cartridge contained only sixty pins, the NES cartridge had seventy-two. A handful of early NES cartridges were also built with Famicom boards rather than NES boards, and these contained sixty- to seventy-two-pin converters. This form of regional lockout helped the company maintain a measure of control over its different international markets—a level of market control affirmed by the fact that Nintendo had no major competitors during this era.[25] In sum, one reason the company dominated the video game market was because of lockout systems that enabled it to control distribution and kept other companies from producing games for the system without Nintendo's approval.[26]

With the arrival of sixteen-bit consoles, that would soon change. The late 1980s and early 1990s saw the launch of Sega's Mega Drive console, known as the Genesis in North America, and Nintendo's Super Famicom / Super Nintendo Entertainment System. These consoles heralded a more concentrated attempt by game companies to develop regional lockout systems that reflected a move beyond the Japan-America axis that up to that point dominated the industry. Sega's experiments with regional lockouts were, in part, a consequence of the company's move into a variety of international markets (and Europe in particular).[27] Because this meant increased potential for parallel imports, the company's consoles were produced in several different models and regional variations, requiring a complicated system of regional lockouts. Indeed, the region-locked status of the Genesis depended on which model one owned.[28] The first two models of the Genesis used a simple form of physical lockout: Japanese cartridges contained two plastic tabs that kept the cartridge from sliding into American consoles. The third model of the Genesis contained no regional lockouts. However, in a move that later consoles would adopt more regularly, some individual Genesis *games* contained regional lockout software even though the console itself contained none.[29] Because of Sega's aggressive international expansion, which helped the company overtake Nintendo for a short period, Nintendo likewise focused more energy on markets beyond Japan and the United States. As a result, the SNES employed a physical lockout system similar to the Genesis: two plastic tabs within the console's cartridge slot that prevented users from inserting Japanese imports into the console. This functioned on top of the PAL/NTSC disagreements that already disallowed American and Japanese systems from playing European games (and vice versa), and together the two systems used a form of regional lockout combining analog measures and incompatibilities.[30] During this period, the renewed focus on international markets set off a period of video game globalization that would only heighten the importance of regional lockout to the game industry.

As a form of technological-geographic control, regional lockout reflects Dyer-Witheford and de Peuter's argument that games characterize the deterritorializing and reterritorializing functions of global capital. Drawn from the work of Gilles Deleuze and Félix Guattari, deterritorialization and reterritorialization in this sense do not necessarily refer to actual geographic territories. Rather, deterritorialization is a metaphorical explanation of how capital "conjures up fresh products and practices, breaks down old habits, and throws all bounded domains—'territories'—of life, geographic, social, and subjective, into upheaval." It then reterritorializes by "enclosing innovations as property, drawing around them new legal boundaries, and policing access so that new technical machines and cultural creations appear as commodities produced and sold for profit."[31] Regional lockout invites us to take "territory" literally here while still retaining the terms' metaphorical usefulness. In other words, regional restrictions represent contemporary media's deterritorializing and reterritorializing functions at the levels of both geography and their relationship to the movements of capital.[32] Because console games developed as a transnational enterprise during periods of intensifying media globalization, the experience of gaming was for many users an encounter with media texts and technologies that gestured toward a broader world. At the same time, games were also reterritorialized through regional lockout, which closed off consumers' ability to symbolically traverse global space through gaming.

Controlling—and Complicating—Compatibility

With the blueprints for controlling global distribution in place, the subsequent adoption of disc-based digital hardware and software helped the game industry implement more complex forms of regional lockout. As discussed in the previous chapter, optical discs enable media industries to implement forms of regional lockout through DRM, which are less visible and detectable than hard-wired forms of lockout like tabs and differently shaped cartridges. The mid-1990s saw the release of the next generation of thirty-two- and sixty-four-bit game consoles from Nintendo, Sega, and a new player on the scene: the major media conglomerate Sony, which released the thirty-two-bit PlayStation console in Japan in 1994 and the United States and Europe in 1995. Using CD-ROM technology, PlayStation software contained one hundred times the maximum capacity of a cartridge yet was cheaper to manufacture.[33] Although the PlayStation commanded much of the limelight in the mid-1990s, Sega had released its latest console just before Sony. After several disappointing Genesis add-ons (Sega CD, Sega 32X), the company shifted gears toward developing a new thirty-two-bit system that would become the Sega Saturn. Both the PlayStation and the Saturn ran on region-locked CD-ROM technology. The Nintendo 64 console, released around the same time, stuck with cartridges as a way to maintain control over its proprietary hardware and software. Much like the NES and SNES, it used plastic tabs to region-lock the system's cartridges.

The general shift to discs resulted in an era of increasing convergence with formats like the CD and the DVD, which would make regional lockouts and incompatibilities more complex. Consoles were now at once more versatile and dependent on the technical specifications and DRM systems embedded on a variety of different formats. This meant that consoles like Sony's PlayStation 2 (PS2) and Microsoft's Xbox, which used DVD technology, had to have multiple regional lockout systems installed: the DVD's CSS/RPC system for playback of movies *and* any separate regional lockout intended for the games. Regional lockout was thus part of a broader congregation of media convergence, console gaming, and technological incompatibility.[34] While console gaming has always been rife with disconnections and frustrations—planned obsolescence, hardware/software disagreements, and malfunctioning cartridges and discs—regional lockout was a kind of intentional incompatibility that the industry used to lock down its systems. In a media environment rife with DRM, "trusted systems," and "tethered appliances," this approach to controlling compatibility through lockout became increasingly normal.[35] In the eyes of consumers, regional lockout could be considered just another one of those technical hiccups that accompanies the gaming experience. This is all to say that the industrial geography of video game distribution exploited the usual problems of compatibility that plagued game consumers, but in ways that attempted to paper over its profit-driven intentions.

While the PS2, Dreamcast, and GameCube maintained now well-known, console-determined regional lockout systems, the Xbox signaled an incoming shift in the logics of regional lockout: the console itself (or, more precisely, the console's DVD-ROM drive that read *game* discs) was technically region-free. This did not mean that the Xbox offered a fully region-free experience, as game publishers could still region-lock individual games if they desired. However, it represented a change in power from console to publisher, which would become the standard for Microsoft and Sony games in the future. Although its release was roughly concurrent with the three region-locked platforms described above, the Xbox's quasi-region-free status pointed to a growing expectation within game cultures that the industry was on a progressive path forward and that regional restrictions would be consigned to the past. In late 2005, there were rumblings among game publications that the PlayStation 3 may not include any region locks whatsoever, with one report suggesting that this move would mark a "significant shift" for Sony.[36] At the 2006 Game Developer's Conference, Sony Computer Entertainment Worldwide Studios president Phil Harrison announced that the PlayStation 3 would, in fact, be region-free.[37] Early reports even suggested that Nintendo, the old stalwart of regional lockout in the game industry, might go region-free with its next console, the Wii.[38] Ultimately, however, Nintendo maintained its usual approach to regional lockout, announcing in October 2006 that the Wii would be region-locked along the same lines as the GameCube.

Like the original Xbox console, the PS3 and the Xbox 360 could still block games based on region, but this would be determined by the publishers of individual games rather than the console manufacturer. As with the Xbox, this meant that while the consoles were nominally region-free, tracking the region-coded status of games was more difficult because it had to be done on a game-by-game basis. For example, the Japanese and American versions of the PS3 and Xbox 360 game *Persona 4 Arena* were each region-locked to their respective countries.[39] The reason for this was the US dollar's weakness against the yen, as the game's publisher, Atlus, was concerned about cheaper American imports flooding the Japanese market.[40] Indeed, with this new, publisher-led form of regional lockout, particular games could be region-locked due to specific dynamics of market or culture. Adding to the complexity was that the same game on different systems could be region-locked according to different guidelines (or not at all). While by all accounts *Persona 4 Arena* is the first and only PS3 game to include regional lockout, the Xbox 360 platform comprises a large number of region-locked games, some of which are only locked in certain territories. For example, *Grand Theft Auto V* is region-free on every platform (both PS3 and Xbox 360) except for the Japanese Xbox 360, where it is region-locked to Japan.[41] Such convolution led to fan-created resources like wikis that list the region compatibility of hundreds of different games.[42]

Adding more confusion, once again, were different color television standards used around the world. While ongoing shifts away from standard-definition television to high-definition television have mitigated the NTSC/PAL/SECAM issues somewhat, they still keep nominally region-free systems like the PlayStation 3 from being universally usable. While HDTV eliminated the difference in the number of lines of video between PAL and NTSC, therefore standardizing frame size around the world, it did not eliminate the difference in frame *rates*: HD televisions in countries that use the NTSC standard still operate at thirty frames per second while those that use the PAL standard operate at twenty-five. Furthermore, the HDTVs for which contemporary consoles are optimized are not common everywhere in the world.[43] As a result, most region-based hiccups that occur on the PlayStation 3 are similar to the earliest forms of regional incompatibilities in consoles like the Atari 2600 in that they result from diverging standards rather than DRM. At the same time, regional lockout on the Xbox 360 and other disc-based consoles show how new DRM mechanisms become culturally legible and legitimate through their association with these older forms of regional incompatibility. For example, the three regions that guide the Xbox's region coding system are GR1: NTSC for North America and South America (i.e., the United States, Canada, Mexico, Chile, and Brazil), GR2: NTSC-J for Asia, and GR3: PAL for Europe, India, Australia, and New Zealand. Seemingly innocuous, this list in fact does some important discursive work. For one, the numerical order indicates a cultural-economic hierarchy in region coding, just like the six-region DVD codes discussed in the previous chapter. Further, while the names of these regions might suggest that the divergent television standards are the cause of any regional incompatibilities, the regional lockout system is in fact buttressed by a separate region code distinct from these standards. To be sure, playing a PAL disc on an NTSC machine and vice versa would produce some compatibility issues, but the disc's region code is a different technical mechanism only related to the PAL/NTSC standards by name. So, when a user puts a disc into a player from the wrong region and a message appears onscreen suggesting that the disc will not play on the console, it may initially seem like an issue of incompatible television standards. In fact, the user is confronting a form of digital rights management.

This is similar to the conflation of PAL/NTSC and DVD region codes discussed in the previous chapter, and it has the same benefit for the game industry: if consumers *think* regional lockout is related to a seemingly inevitable technological hurdle, they may be less likely to protest. Indeed, a survey of both consumers and video game industry workers indicates that this conflation seems to be working. While many users think that the PAL/NTSC distinction is a significant factor in why the game industry employs regional lockout, industry workers indicate that it is not a factor at all. One developer even admits that the PAL/NTSC issue is a smokescreen put up to mask publishers and distributors' control of market rollout. Rather, the developer delivers a master disc to the publisher that has all languages and region codes on it, and the publisher implements the appropriate ones as it sees fit.[44] In his hacker instruction manual *Gaming Hacks*, Simon Carless distinguishes between "regional differences" and "regional lockouts."[45] The former are unintentional incompatibilities over which developers, publishers, and console manufacturers have little control. The latter are intentionally installed DRM systems meant to control the distribution of games. By blurring this distinction, the game industry asks consumers to view regional lockout as a natural outcome of convergence rather than a consciously developed form of control.

New DRM Debates

Contemporary debates over region-locked consoles have at once shifted into new technological terrain (specifically, region-locked portable consoles and digital distribution systems) and recalled some of the earliest public invocations of regional lockout through new protests against Nintendo. The tendency for some recent consoles to reject regional lockout allayed public concerns about geographic restrictions somewhat, but not before some contentious back-and-forth between the two largest console manufacturers. Industry and public discussions about regional lockout in Microsoft's Xbox One and Sony's PlayStation 4 (both rolled out throughout 2013 and 2014) were part of a broader series of controversies in mid-2013 about DRM in the two consoles. In spring of that year, Microsoft announced that the Xbox One would contain a number of strict DRM measures, including limits on how often you could share a disc-based game as well as a requirement that the console would need to connect to the internet once every twenty-four hours in order to authenticate the system and keep its DRM updated and in place.[46] In addition, the company announced that the console would feature region locks due to "country-specific regulatory guidelines."[47] This brought about a good deal of anger from game consumers and gaming publications. At the time, Microsoft also indicated that the console's initial launch would only include twenty-one countries, leaving out Japan and parts of Europe (in addition to territories across the Global South that the major console industries generally did not bother with anyway).[48] Because the console was to be region-locked, this would effectively preclude these territories from purchasing consoles and games from one of the launch regions. This resulted in public backlash against Microsoft, to which

Sony responded by quickly announcing that the PlayStation 4 would *not* incorporate similar DRM systems. Although it was initially unclear whether this would include region coding, Shuhei Yoshida, president of Sony Worldwide Studios, eventually confirmed that the console would be region-free.[49] In response to Sony's announcement as well as consumer anger, Microsoft reversed course and announced that the Xbox One would no longer contain the announced DRM measures.[50] The introduction of Nintendo's Wii U system would only inflame these debates over corporate and consumer control. While Sony and Microsoft were tussling over DRM, Nintendo announced that its console would be region-locked along the same lines as its predecessor, the Wii. Hinting at the company's long history of proprietary control and the fact that regional lockout had become standard industrial practice by that point, Nintendo executives also suggested that that the Wii U would be region-locked in part because Nintendo had traditionally engaged in the practice.[51]

Much of the public ire directed at Microsoft and Nintendo relied on the premise that new technologies should fix the problems of "old" media. As one video game writer puts it, regional lockout is now an "unwanted relic from gaming's past."[52] Another writer points out that due to the region-free nature of the PS4 and the Xbox One, the "tide is turning" toward a video game culture that cedes more control to consumers.[53] These arguments suggest that the internet should make regional lockout obsolete. But this is a two-way street. While many consumers feel that digitally connected consoles are fundamentally incompatible with the idea of regional lockout, console companies' ability to connect and communicate with consoles through the internet can make top-down control even easier. Manufacturers' ability to update a console's functions quickly through online updates to software stored in read-only memory (otherwise known as firmware) was the centerpiece of a recent coordinated protest against regional lockout. In the wake of Nintendo's announcement that the Wii U would be region-locked, users started campaigns on social media as well as in the Miiverse, the Wii U's own social networking and communication service, attempting to convince Nintendo to reverse its stance.[54] A post on gaming forum NeoGaf outlines a massive and comprehensive overview of this consumer-driven push, including instructions on how to contact Nintendo; links to dozens of Miiverse posts, news articles, YouTube videos, and Reddit threads calling for an end to regional lockout; and a call to post protests using the hashtag #EndRegionLocking.[55] One user even started a Change.org petition asking Nintendo to release firmware updates for the Wii U and the portable 3DS (which, unlike earlier portable consoles, was region-locked) in order to make them region-free.[56] By attempting to convince Nintendo to eliminate regional lockout through firmware updates, users tried to take a form of technological control and instead use it to open up the console.[57] At the same time, fighting regional lockout via petition represents a more formal attempt at lockout circumvention than the more illicit and unauthorized approaches (e.g., hacking) I will discuss below. It also indicates that regional lockout through firmware could be a more effective form of control for the console industries due to the difficulty of altering such firmware. Despite all this, the Wii U remained region-locked, though Nintendo eventually abandoned regional lockout in its most recent console, the Switch.

As consoles continue to intersect with different networked media technologies, the question of whether they are or are not region-locked becomes increasingly difficult to answer. The next chapter will dive more deeply into how regional lockout changed with the popularization of high-speed internet and streaming media, but a recent shift in the game industry toward digital distribution and online game purchases through services like the PlayStation Store, the Xbox Games Store, and the Nintendo eShop added another layer to the regional lockout question. Namely, online distribution has allowed platform owners to install a two-step form of regional lockout, where platforms are both geoblocked from the network (i.e., blocked in certain areas based on the user's IP address) *and* require a credit card from the accepted region. At the same time, the rise of online distribution has intensified talk about the archaic nature of regional lockout. In 2009, *Kotaku* asked its readers if they believed digitally distributed games should be region-locked. Responses ranged mostly from mild annoyance at the practice to rather passionate anger.[58] Following the perhaps overly simplistic futurism described above, the question rests on an assumption that online distribution *should* be freer from the shackles of regional lockout. As more of the gaming experience takes place online, users associate regional lockout with the supposed inadequacies of more obviously physical media like discs and cartridges. Regional lockout in digital distribution indicates that the console companies are still trying to figure out a balance between excluding players from prohibited regions and easing headaches for users who live in increasingly interconnected environments. Part of this involves a growing recognition of the industrial construction of the "casual" gamer, or quite simply the idea that not all video game consumers represent the archetype of the hardcore gamer. When discussing the reasoning behind the Xbox One's regional flexibility for digital downloads, Microsoft's Albert Penello pointed to a rather banal tendency of everyday life: "Lots of people in Europe specifically travel, move, and visit family."[59] However, even if the game industry began to see cross-border travel—whether literal or metaphorical through internet connections—as a recent phenomenon, video game consumers traveled before the release of the Xbox One. More to the matter at hand, importing games from around the world has always been a major part of video game consumption, at least for the medium's most ardent devotees.

Creating and Selling Gamer Culture through Circumvention

In order to track regional compatibility and bypass DRM systems, users need to know a great deal about video game distribution and technology. And although regional lockout has assuredly frustrated many users around the world, it has also engendered a robust community of lockout circumventors as well as a cottage industry of products that cater to them. Informal economies specializing in unauthorized copies of games exist across the Global South, for instance, while all over the world gamers exert some measure of control over game production and distribution through practices like hacking lockout systems and playing versions of imported games on unauthorized desktop emulators.[60] Methods of lockout circumvention often reflect a great deal of ingenuity, ranging from altering code to physically manipulating the hardware and software by soldering wires, removing tabs that keep unauthorized cartridges from fitting into consoles, and literally cutting, shaving, and sanding cartridges to get them to fit into consoles for which they were not intended. One online tutorial on playing Famicom game cartridges on NES consoles instructs the user to pry open the plastic cartridge, melt plastic tabs inside the NES cartridge case using a screwdriver warmed up with a butane torch, and switch out the boards from one cartridge to another.[61] Another helps users track down sixty- to seventy-two-pin converter boards by listing which games have been known to contain these boards and outlining how to determine whether certain copies will include them based on the cartridge's weight as well as the number and position of the screws on the back.[62] These methods exemplify what Saugata Bhaduri calls "creative and subversive appropriation" in game cultures, as they represent a measure of user agency over the technology. They also illustrate high quantities of gaming capital, since they require knowledge and literacy of video game practices, subcultures, and technologies.[63] Regional lockout represents one way the transnationalism of game culture might be foreclosed, but it also opens up moments when users might, to coin an admittedly cumbersome term, "re-deterritorialize" games by circumventing regional lockout and violating the industry's trade routes. In other words, circumvention enables gamers to take technologies that video game corporations have artificially territorialized and travel past the geographic borders implanted in them.

Such practices inspired an industry built on helping gamers get past regional lockout. As Consalvo has shown, the game industry is surrounded by a variety of ancillary industries geared toward the circulation of gaming capital—industries comprising what Matthew Payne refers to as "companies that seek to profit from selling the information that gamers value."[64] Regarding regional lockout, this has manifested over the years in message boards, blogs, books, magazines, and mail-order catalogs that instruct users on workarounds for lockout systems and sell products like modchips and imported games. Books such as Carless's *Gaming Hacks* and websites like Games X, Racket Boy, and Modchip Central explain and sell the tools users need to circumvent various forms of DRM. For instance, this industry has long produced "passthrough converters" for cartridge-based consoles, where the cartridge is placed in one end of an adapter, and the other end is placed in the console. Additionally, it is now possible to purchase unauthorized clones of older consoles like the Famicom, which will play imported games.[65] As Consalvo argues, paratextual industries like these help users experience games in ways that do not always align with the desires of developers or console companies, "daring players to ask who should control what legitimately purchased games they can play on their own videogame console."[66] Since they operate outside dominant, sanctioned modes of practice, these shadow industries of lockout circumvention are, of course, generally frowned on by mainstream game institutions.

Because these informal economies undermine the goal of controlling distribution, the game industry has sought to punish users who engage in circumvention practices. One such measure has been to lobby legislatures to pass anti-circumvention laws, as in the example of the Digital Millennium Copyright Act discussed in the previous chapter. At the individual level, however, console companies dissuade users from circumventing lockout systems by prohibiting them from using certain services. For instance, tampering with a console, as in modding it in order to disable a lockout system, voids its warranty. Additionally, modded consoles are often automatically barred from supplementary services such as the online Xbox Live platform. While Microsoft implemented these measures primarily to keep users from cheating while using the service, it has the effect of banning users who mod their consoles to play games from other regions.[67] This strategy of using consoles' online marketplaces and social networks to track modded consoles engendered new fears of surveillance that previous circumventors did not need to worry about. One Xbox magazine ran a feature called "The Myths of Modding," investigating the belief that "If you play Xbox Live with a modded Xbox, the FBI will bust down your door and arrest you with a warm controller still in your hand."[68] The subversive thrill of engaging in activities that invoke fears of the FBI (even in the context of debunking those fears) is assuredly part of the appeal for some. Lockout circumvention is in some ways part of the standard gamer practice of breaking rules, as there are ludic elements in not only gameplay but also the hacking of a console itself. As Dyer-Witheford and de Peuter suggest, game hacking cultures embody "an audacity that sees repurposing code as just another dimension of play."[69] In this sense, we can think of regional lockout itself as an extratextual rule meant to be followed in order to play games properly. If the rules of a game are contained within the game's code, the "rule" of regional lockout is likewise part of the code of the game or console.[70] Consalvo notes that gamers can take three positions in relation to rules: following them, explicitly rejecting them, or "secretly not abiding by [them] . . . and thus cheating."[71] User responses to regional lockout follow in line with these three positions, with many players rejecting these rules and choosing to "cheat" regional lockout systems.

Just as cheating helps gamers succeed within a game, hacking regional lockout helps gamers achieve greater gaming capital outside of it. Thus, like the circumvention practices described above, it would be overly simplistic to see these paratextual industries and circumvention cultures as purely antagonistic to normative gaming. After all, they represent ways users can further immerse themselves in video game culture. Indeed, purveyors of informal circumvention technologies pitch their products to an imagined gamer with a great deal of gaming capital and a willingness to bend the rules. This is just one part of how regional lockout and regional circumvention have helped shape the self-identities and subjectivities of what Dyer-Witheford, de Peuter, and others have called the "hardcore gamer." Mikolaj Dymek describes this demographic as a "dedicated gamer" who is "technologically savvy, willing to pay for gaming hardware/software, plays many and long sessions, is part of the gaming community (online and offline) and is interested in the latest information and news from the video game industry."[72] The hardcore gamer acquires gaming capital through knowledge of how game consoles work, the contours of the game industry's distribution practices, lists of import games, and the means to circumvent regional lockout. In *Gaming Hacks*, Carless draws an explicit link between circumvention and this consumer group when he writes, "I can see it in your eyes. You're hardcore. Not only will you wait no longer than necessary for your games, you want the best versions available, without censorship or missing features. You also want to play the games that you could only dream about as a child—Japan-exclusive titles that never made it to the NES or Genesis."[73] Those who have the knowledge to seek out and practice circumvention techniques embody gaming capital through their expressed expertise over the machine. After all, using the technology in ways counter to the intentions of console corporations expresses a greater amount of knowledge about the system than even the company that made it.

The irony is that the game industry created and catered to the demographic of the hardcore gamer even as this group undermined the industry by pirating games and hacking regional lockouts. These users have an ambivalent relationship to the institutions that create the media texts and technologies they want to consume—an attitude that characterizes much of the frustration with regional lockout across media. On the one hand, anti-regional-lockout discourse expresses irritation at massive corporations for controlling gaming culture in ways that do not always seem just to users. On the other hand, this frustration is premised on the disappointment that these users cannot consume as many of the corporation's products as they would like. Because many users attempting to circumvent lockout are interested in buying *more* games from legitimate, "formal" businesses, the act of purchasing import games still contributes capital to developers, publishers, distributors, and console companies (particularly from those users who seek out multiple international versions of the same game). Thus, circumvention is not always a form of protest positioned in direct opposition to these corporations, despite its expression of irritation at them. Likewise, while anger at regional lockout is often expressed in terms of internet freedom or free speech, it blends these with discourses of consumer rights and access to commodities. As one editorial opposing regional lockout in the Wii U suggests, "The anti–region locking argument is ultimately about consumer choice . . . Being region free leaves gamers to play whatever they want, and gives that choice."[74] This particular kind of "choice" promoted here and elsewhere is wrapped up in a complicated mix of anticorporate free speech activism and a will steeped in ideologies of free enterprise capitalism to buy and consume whatever we desire.

That circumvention blends dominant and resistant cultural politics is also apparent in its expressions of gender. Gaming capital is often unevenly distributed across different genders, and those who most visibly take part in and promote the practices of lockout circumvention reflect a commonly circulated vision of gamer identity: male, and with a great deal of technological knowledge and acumen. As Dyer-Witheford and de Peuter put it, "Hardcore players identify with a specific subject position: *the man of action*."[75] "Man" points overtly to the long-held idea that gaming is a predominately masculine space, and "action" implies masculinized tropes of agency and control over complex technologies that have long characterized hacking cultures.[76] Indeed, many of the vloggers and bloggers illustrating circumvention tactics are young men, and several of the tutorials discussed above involve activities often coded as masculine (whether these are manipulating physical hardware like torches, pliers, and soldering irons or manipulating software by messing with code). Furthermore, all eighteen contributors of game mods and hacks in Carless's *Gaming Hacks* appear to be men. Taken together, this indicates that the formal game industry's overwhelming masculinity, which is in part rooted in the presumption that to work in the business it helps if you are a stereotypical "gamer," extends to the informal para-textual industries that sell lockout circumvention tools.[77] It also draws lines around the industry- and consumer-constructed category of the "casual" gamer (often gendered female) and the "real" gamer, who is part of a subculture bound by gaming capital and oppositional practices (hacking, piracy, modding, and so forth).[78] By co-opting discourses of nondominant cultural practices, the game industry uses subcultural cachet to construct and attract an ideal consumer.

Beyond the construction of the gamer as an industrial imaginary, the gendering of lockout circumvention follows deeper-seated cultural meanings of masculinity and technological control. Within cultures of lockout circumvention, the gaming capital represented by access to global games and knowledge about game culture commingles with ideas of global travel and the transcendence of geographic space that are often gendered male. As Dyer-Witheford and de Peuter argue, the nomadic subjectivity embodied in gamers engaging in piracy, hacking, and modding is one that is "imbued with masculine techno-expertise."[79] Insofar as hardcore gaming culture incorporates the circumvention of regional lockouts, the intersections between hardcore gamers and masculinity point to a broader coalescence of technological control, mobility, and mastery over geographic space. As David Morley points out, traditional understandings of private and public spaces have privileged masculine mobility over feminine privacy and domesticity.[80] By promoting a kind of gaming practice where users—whom, again, the game industry works to discursively construct as predominately male—can metaphorically transgress global spaces, hardcore gaming culture continues this cultural association between the global and the masculine. The "man of action" has agency not only to best the technology, but also to do so in order to traverse physical, geographical borders.

Circumvention, Access, and Global Difference

To the degree that lockout circumvention *is* a resistant practice, it offers gamers a chance to recognize and reject the potentially unfair consequences of the game industry's logics of capitalist accumulation and geographic control. In this way, it exemplifies what Dyer-Witheford and de Peuter characterize as a Deleuzian "nomadic" community that engages in "mobile, subversive uses of technology" like piracy, modding, and other uses that violate the preferred practices of dominant gaming industries.[81] Like deterritorialization and reterritorialization, nomadism can be literalized in the context of regional lockout, as users transgress the geographic boundaries inscribed in the industry's preferred circulation routes. This is not to suggest that circumvention necessarily represents taking up arms against the "planetary, militarized hypercapitalism" represented by the global game industry.[82] Rather, it is usually a more banal case of users simply trying to play the games they want to play. At the same time, if we understand regional lockout as a phenomenon that affects global spatial and cultural flows and hierarchies of geographic value, the iterations of gaming capital expressed in challenges against regional lockout often manifest as anger at the large corporations that shape them.

Even still, while gaming culture is rich with modding, hacking, cheating, and collective intelligence about regional lockout, the degree to which video game consumers are likely to think or care that much about such issues will vary widely. Many people (especially in privileged markets like Japan and the United States) never know about regional lockout. Quite simply, they buy the games accessible in their area and do not think twice about what might be available elsewhere. However, while the video game industry has made inroads in recent years throughout the Global South, gamers in these territories can still find it difficult to access desired games and consoles in formal markets. In Latin America, Africa, the Middle East, and South and Southeast Asia, or territories with less geocultural capital within global video game flows, regional lockout's consequences strike consumers as more consistently frustrating and baldly discriminatory. As in user discourse about DVDs discussed in the previous chapter, these frustrations often invoke familiar global hierarchies. For instance, the British blog *RegionFreeGamer* carries the subtitle "Because Europe Shouldn't Be a 3rd Class Gaming Region." And if the UK is still a privileged market compared to parts of the Global South, elsewhere we can see frustrations borne out of long histories of neglect by dominant media industries. For example, the above-cited poster on IGN's community blogs suggests that region codes put a particular burden on users across the Global South: "I have to provide a voice for those often forgotten gamers found elsewhere. Gamers in Latin America, Australia, and every other place that isn't part of the big three regions I've mentioned have more reason to complain than any of us and would benefit most from a region free world."[83]

Such statements illustrate geocultural capital in their irritation at how geographic territories are placed within a hierarchy of value based on media access. In one example of this, a blogger named Rashed Mokdad, who goes by the name the Arab Gamer, voices his frustrations in a YouTube video called "The Wrath of Region Codes."[84] In the video, he laments that the Middle East is "lumped in with Europe" as a video game market and discusses the irritations of regional lockout for gamers in the region (even dramatizing and acting out the experience of bringing a region-locked game home and finding out that it doesn't work). Invoking the complex intermingling of formal and informal industries in the region, he also mentions that many shops in the Middle East ignore staggered release dates and sell parallel imports of American copies of games anyway—a practice that becomes problematic for gamers in the region because of their consoles' regional lockouts. The video has a certain homemade quality that places the Arab Gamer firmly within participatory culture, existing partway between the consumer/amateur and the producer/expert. At the same time, his gaming expertise and not-insignificant number of followers and viewers ensure that his populist appeals to players in the Global South also reflect a great deal of gaming capital.

By articulating these frustrations to the broader concerns of a globally marginalized community, the Arab Gamer and others remind us that in order to comprehend the cultural impact of regional lockout, we need to be clear about its directional flows. That is to say, the vectors of its cultural and political power will operate differently depending on geopolitical context. Regional lockout means something different to users in the United States than it does to users living in Yemen, for instance. In American and European gaming markets, importing games from different regions usually manifests as part of a niche fandom of Japanese media—an American rendition of the *otaku* cultures embodied by diverse, transnational, intense engagement with Japanese popular culture like anime, manga, and video games.[85] Ranging from sincere engagement to Orientalist fetishism (and often including complex shades of both), these fandoms have always been marked by particularly strong forms of participatory culture, which digital media have only exacerbated.[86] In its gamer-culture iterations, *otaku*'s participatory culture and collective intelligence manifest as a shared fandom for the Japanese games that regional lockout attempts to keep from these regions. Online resources like *Kotaku*'s reader-created "A Beginner's Guide to Importing Games" offer overviews of the region-locked (or region-free) status of consoles as well as suggestions on where and how to purchase Japanese games, and fans regularly share information on importing and playing Japanese titles.[87] While Koichi Iwabuchi argues that video games are not "culturally odorous" Japanese exports, in that they bear few obvious traces of their Japanese provenance, this is not the case for gamers who seek out international consoles and software (whether these are *otaku* fandoms in the United States seeking out Japanese games or gamers in the Global South searching for American games).[88] In other words, the "Japanese-ness" of video games for some American gamers is central to their enjoyment—an attitude that grew as NES, Genesis, and SNES consumers sought out titles from across the Pacific.[89]

Whether Middle Eastern gamers pushing back against decades of media industry neglect or American fans of Japanese games trying to collect them all, these practices all confront the realities of geography getting in the way of media accessibility. Beyond simply putting knowledge about gaming culture to use, circumvention is also about recognizing one's place within global hierarchies of media access. Here, we can see how different kinds of capital—subcultural, gaming, financial, and geocultural—are all layered on top of one another. The Arab Gamer's video points to the gulf between gaming capital and geocultural capital. It shows that while people can have a great deal of knowledge and competency regarding video games, for many in certain parts of the world this does not translate to an ability to access the games they want. While for US-based gamers frustration may come out of an uncharacteristic

The Arab Gamer Episode 3 - The Wrath of Region Codes

Rashy

Subscribe 1,698

2,850 views

+ Add to   Share   ••• More   👍 119   👎 6

Figure 2.1. "The Arab Gamer" performs his anger at regional lockout. Screenshot: Rashy, "Arab Gamer Episode 3."

inability to access whatever, wherever, whenever, users in the Global South express anger at once again being ignored or shortchanged by the shepherds of global media distribution. North American and Japanese consumers who have ready and early access to a wealth of consoles and games live in places with much geocultural capital. Not so for consumers in the Middle East and Latin America, who have to contend with regional lockout more regularly. For these users, circumventing regional lockout represents a way of resisting this structure of power and capital.

Tracing these dynamics becomes increasingly difficult as many parts of the world transition into an era marked by online media access. With the DVD region code, one could look at the map, with its hierarchically ordered regions, and deduce rather easily which territories the media industries valued more highly. Furthermore, because this was a centralized form of control, DVD consumers around the world were all subject to the same regulatory system. As is clear from the sketch above, navigating regional lockout in video game culture requires users to keep track of which consoles and games are locked out where, and how such dynamics change with the new generation of hardware. Furthermore, consoles' increasingly convergent incorporation of other media formats and streaming capabilities made this even more complicated. Given the ways its histories have incorporated DVD, Blu-ray, and streaming platforms, regional lockout in console games serves as a bridge between the first chapter and the third. The next chapter, on geoblocking and video-on-demand platforms, engages these unequal levels of access as well as how they reveal different vectors of cultural politics in the global VOD environment. The move toward online video via platforms like Netflix and the BBC iPlayer raised new questions and problems regarding the logistics and appropriateness of regional lockout. As I will show, the debates over regional lockout continued well after what many perceived to be a shift away from "physical" media and toward a supposedly—but not actually—borderless medium.

3

Video on Demand

Geoblocking, Borders, and Geocultural Anxieties

In January 2016, Netflix CEO Reed Hastings delivered a keynote address at the Consumer Electronics Show (CES) in Las Vegas. The presentation was, in many ways, standard tech CEO fare: a blazer-and-jeans-clad Hastings expounding on internet TV's revolution of consumer choice and technological progress. Notable about this particular speech, however, was his assertion of Silicon Valley–based Netflix as a newly *global* delivery system for that choice and progress. Toward the beginning of the talk, Hastings celebrates Netflix's international reach as not just good business and proof of the platform's success, but as something deeper: an emblem of global connectivity. Promising to "put consumers around the world in the driver's seat" vis-à-vis their viewing, Hastings promotes Netflix as a way of "building connections between cultures and people."[1] These promises of consumer empowerment reverberate from the individual to the global. Not only do consumers around the world get to watch *Orange Is the New Black* no matter where they are, in so doing they are offered the opportunity to participate in a shared media ritual that extends across continents. At the presentation's climax, Hastings makes a dramatic announcement in front of a screen adorned with several national flags: "Today, I am delighted to announce that while we have been here on stage at CES, we switched Netflix on in Azerbaijan, in Vietnam, in India, in Nigeria, in Poland, in Russia, in Saudi Arabia, in Singapore, in South Korea, in Turkey, in Indonesia, and in 130 new countries." The crowd bursts into applause, and Hastings continues, his voice raised: "Today, right now, you are witnessing the birth of a global TV network!" Onscreen, we see a map of the world comprising tiny rectangular video screens and a hashtag: #netflixeverywhere. As Ramon Lobato says, Hastings's presentation signaled that "Netflix had become a global media company—available almost everywhere, with a potential foothold in almost all the major national markets."[2] The company would no longer be defined in national terms (a series of different Netflix*es*), but in terms of global ubiquity and unification.

Hastings's presentation is quite savvy in its spoken and visual rhetoric. The nations he stresses in his announcement are carefully chosen to include a sampling of powerful and growing national media markets, thus implying that the platform will be a major player in both established and burgeoning media economies. At the same time, the flags onscreen collectively signify a holistic sense of globalness. This reminds us of all the places Netflix will now be available while at the same time turning our attention to the world as a broader connected space rather than a series of disconnected territories. In promoting Netflix as a new network, Hastings implies that the same opportunities and products will be available to everyone—viewers across all seven continents (yes, even Antarctica) can all feel like they are experiencing something together. Perhaps Marshall McLuhan's global village, long promised by digital evangelists and deferred by the disjunctive realities of digital politics and infrastructure, would manifest as collective global binge watching.

The keynote commemorates the supposed end of a specific genre of regional lockout: online video geoblocking. Hastings obliquely references this irritating experience, promising consumers, "No more waiting . . . no more frustration. Just Netflix how, when, and wherever you are in the world." However, it will likely not come as a surprise to find out that he is overstating things. While the Netflix platform and subscriptions to its streaming services are available around the world, prices and content libraries still differ from place to place.[3] Furthermore, despite Hastings's promises of global access, Netflix is not even available everywhere: North Korea, Syria, and Crimea are barred access due to sanctions. In addition, Hastings's breathless announcement was undercut slightly by a caveat: "While you have been listening to me talk, the Netflix service has gone live in nearly every country of the world but China, where we hope to also be in the future." The CES crowd chuckles at this last line, likely familiar with having to navigate that country's tight restrictions on cultural imports and digital access. Furthermore, as Lobato points out, Netflix's global expansion has been a bumpy road, rife with protests against explicit content, blocks by local telecoms, and difficulties regarding content quotas.[4] While Hastings's announcement

Figure 3.1. "A new global TV network," says Hastings. Screenshot: Netflix, "Netflix CES 2016 Keynote."

posits a dramatic erasure of online video's borders, a look across the global digital entertainment landscape reveals a media environment still replete with purposeful disconnection.

Although Hastings's presentation is loaded with now-familiar rhetoric of democratized global interconnection—what David Morley and Kevin Robins call the "mythology of global media"—this book has shown that digital borders exist even in an era when the internet shapes more and more of the world's cultural experiences.[5] The CES keynote, intended to be a moment of shared revelry in Netflix's brand-new global openness, is undercut with reminders of territories still left in the dark. Indeed, regional lockout is still very much in place, showing signs of adaptation to new conditions rather than what many assumed would be its gradual elimination. Regional lockout's borders are still based on established distribution business models of global geographic market segmentation, and they are put in place through complex alignments among content industries, digital media manufacturers, and industrial consortia. These borders are theoretically good for entertainment industries looking to maximize profits but occasionally a thorn in the side of platform-owners hoping to expand their markets. Just before making this final announcement, Hastings laments the conditions that have slowed Netflix's global reach, complaining that "content rights are sliced and diced" in ways that make it difficult to offer the same products to everyone. As this suggests, regional lockout also still regularly frustrates consumers.

This chapter moves from the cartridge- and disc-based media explored in the first two chapters and into the more fragmented and less obviously physical realm of online video-on-demand (VOD). For many around the world—though by no means everyone—the distribution of film and television is transitioning to an era of online delivery.[6] Viewers increasingly access film and television through online streaming, rental, or electronic sell-through platforms while moving away from DVDs and Blu-ray discs. As online platforms have developed and proliferated, regional lockout practices have shifted from region codes (whether in differently coded DVDs or video game discs) to what is usually referred to as "geoblocking," or the prohibition of access to an online platform or service based on one's geographic location. Part of what distinguishes geoblocking in online VOD from the earlier forms of regional lockout explored in the last two chapters is that popular perceptions of the internet as a borderless medium have animated even more intense debate over the appropriateness of regional control. Of course, such utopian ideas have long ignored that the internet offers more opportunities for back-end control, user surveillance, and invisible DRM systems than a DVD or video game cartridge ever did.

This chapter argues that geoblocking in VOD is an arena wherein users, industries, regulators, and intermediaries engage in a tug-of-war between fantasies of a borderless, open internet and the sovereignty of nations and regions. This tug-of-war is characterized by a tension between frustration that borders are still important in a digital age as well as attempts to assert the importance of retaining and protecting these borders. Geoblocking therefore offers a particularly rich illustration of the kind of status via media access that I have been calling geocultural capital. As I will show, various stakeholders who discuss and debate geoblocking use it to fight battles over issues like national identity and economic protectionism. These debates are occasionally more complicated than the commonly assumed idea that media companies would be in favor of geoblocking and consumers against it. For instance, this chapter's primary case study of the geoblocked BBC iPlayer shows how consumers throughout the world covet access to the UK-only platform and how this brings about feelings of nationalist pride and protection in British viewers who are opposed to unauthorized iPlayer access. This pride expresses itself as geocultural capital, because these British viewers want to assure that the scarce resource of access to the BBC remains available within their borders. This chapter's case studies focus largely on examples throughout the UK and Europe (with a brief detour back to Oceania), as these are spaces wherein the ongoing tensions among nation, region, and world are particularly acute and easily observed. With that said, the particular dynamics blending national/regional identity, distinction, geopolitics, and questions of access look different depending on context.

From Region Codes to Geoblocking

Although geoblocking is philosophically similar to region codes in its attempts at geographic control, technologically it is quite different. Instead of relying on codes and encryption, geoblocking generally operates through technologies that block users' access to a platform based on their Internet Protocol (IP) address, the unique number assigned to each device connected to the internet. Because IP addresses indicate users' geographic locations, platforms can measure them against databases of IP addresses to determine how to respond. If the IP address indicates that the user is connecting from a country where the platform is allowed, the user gains access; if not, the user is blocked.[7] Platforms also use IP address detection to alter prices and libraries based on territory, practices often lumped in with geoblocking as a geographically informed frustration. However, IP detection is not the only method platforms use to block access. Netflix, for instance, requires that users trying to access the United States' version of the platform not only connect from a US IP address but sign up for the service using an American credit card as well. As a broader phenomenon, geoblocking can manifest through the power of the state (through internet censorship), private media industries (through geoblocking in online video contexts), or somewhere in between.[8] While states and international regulators grease the wheels for cultural industries and multinational corporations to perpetuate geoblocking, the industries and corporations are the ones that introduce and monitor geoblocking systems. Digital platform developers, media industries, and intermediaries set the conditions for the kind of geoblocking explored in this book more so than oppressive states do.

As a way of controlling film and television's distribution windows, geoblocking follows similar industrial logics as DVD region codes. However, it is not precisely a *next step* in a linear history of regulating digital platforms. While earlier tussles over DVD and video game region codes helped shape subsequent debates surrounding the geoblocking of VOD platforms, the latter is harder to pin down. It does not abide by a single standard like the DVD region code, it shapes media flows across a diverse and constantly changing VOD landscape, and it can be enforced through several different technological mechanisms. Whereas a bit of digging could lead a consumer to learn about the DVD CCA and the reasons a Region One DVD would not play in her Region Two DVD player, geoblocking remains a contingent and often confusing process informed by the practices of individual platforms rather than one transnational body that determines the standards and shape of geoblocking around the world.

On a basic technological level, geoblocking is one example of an everincreasing number of digital geolocative technologies that use satellites or IP addresses to pinpoint a user's location. These exist well beyond the realm of entertainment delivery and permeate everyday life for digital media users: cellular phones, the Global Positioning System (GPS), and internet-connected computers are all geolocative. Often, these technologies use geolocation in order to customize the user's experience on the platform, allowing platform owners and advertisers to collect identifiable information for a variety of reasons. Thus, geoblocking is related to the surveillance and customization systems of major digital platforms. However, while such uses take advantage of a technology's geolocative properties to the user's supposed benefit (even if the reality is, at best, far more ambivalent), the firms that own and control VOD or other online platforms use geolocation to prohibit people from using a technology or platform. They do so with IP detection and blocking software developed by a company like Neustar, which licenses its IP Intelligence geolocation program to platforms so that they can comply with content industries' international licensing deals. Content industries and their intermediaries can thus use digital media's locative nature to restrict or control the activities of users as much as they can to enrich them.

Despite this, many VOD optimists argued that streaming video would usher in an era of widespread media accessibility. For them, online distribution would enable a greater accessibility of films and television programs around the world.[9] These arguments articulate familiar celebrations of the internet as an entertainment cornucopia. As the logic goes, because online media platforms were supposed to have opened up borders, regional lockout should be a relic of an earlier era more reliant on the limitations of analog infrastructures and "physical" media. Examples abound of global op-eds and trade publications characterizing geoblocking as undemocratic and anachronistic. An Australian consumer reports journal protests, "The internet is a borderless world—news, shopping and social interaction with people from all over the world is at our fingertips. But some online retailers haven't yet embraced this fact."[10] One report about Singaporean streaming services likewise argues, "Geographical restrictions on content distribution have their roots in a business model built long before the Internet and digitization made it possible for content to be distributed around the world at a low incremental cost. And, as with all industries disrupted by technology, the movie and TV industry continues to resist change."[11] A Sydney newspaper suggests that regional lockout should have been consigned to history and compares it to DVD region codes: "Just when you thought geographical restrictions were a thing of the past, along came geoblocking, a kind of regional encoding for the era of digital downloads and streaming."[12] These are just a few representative examples. As such arguments would have it, while the internet inevitably moves society toward a condition based in increased openness and less reliance on geographic boundaries, the business models of film and television production and distribution companies should follow suit and adapt to these new conditions.

Such arguments rely on a couple of assumptions: first, that the internet offers an easier, freer, and more equalizing user experience than discs and cartridges, and second, that new media somehow erase spatial boundaries rather than reinforce or reflect them. Rather, Chuck Tryon posits geoblocking as a material limitation on the sort of mobility and consumer freedom that on-demand platforms promise, pointing to a disconnection between the discourses of ease and fluidity and the often disjunctive reality of the streaming VOD experience.[13] As Peter Urquhart and Ira Wagman argue, for instance, confrontations with geoblocked technologies remind Canadians of the "power of place" even while the rhetoric of the borderless web surrounds VOD.[14] As they suggest, the ubiquity of geoblocking throughout Canada requires considering the ways global media distribution shapes global culture and complicates the rhetoric of borderlessness. When we move beyond the PR hype of digital media industries, it becomes clear that geoblocking and streaming platforms' putative flexibility are not countervailing forces but phenomena that operate on the same logic of panoptic customization and control. VOD platforms like Netflix mask their careful control of content availability and the user experience beneath a veneer of improved customization and the promotion of entertainment's increased convenience and ubiquity. Over time, it has become clear that algorithmic culture and its attendant practices of data tracking and user surveillance are as much about back-end control as they are about consumer flexibility and freedom. Geoblocking must be considered in this broader context, as the geolocative dimensions of algorithmic culture—how recommendations and libraries are based on one's geographic location—can be wielded in order to keep users out.

These issues are indicative of broader forces of market and infrastructure, but they also bring out more banal feelings of frustration and discrimination. Urquhart and Wagman's argument gestures at some of geoblocking's softer, complex, and identity-based dimensions—namely, how regional lockout reminds people of where they stand in global cultural hierarchies. Following this move beyond issues of hard regulatory power and digital utopias and dystopias, we might better understand how geoblocking intersects with geographic and cultural difference, identity, belonging, and status.

Geocultural Capital and Geoblocking in Oceania

To explore these issues, let us return briefly to Australia and New Zealand, where we spent some time in chapter 1 and where concerns of equitable access have been central to digital film distribution.[15] The discourses surrounding anti-geoblocking sentiment regularly involve geocultural capital—which territories have more of it than Australia and New Zealand, how to attain it through greater access to cultural resources, and so on. Mark Stewart has argued that New Zealand's television viewers exist in a "cultural silo" due to a lack of access to television on-demand services and spaces of television talk.[16] Furthermore, the idea that Australians are "second-class citizens" in the global media economy is a common theme in complaints about lack of access.[17] While the higher prices that Australians in particular pay for digital services (often referred to as the "Australia tax") suggest that these struggles are in part about economic capital, they also reflect more abstract questions of a territory's cultural status.[18] This comes about in moments when the public as well as policy makers invoke the United States as both the villain (by disallowing access to its platforms and forcing versions of its own intellectual property laws on the rest of the world) and the standard by which Australia's own consumer-cultural landscape should be shaped.[19] Feeling left out of the global mediascape, Australian consumers and politicians alike have a long history of expressing their feelings of exclusion from the higher ranks of the world's cultural markets.

Debates over geoblocking—as well as discussions about how to get around it—exist among a wide variety of Oceanic players: consumers, consumer rights groups, regulators, and stakeholders in the media and tech industries. As Ramon Lobato and James Meese have shown, geoblocking circumvention is a relatively mainstream practice in Australia.[20] It is so mainstream, in fact, that papers like the *Sydney Morning Herald* have published circumvention instructions and consumer reports on different virtual private network (VPN) and proxy services, which mask a user's IP address and trick a platform into thinking that she is connecting from an approved country. Even telecommunications companies get involved in circumvention. In 2013, New Zealand ISP CallPlus offered its customers an add-on service called Global Mode, which was essentially a built-in VPN that gave users access to geoblocked platforms.[21] This would allow users to connect to geoblocked VOD platforms like Netflix and the BBC iPlayer, effectively sanctioning geoblocking circumvention at the service-provider level.[22] Global Mode no longer exists in New Zealand, as CallPlus and Bypass Network Services, the developer of Global Mode, settled with a number of media corporations (including Sky TV) who had sued to stop ISPs from offering the service.[23] Still, during its brief lifetime, Global Mode's promotional rhetoric was redolent with suggestions of unequally distributed geocultural capital: "We don't want your guests being treated like second-class citizens just because they are staying in New Zealand. Instead, we want them to have the same rich online experiences as they do in their own country."[24] The use of terms like "second-class" and "rich" to describe differential access to entertainment and media is not simply a melodramatic analogy; rather, it shows that people think of media accessibility as related to capital and status.

At the same time, geoblocking debates in the region are not merely altruistic paeans for equality. Just as often, politicians use geoblocking to foment nationalist sentiment and push for free-market trade regulation and deregulation.[25] In July 2013, an Australian House of Representatives Standing Committee on Infrastructure and Communications published a report on IT pricing, in particular tackling online price-discrimination practices for which geoblocking sets the technological conditions. They called for the end of geoblocking, referring to it as "a significant constraint on consumer choice."[26] Much of the committee criticized the fact that Australians often had to pay higher prices for entertainment and computing technology because of territorial markets. As committee chair Nick Champion suggested, Australian consumers were "clearly perplexed, frustrated, and angered by the experience of paying higher prices for IT products than consumers in comparable countries."[27] The government's condemnation of geoblocking offered a rather strong rebuke of the world's most powerful intellectual property regulators, but it also represented an argument for the equitable treatment of global territories (or at least Australia) by major media corporations. Champion's invocation of "comparable countries" is, itself, a plea resting on the premise that the world is divided into unequal, hierarchically organized territories and that Australia belongs higher up in the hierarchy. Through geoblocking, issues regarding market power, cultural access, national identity, and feelings of inadequacy all swirl together.

This becomes clear in the debates that have circulated around Netflix in particular, which was finally introduced to Australia in 2015—albeit with a smaller library that still inspired viewers to seek out the larger American version. In April 2013, the Australian consumer reports publication *Choice* prepared a report on why Netflix was not available in the country and attempted to contact the company in order to get answers. This was motivated by the upcoming Netflix-exclusive release of the fourth season of the American cult comedy favorite *Arrested Development*, which Australian Netflix users would not be able to access.[28] After receiving no response from the company, *Choice* published a copy of their letter to Netflix on its Facebook page. Noting that since the first three seasons of *Arrested Development* had already aired in Australia and thus had a significant fan base in that country, *Choice's* letter asked the following questions:

Will Australian consumers be able to legally access season four of *Arrested Development* at the same time it is made available to US consumers?

Will Australian consumers be able to legally access season four of *Arrested Development* in the same format as US consumers? For example, will they be able to access all 15 episodes at once, and watch them when they choose?

Will Australian consumers be able to access season four of *Arrested Development* from the Netflix site, from an Australian IP address with an Australian credit card?[29]

Such questions indicate that this is not a mere issue of access to a television *text* but is also about access to a similar viewing *experience*. As the argument goes, not only should Australian viewers be able to see this season of *Arrested Development* at some point, they should be able to watch it and potentially binge it at the same time as North American viewers.

On one level, these issues are banal. Questions of whether viewers get to watch *Arrested Development* in the same way pale in comparison to more obviously important concerns over international trade and intellectual property regulation in both the private and public spheres, not to mention more urgent matters like unequal access to food or potable water. However, as the publication argues in a subsequent post, the letter is about more than just *Arrested Development*: "*Choice* isn't campaigning for an Australia with Netflix; we are campaigning for an Australia where consumers can access the content they want, the way that they want, at a price that is fair and reasonable, without resorting to criminal activity."[30] Such statements invoke issues that extend well beyond the simple question of what to watch on a lazy Sunday. Geoblocking provides a gateway to broader questions regarding the role of both private and state organizations in shaping how we use digital technologies, how we understand our own agency in relation to our devices, and how these issues tie to our ability to participate on a more-or-less equal playing field in the digital mediascape.

National Culture and Circumvention: The BBC iPlayer

Because geoblocking and geocultural capital are wedded to place and access, they often articulate expressions of national identity. These may not always take the same shape—consider the distinctions among politicians' free-market nationalism and consumers' more personalized expressions of national discrimination. Either way, geoblocking (and regional lockout more broadly) enacts its "boundary work" both by tracing literal geographic borders and by sustaining lines of difference and inequality among media viewers living in different countries.[31] Users might consider access to be a barometer of cultural power and status attained via geocultural capital. The knowledge that a certain platform is available in one area but unavailable in another can engender feelings of inclusion, exclusion, pride, and envy. Take the BBC's iPlayer platform, for example. As a national public broadcasting system that carries programs with global appeal, the geoblocked iPlayer illustrates familiar tensions between television as a national form and transnational digital media distribution. While on the one hand national broadcasting institutions experiment with multi-platform engagement, global digital presences, and the fragmentation putatively wrought by media globalization and on-demand platforms, on the other, users, industries, and states often still imagine public broadcasting's audience in terms of a nationally defined public.[32] The iPlayer thus exemplifies how broadcasting as a spatially limited technology conflicts with commonly held notions of the internet as a fundamentally *global* medium.

These tensions bring out arguments for and against geoblocking that rest on differences in geocultural capital. Here, the nationally geoblocked status of the iPlayer becomes a flashpoint for debates over BBC access—who should have it, who should not, and how access is a resource that marks national distinction. British viewers have a significant investment in the BBC—literally, through the license fee they pay, and figuratively, as a political and emotional emblem of national identity. When consumers from outside the UK use VPNs in order to access the geoblocked platform, this raises ire among consumers and industry types alike. iPlayer access is a cultural resource that many aim to keep scarce, which assures that the UK maintains the geocultural capital that comes with full access to a premier broadcasting institution. It makes sense that the BBC, whose operations depend in part on controlling viewer numbers and meting out access to the platform, would want to geoblock the iPlayer. Still, that *viewers* might want the platform to remain geoblocked seems counterintuitive. Because many public discussions about geoblocking reflect the idea that we all want and expect equal access to platforms in a streaming era, it would be easy to assume that the battles break down with consumers on the anti-geoblocking side and media industries on the pro-geoblocking side. However, this would ignore how issues of international distinction and geocultural capital complicate these debates. For some British users, the status that comes with national ownership of the BBC outweighs any benefits of opening it up to the rest of the world.

The BBC iPlayer is a streaming and download platform providing television and radio programs from the Corporation's various channels. The platform's television programming is geoblocked outside the UK, the logic being that citizens who pay the nation's television license fee, which funds the BBC, should have access to both the platform's livestreamed and on-demand programming. While anyone connecting from within the nation's borders can access the on-demand service, one needs a TV license to access the iPlayer's livestreaming capabilities. Although one might assume that the BBC is solely responsible for ensuring that the platform remains geoblocked, the reality is more complicated. BBC Worldwide, the commercial, international distribution wing of the Corporation, has paid lip service to extending the iPlayer's access abroad. In 2011, the iPlayer expanded onto a limited subscription and ad-supported mobile app version called Global iPlayer, which was made available in several European countries, Canada, and Australia before shuttering in 2015.[33] Soon after the Global iPlayer's launch, the BBC announced that the platform would be made available in the United States, but that was put on hold after threats from cable companies that were worried the iPlayer would carry shows already aired by the US cable network BBC America.[34] Thus, the tussles over the iPlayer's access in the United States remains a point of contention between the two nations' media systems, with the US media industries ensuring that the British app remains blocked.

One outcome of television's convergence with the internet is the rise of proprietary curatorial platforms—what Amanda Lotz calls "portals"— each of which operate under different, constantly changing sets of licensing agreements with content companies.[35] Portals like the iPlayer (and Netflix, Amazon Prime Video, and the host of others that deliver movies and TV programs to viewers around the world) operate separately from one another as business entities, brands, and spaces of user experience. The platform is important both as an industrial and technological system that delivers media to us *and* as a set of discourses about what those systems can offer us.[36] The iPlayer in particular is redolent with meanings of Britishness and British identity due to its geographically limited remediation of British state media. Even in an era of media globalization, the presentation of media through a national frame still carries a great deal of purchase. Nationally scaled media industries assert ideological and cultural power at the level of subjectivity and identity. By generating "affective proximity across disperse locations," to use Nitin Govil's words, media help produce an idea of nationhood in which the audience invests.[37] In the British context, Stuart Hall argued that the BBC was "a 'machine' through which the nation was constituted. It produced the nation which it addressed; it constituted its audience by the ways in which it represented them."[38] Thus, while on the one hand the iPlayer's practice of locking out non-UK users is just one of many geographical constraints placed on the internet's architecture, on the other hand it extends the BBC's role in addressing and constructing a distinctly British audience. The iPlayer thus remediates the goals of public service that have informed the BBC since its founding. Indeed, one group of scholars argues that the BBC as a multi-platform project presents opportunities for different, potentially richer media experiences while maintaining and extending the Corporation's public service compact.[39] Of course, this compact generally articulates to a sense of British nationality and even nationalism, both in its industrial ontology as a national public broadcaster and the emotional and political relationship that viewers might have with the network.

At the same time, BBC television programming has long had appeal well beyond the UK's borders, in part due to the network's history of exporting programs and developing international networks.[40] British television is valuable abroad—not just in economic terms, but also in how people appreciate it as a harder-to-access commodity that aligns with particular cult and sophisticated tastes. Given this, it made sense that fans would try to view episodes before they were available in the United States. Unauthorized attempts to access the iPlayer also become particularly widespread during major global sporting events like the Olympic Games or the World Cup.[41] Viewers discontent with local time-shifting of the Olympics or the quality of home broadcasts look for ways to access the BBC's coverage, which are relatively easy to find. A 2010 article on the tech blog *Lifehacker* (one of many such posts on this site and others) instructs users on how to connect to the iPlayer via proxy or VPN. The impetus for this particular *Lifehacker* piece is the gap between *Doctor Who*'s British airdate and its broadcast on BBC America two weeks later, though similar articles abound that highlight a jones for Olympic gymnastics or Premier League football. Indicating that regional lockout is as much about time as it is about space, this particular article shows *Doctor Who* fans in the United States how they might access the iPlayer in order to maintain the same temporal relationship to the program as their British counterparts. This becomes crystal clear in the comment threads, as one American commenter notes, "We don't want to have to wait two weeks (for BBC America) or six months to a year (Netflix) for the show to actually become available for us to watch . . . And unfortunately, the only way for us to watch it in a timely fashion is to do so illegally."[42] Articles like this, and many comments in response, reject the bordered logics that keep the global VOD environment segmented along national lines. In doing so, they treat the iPlayer like a platform violating the internet's ideally global state rather than an online manifestation of a national broadcaster.

Of course, not everyone feels the same way. Some British users have made it clear that they are less than thrilled with the fact that audience members in the States are looking to access BBC material for free. Often, they express this irritation in the comment sections of articles and blog posts that promote circumvention via VPNs. And while comment sections may not seem like the ideal place to find arguments built around complex, intertwined dynamics of national identity, cultural policy, and digital regulation, many of their points show how some British citizens associate the BBC with a sense of national pride and ownership. For them, opening up access dilutes the BBC's national character. Commenters make statements such as "If you're not paying the UK license fee you're stealing from me and all others who do fork out $228 a year for the service . . . All things considered, this is clearly a way to rip off honest license payers in the UK."[43] In the aforementioned *Lifehacker* article, one commenter complains, "I don't like this. Why? Because I (along with everyone else in the UK) PAY £145 a year to watch TV IN-CLUDING iPlayer. It's not cool, you're basically stealing our great television that we pay for. *That's why British TV is the best,* WE PAY FOR IT. So this is annoying."[44] These viewers are not simply angry about theft. They also associate the national, publicly funded model of the BBC with the quality of the programming. As the logic goes, if freeloaders access the platform and that association degrades, the BBC will be no better than other, lesser forms of popular media. Another reacts similarly: "Great. So just as the BBC is being forced to cut services we now have even more of those who don't pay the license fee ($213 a year!) watching the shows for nothing! If you want the benefits of a 'socialist' system then you'll have to pay for it!"[45] Yet another commenter uses the piece to assert support for the publicly funded BBC against transnational, private corporations: "Doing this harms the BBC and threatens future access to content, there are already very powerful media figures (Rupert Murdoch and his Sky network) working very hard to take down the BBC—this isn't helping."[46] Again, the national character of public media contrasts with the transnational character of corporate, private media conglomerates. Others suggest that they plan to send the article to the BBC, with the presumed goal of encouraging some form of disciplinary or legal action against *Lifehacker*.

The ongoing relationships between the BBC and British identity, as well as the ways people negotiate such issues when television goes global, reveal a particular international dynamic at play in these threads. For one, the threads are populated by many American commenters. Perhaps used to the relative wealth of media access associated with the United States' generally high levels of geocultural capital, these consumers argue for various reasons that they should have access to the platform.[47] Occasionally, such users suggest that they would happily pay the BBC license fee for access to the iPlayer, enacting a consumer logic whereby the license fee functions as the price of a globally distributed product rather than a national tax. The distinctly *national* dimensions of the iPlayer are more apparent in the discourse of British commenters, who express pride and protectiveness through the iPlayer and its license fee. This manifests in part as pushback against the kind of American privilege that suggests US viewers necessarily deserve access to the platform. For these British viewers, the license fee is not simply the pay-to-play price for the iPlayer—it is a contribution that helps ensure the higher quality of the BBC's programming and the obligation of a good viewing citizen who recognizes the Corporation as a public utility.[48] Even as the BBC's professed goals of global expansion and individualized, customizable programming seemed to undercut its national associations somewhat in the mid-2010s, the trend has moved back toward making the iPlayer available only to tax-paying Britons. As mentioned above, the Global iPlayer is no more, and in 2016 the BBC began requiring that all iPlayer users must pay the license fee in order to watch live *and* on-demand programming. This not only curbs free viewing by those living in the UK, it also makes it harder for non-British viewers to access the platform through VPNs.[49] While pro-circumvention publications and consumers argue their case through the logics of internet freedom or consumer economics, British viewers argue that the iPlayer's geoblock is steeped in the BBC's fundamentally national identity. In doing so, they maintain a kind of ownership over the platform. In a 2013 statement, BBC director-general Tony Hall made clear the relationship between this sense of national ownership and "proper" access to the network: "We should be treating [viewers] like owners, not just as license fee payers. People should not be saying 'the BBC,' but 'my BBC,' 'our BBC.'"[50]

Thus, the iPlayer is not simply another way of delivering radio and TV programs. It remediates the national, and nationalist, associations between the BBC and the UK. A view of geoblocking as simply the oppressive, top-down practice of shadowy oligopolies ignores moments when users unexpectedly promote geoblocking—in this case, by drawing on ideas regarding the BBC as something special to British viewers. Broadly, such arguments are steeped in questions about what television is worth in a digital age, when access is increasingly unmoored from perceived obligations of payment.[51] More specifically, the iPlayer represents to many British viewers the ability to access a precious cultural resource—one that lends the UK rare stores of geocultural capital. Those who hold the platform dear perceive "stolen" access to it as a way that another region (in this case, the United States) attains unearned geocultural capital. By this logic, unauthorized access not only reinforces US viewers' relative privilege in the global mediascape, it also dilutes the UK's geocultural capital by making a particular cultural resource less scarce. Such an example shows that users' feelings are more complicated than the simple assumption that they would and should be opposed to geoblocking. Rather, the alignments between regional lockout and geocultural privilege can bring about complex blends of feelings related to competitiveness and superiority. As a *Wired* article about the launch of Global iPlayer in Europe puts it, the platform "fills the gap for smug Europeans left by Spotify launching in the U.S."[52] While the comment is of course a joke, it speaks to the capital that comes with owning something exclusive. Further complicating our assumptions about geoblocking's global effects, the iPlayer indicates how a nation or region's geocultural capital does not *always* follow a preestablished global hierarchy of economic or state power. If the iPlayer is the cultural resource so highly coveted, then the UK has a greater amount of geocultural capital than does the United States in this instance. Such complicated dynamics of power, status, and difference become apparent when governing bodies attempt to ban geoblocking. The difficulty in doing so speaks to the influence of the various stakeholders involved.

A Digital Single Market?

By arguing that the iPlayer should remain geoblocked, industry players and viewers in the UK sought to protect British culture, identity, and economy from encroaching hordes of nonpaying viewers. Across the sea, the European Commission would soon propose an alternate path, one marked by the easing of digital borders. It would do so through the initiative I discussed at the beginning of this book: the Digital Single Market (DSM). After a years-long debate, the Commission approved the DSM in 2015. Encompassing a broad set of transnational copyright and trade proposals, the initiative seeks to combine the EU's countries into one larger market to ease cross-border digital trade, end price discrimination for digital products, and curb geoblocking among member states. As part of a broader push to ban geoblocking among EU countries, the DSM sought to open up iPlayer access across Europe. The BBC was initially noncommittal, suggesting in 2015 that it would "look at the technical and legislative implications" of making the platform available throughout the EU, but this raised the question of who would be in charge of such issues: the platform or the legislative bodies that govern where the platform had a presence.[53] As it turned out, the split between UK sovereignty and EU governance represented in 2016's Brexit vote had an analogue in the question of iPlayer access. Indeed, the UK's impending exit from the EU—and, as a result, the Digital Single Market—meant that any anti-geoblocking measure put in place by the latter would not apply to British viewers.[54]

Even still, the EU has promoted the DSM as a potentially barrier-breaking approach to cross-border digital trade over the past several years, although the process of implementing it has often been fraught. During a May 2015 press conference, European Commission vice president Andrus Ansip promoted the DSM's goals of improving "price transparency" and "tackl[ing] unjustified geoblocking."[55] The Commission defines unjustified geoblocking as "discrimination between E.U. customers based on the desire to segment markets along national borders, in order to increase profits to the detriment of foreign customers."[56] Although the initiative stretches well beyond video-on-demand, VOD services were initially significant targets of the geoblocking ban. Indeed, the DSM is only the latest instance of the Union's ongoing attempts to restrict regional lockout among European territories. In 2001, it opened an antitrust investigation into DVD region codes, threatening a possible penalty of 10 percent on all disc revenue if Hollywood studios were found guilty of price-fixing.[57] Ultimately, this investigation went nowhere, with the EU report concluding, "There has been a convergence in prices between these two regions and the Commission therefore decided not to actively pursue this case any further."[58] Since then, price discrimination and regional lockout have remained significant issues within the European mediascape, and the DSM is the highest-profile attempt thus far to do away with them.

Much of the pro-DSM rhetoric reflects by-now familiar assumptions about how digital media should work—assumptions routinely upended during moments of disconnection or inaccessibility. Similar to many other arguments against geoblocking, pro-DSM forces often argued that regional lockout violated the internet's fundamentally and ideally open condition. Take these words from a Commission website: "It's time to make the EU's single market fit for the digital age—tearing down regulatory walls and moving from 28 national markets to a single one."[59] The commission's rhetoric presents the geoblocked internet as incongruous with the putatively borderless digital age. Indicating both the proposal's alignment with traditional tech dogma as well as its attempts to boost the EU as a powerful digital market, many in Silicon Valley celebrated the potential for opening the EU digital borders. In 2014, Google's executive chairman Eric Schmidt wrote a World Economic Forum editorial titled "Why Europe Needs a Digital Single Market." Schmidt argues in favor of open digital borders, drawing on the now-common Silicon Valley–espoused blend of utopian digital freedom and free-market capitalism.[60]

Indeed, boiling the issue down to a clash between open internet activists versus copyright-obsessed corporations ignores the degree to which the DSM is as much about liberal capitalism as it is about digital freedom—if not more so. While all sides invoked the potential losses for consumers regardless of how the regulation turned out, the DSM debate amounted to a battle among different sectors of the media and entertainment industries. Attitudes like Schmidt's clashed, as they often do, with the goals of global and local media distributors invested in maintaining territorial distribution routes. Trade publications representing the entertainment industries, such as the *Hollywood Reporter*, often framed the issue through the perspectives of studio executives, film distributors, and theatrical exhibitors. Such pieces leaned heavily on quoted fears that the proposal would "kill European audiovisual culture and diversity" and represent the "death knell" of independent film due to the elimination of territorial exclusivity, which indie studios draw on for financing.[61] Ironically, given geoblocking's long-standing association with Hollywood, such warnings pointed to the possibility that a single EU market could result in the major Hollywood studios dominating that market while European and indie studios get squeezed out. Of course, given that "independent" in these stories referred to Hollywood-indie studios like Lionsgate (which produced the global hit *The Hunger Games* and sold its European rights by territory), this argument comes across as rather disingenuous.

The influence of private media industries initially resulted in a more compromised agenda as the EU announced in 2016 that "copyrighted audiovisual content" would be exempt from the DSM's anti-geoblocking rules.[62] While the EU aimed to break down digital borders for all entertainment throughout Europe, it seemed that territorial television and film distribution licenses would continue to shape the libraries of VOD platforms like Netflix and Amazon Prime Video. Later on, however, EU negotiators agreed on a version of the anti-geoblocking rules that would allow users access to their home country's version of the platform while traveling elsewhere in the EU. The DSM's "portability regulation" aimed to curtail a particular kind of frustration: a business or vacation traveler discovering that she is blocked from her Netflix account. The result is thus more of a softening of geoblocking rather than an outright ban. By still ensuring that consumers had to keep an account based in their home countries, the proposal exposes the continued importance of the nation while at the same time speaking to the desire for media experiences that fit into a world marked by easier transnational travel and interconnection (for some of us, at least).

As cultural policy, the DSM privileges the EU's broader regional borders over the national media markets within it, while at the same time drawing new borders around media experience. In doing so, it implies that regional lockout has since become even *more* fragmented than it was in the days of DVD region codes, which placed most of the continent within Region Two. In a 2007 piece cheekily titled "Notes from Region 2," Rob Stone wrote of the "lofty ideal of European cinema as a borderless network of film-makers in which countless individuals make decisions that energize a borderless market."[63] Writing even earlier, David Morley captured some implications of such a move: "We have seen a concerted attempt by the European Union to construct the equivalent of a transnational EuroCulture, enshrined in concepts and cultural institutions such as the European Audiovisual Sphere, based on a geographically expanded version of the conventional model of national broadcasting. These cultural strategies have been intended to create a synthetic pan-European identity which will transcend the narrow limits of national particularisms."[64] Years later, the DSM is applying this logic to a broader audiovisual sphere. Indeed, the rhetoric surrounding the DSM presents it as one step toward smoothing what William Uricchio has referred to as the "tangible fault lines, fissures, and ruptures" that have characterized collective European life and identity.[65] At the same time, the regulation represents cosmopolitan, liberal capitalism wrapped in the rhetorical packaging of equitable human treatment. It is the Digital Single *Market* and not the Digital Single *Territory* or something similar, because its top priority is to smooth the flow of capital across borders.

These tussles between exclusive national borders and open, cross-border movement felt remarkably of the moment in the latter half of the 2010s. Without equating the frustration of a geoblocked Netflix with more urgent matters like refugee crises and violent nationalism, the Digital Single Market issue is nevertheless part of a broader cluster of policy debates over the primacy of national gatekeeping versus a freer flow and intermingling of culture. While the EU and tech companies consider such issues through a blend of cosmopolitan liberalism and free-market capitalism, for many users the issue is much simpler: geoblocking is frustrating because it represents an intrusion of materiality on media texts and experiences that we often think of as somewhat divorced from the material world. However, decades of evidence have shown us that the digital world will not escape the real world's cultural and geographic clashes. The next chapter explores these issues in the context of digital music—a media practice that seems even less material than VOD given its close association with mobile technologies and its related lack of an obvious visual element that keeps us tied to our screens.

4

Digital Music

Regional Lockout and Online Listening

At the end of 2013, Swedish streaming music platform Spotify launched an ad campaign for its free mobile service built around the refrain "Music for Everyone." One such ad portrays Spotify as integral to a cosmopolitan life of global travel. Scored to "Elevate" by indie pop musician St. Lucia, it begins with two establishing shots of a forest before cutting to two shots of a young, bearded, backlit man pressing play on his Spotify mobile app. The rest of the minute-long clip portrays hip, attractive, young men and women traveling the globe, listening to Spotify, and having fun. We see them riding in the back of a taxicab, swimming in the ocean, diving into a river, riding a train, and riding a motorcycle in a tropical location—all presumably soundtracked to Spotify playlists. The ad alternates between these moments and beautifully composed shots of various landscapes signifying a general "globalness"—mountains, city streets, palm trees, rivers, jungles, and lakes. Over these images, we see a series of superimposed titles that proclaim, "Music for everyone. Now free everywhere. The perfect playlist. Your next favorite song. The artists you love. Play everywhere for free." The final shot of the ad is a view of the Lower Manhattan skyline from a subway platform, superimposed with the hashtag "#freeyourmusic."[1]

The ad is part of what Jeremy Morris and Devon Powers refer to as Spotify's "branded musical experience," the streaming platform's holistic attempt to suggest to users that they are participating in something distinctive and special rather than just another corporate-run digital platform.[2] As represented in this ad, the branded musical experience promises freedom, cosmopolitan mobility, and the agency to tailor a soundtrack to one's global adventures. Spotify's limited worldwide availability, however, gives the lie to this "Music for Everyone" aphorism. As of mid-2019, the platform is available in seventy-nine countries, mostly throughout Europe, Latin America, North America, the Middle East, Oceania, and Southeast Asia, leaving much of Africa, South Asia, and a smattering of other countries geoblocked. Especially in 2013, when the ad was released and the platform was available in far fewer places, its hip, urbane global travelers would likely encounter trouble when trying to listen to their Spotify libraries during their travels—inability to access the platform, running into "This song is not available in your country" messages, and so forth. As Morris and Powers point out, streaming platforms' branded musical experiences often promise ease of use and fluidity that mask tiered access and imperceptible systems of control.[3] A service like Spotify trades on the contemporary associations between music and mobility in order to paper over such inconsistencies. Streaming music platforms sell a listening experience to users that is at once hyper-individualized and unbounded—tailored to one's specific tastes yet mobile and potentially globally connective. However, as this chapter argues, such promises conflate localized, *experiential* mobility (i.e., the ability to listen to music on the go, during a commute, etc.) with larger-scale, transborder travel. This conflation smooths over a seeming contradiction: that the techno-cultural systems enabling the creation of an individually tailored soundtrack to one's mobile life—data tracking, surveillance—are the same that impose traditional, large-scale geographic borders through geoblocking. Furthermore, because streaming platforms base their recommended and promoted music on mounds of user information, the compilation of this data from a limited segment of the world perpetuates and even deepens a familiar haves-and-have-nots dynamic within the global music industry. This chapter explores this contradiction through a history of regional lockout in music and a closer reading of Spotify.

In his writing on streaming music platforms, Eric Harvey captures a central tension of this chapter when he asks, "Are we living in a techno-logical golden age of creative possibility, cross-cultural communication, and sheer abundance, or a surveillance state controlled by privately-held brands promising endless access at the expense of imperceptible control?"[4] The truth is that streaming music platforms are built on technological systems that enable both. Geoblocking is a good example

Figure 4.1. Spotify presents a brand of hip, cosmopolitan mobility. Screenshot: SpotifyVideoChannel, "Spotify."

of this—the technology of geolocation can be used to, say, recommend certain songs based on the current weather in a listener's city, but it is also used to block people in certain countries from accessing the platform and to present different libraries based on a song or artist's territorial licensing agreements. This seeming paradox is part of what makes the historical trajectory of geoblocking in music distinct from movies, TV, and games: as music became increasingly mobile, the geographic contours of its distribution became *more* stringent. Records, cassettes, and CDs contained no rights-managing regional restrictions, so regional lockout represents a relatively new phenomenon in global music. Contrast this against the DVD region code's attempts to retain segmented windows for film distribution and streaming video platforms' use of geoblocking in order to do the same. For film and TV distributors, regional lockout is a way to maintain distribution practices that existed long before the digital age, whereas for music distributors it is a solution to a relatively recent problem *caused* by digitally networked technologies. In streaming platforms, the music industry discovered a way to further encourage associations between music, mobility, and freedom (in multiple senses of the word) while building systems that could more tightly control its distribution.

Digital Music, Geography, and Control

Popular music's digitization came at a time when the record industry intensified its embrace of global commercialization, conglomeration, and global expansion.[5] Digital outlets like sell-through and streaming platforms have become increasingly central to the operations of the three dominant record companies—Sony Music Entertainment, Universal Music Group, and Warner Music Group—with the International Federation of the Phonographic Industry reporting a 41.1 percent increase in streaming revenues in 2017.[6] The shift to digital formats has been accompanied by an intensified focus on "global markets," or territories around the world that the multinational record corporations seek to exploit and keep distinct. Geoblocking manages and controls forays into these new markets by keeping them segmented. This is important for the music industry, which has long relied on both broadly scaled and fine-grained forms of segmentation and market research. For example, Keith Negus shows how record corporations employ "experts" on local territories that other arms of the corporation consult in order to better understand and exploit these territories as markets. As he suggests, the music industry's market-segmentation initiatives are part of its broader practice of cultivating and promoting knowledge about music production and consumption in order to guide global business practices.[7] Although Negus refers primarily to markets defined through genre, the broadly scaled national and regional markets that inform geoblocking operate according to a similar logic. Rather than mere rational economic decisions, markets are industrial organizations built around industry-constructed knowledge about people and places. All this knowledge is an attempt to respond to the speculation, uncertainty, and risk that saturate the global record industries. The music industry's profits are driven by hits, which subsidize the less successful artists signed to a given label, and these hits are difficult to predict.[8] The expansion of distribution operations around the world is a way of managing that risk. If a single, album, or artist can become successful around the world, it will bring in even more revenue, particularly because the cost of distributing a record to more markets is far less than the profit that can be made from it.[9]

As popular music migrated to digital forms of delivery throughout the 1990s, 2000s, and 2010s, the music industry encountered a problem that should by now be familiar to readers: the potential abundance of digital media clashed with the need to monetize product through carefully controlled distribution. Despite this, the two dominant digital formats for music listening before the streaming era—the CD and the MP3—were both free of regional restrictions. This period of relative geographic openness was not only surprising in relation to the early implementation of regional lockout in digital video and games, it also seems out of place within a regulatory environment that otherwise increasingly used intellectual property law as a mechanism to clamp down on the possible uses and affordances of digital music technologies. Thus, regional lockout is a relatively recent phenomenon in music consumption. Pre-digital forms of music delivery were all essentially compatible; a vinyl record could play on any turntable around the world, and a cassette could play on any tape player. The CD, product of a long series of experiments by various companies and an eventual standard-setting collaboration between Sony and Philips, contained no regional restrictions within its technical standards.[10] These specifications, known informally as the *Red Book* due to the color of the document's cover, indicate that a CD manufactured anywhere in the world must be playable on a CD player from anywhere in the world. This is not to say that the *Red Book* standard was unconcerned with issues of geography, as it also included metadata called the International Standard Recording Code, which contained, among other things, information about where the recording originated.[11] However, these metadata were mainly for industry uses and had little bearing on the average listener's experience with the CD.

It was due to the economics of international distribution in the record industry that CDs did not include region codes. Recall that, in contrast, DVDs contained region codes primarily to protect the windowing operations of the film industries (and particularly Hollywood) at a time when films were released on a staggered schedule. While records were routinely released at different times in different territorial markets, the multistep windowing process familiar to film distribution—that is, first-run theaters, second-run theaters, home video, television—did not exist in the recording industries. At the time of the CD's development, the issue of parallel imports was not as pressing for the recording industries as it was for the home video industries (again, because they did not have to abide by these same windowing agreements). Furthermore, at the time of the CD's adoption, the major record labels did not anticipate the potential for the format to be copied.[12] As Barry Kernfeld points out in his history of music piracy, the manufacture of compact discs was at first a specialized process (even more so than manufacturing vinyl records) and copies could generally only be made through illicit access to CD manufacturing plants.[13] Therefore, the inability to foresee the potential for unauthorized copies to not only be made but also *distributed* meant that CDs did not have the content- and region-protection forms of encryption that later disc formats would. Eventually, however, the development of digital ripping software enabled relatively easy copying and, in turn, transgression of the geographic borders determined by those in control of global market segmentation. Much of this took place within informal and bootleg media networks, but even sectors in some ways connected to formal media economies engaged in unauthorized copying. For instance, many CD manufacturing plants were based in territories like Taiwan, far from the surveying watch of North America and Europe's major record companies, and these plants would occasionally "accept illicit orders" for pirated discs.[14]

The problem of controlling music's global circulation became even more apparent for the record industry after the development of the MPEG Audio Layer III (MP3) format. On its own, the MP3 is not obviously central to a history of regional lockout in the music industry since, like the CD, its technical standards do not contain such mechanisms.[15] However, the easily shareable nature of the MP3 as well as other region-free audio container formats like WAV and FLAC—alongside the rise of file-sharing services like Napster and the Pirate Bay—led the record industry to encourage digital distribution platforms that promised greater degrees of control. Specifically, major and independent record labels began partnerships with tech companies to sell individual songs and albums via online sell-through outlets like the iTunes Music Store (launched by Apple in 2003) and Amazon Music (launched in 2007). Bowing to pressure from the record industry, many of these platforms encoded the digital files they sold with forms of DRM, ensuring that users could only play them on certain platforms, on certain computers, or in certain parts of the world. Indeed, in addition to locking down users' files through DRM, many of these platforms were also geoblocked. With the implementation of DRM on digital music files, distributors could more easily route music's global circulation (at least in legal consumption practices).

The centrality of geoblocking in digital music—both functionally and in broader discourse—intensified with the arrival of streaming music. Such platforms, like Spotify, Pandora, Apple Music, and Tidal, at once feed a broader cultural expectation of free, cheap, and/or à la carte entertainment while keeping content distribution controlled along geographic lines. These platforms are geoblocked for two primary reasons. First, like the streaming rights for a film or television program, music licenses function on a territorial basis. To make a recording available to consumers, the platform owners must negotiate distribution and licensing terms either with local rightsholders and record labels or with aggregators that make distribution deals with smaller, independent record labels. The ability to employ regional lockout as a way of regulating music's global distribution is part of what makes streaming platforms appealing to the recording industries. Through a platform like Spotify, the labels can offer consumers free or subscription music along paths that align with the industry's preferred organization of spatial distribution (as opposed to a practice like peer-to-peer file sharing, which transgresses these borders). Although record executives were initially concerned about free streaming services, labels now use them in part to discourage such peer-to-peer file sharing. A second reason for streaming platforms' unavailability in certain territories is that they are careful not to expand too quickly. Music licensing is expensive, and moving into new territories means balancing revenues from new subscribers and local advertisers against the new licensing deals that will come with entering that area.[16] Like many of the video-on-demand services discussed in the previous chapter, streaming music platforms balance a desire for global expansion and greater economies of scale with the dual requirements of contending with territorial licensing agreements and not expanding too fast.

Platforms can be geoblocked full stop, or they can employ "soft" geoblocking, where users have nominal access to the platform but with differences in price and content based on location. In a 2012 post that sparked a debate over Spotify's geoblocked nature, one user converted the cost of Spotify Premium in different countries to US dollars, finding that the platform was, in fact, cheapest in the United States ($9.99/

month) and most expensive in Norway ($17/month).[17] Although differing prices between markets is hardly a new phenomenon, as prices are generally set by local market factors and dynamics of supply and demand, some users see them as less necessary or more artificial when the product is a subscription to a platform rather than a single commodity. This is compounded by the fact that major record companies have long been dogged by accusations of cartel price fixing.[18] Even when platforms are made available, certain songs or albums may remain unlicensed in certain territories. Content libraries can be different from place to place, though Spotify has occasionally been cagey with journalists and tech writers on this issue.[19] Spotify's online message board is rife with examples of listeners lamenting their inability to access particular songs and artists, even if they do have access to the platform itself. Thus, much like the streaming video platforms discussed in the previous chapter, geoblocking is a multitiered system built on prohibiting access to platforms, particular content, and/or lower-priced access to the same content.

Geoblocked music is particularly complicated—for both users and industrial players—because of how services like Spotify are tied into other proprietary platforms and technologies. In the company's early days, even before its introduction in the United States, speculation grew as to whether Spotify would be available on Apple's iPhone. On the one hand, Spotify's presence would potentially cut into Apple's profits from the iTunes Music Store. On the other hand, Apple's financial damage could be mitigated by the company's revenue-sharing policy, wherein a percentage of Spotify's in-app subscription purchases flows back to Apple. Spotify's App Store availability could also help drive iPhone sales. This is relevant to issues of regional availability because even if a *platform* is technically available in a certain location, the *technology* allowing users to access it as well as particular forms of payment may not be readily accessible. As this suggests, Spotify must adjust its expectations of use from territory to territory based on common and available media practices. For instance, Spotify sees the potential for success in Asia because of the popularity of mobile phone use throughout the region.[20] Similarly, the company has entered agreements with telecom companies throughout Latin America to provide Spotify subscriptions within mobile phone contracts so that users do not have to sign up using a credit card.[21] These are basic business strategies, but they also indicate that a music platform's relative ease of access is shaped by the quality of local broadband and mobile service.

Streaming music platforms can also be geoblocked because of internet radio's licensing and royalty payment structure. One example: Pandora, an online streaming music platform only available in the United States, Australia, and New Zealand, allows users to customize certain "stations," which play music selected based on an algorithmic recommendation system called the Music Genome Project.[22] Pandora's payment mechanism is different from terrestrial radio, and the platform has found it difficult to negotiate licensing terms outside the three nations where it is currently available.[23] Harvey explains, "Whereas broadcast radio stations pay royalties via ASCAP and BMI only to composers and publishers . . . Pandora is required to pay performers, who collect directly via the non-profit performance rights organization SoundExchange."[24] Consequently, Pandora has to pay far more in royalty fees than do terrestrial and satellite radio, with various quarterly reports showing that the company regularly shells out over half its revenue to SoundExchange.[25] Some do not buy this line of reasoning, however, suggesting that the platform could still be lucrative around the world if it focused on expanding its operations. One tech reporter asks, "Instead of cashing out millions every month, shouldn't Pandora executives put some of that money back into licensing? For the US, and beyond?"[26] This is one version of a common and not entirely unreasonable argument against geoblocking—that through regional lockout, some platforms are ignoring the desires of their customers in order to collect higher profits from fewer territories. At the same time, Pandora shows how geoblocking is not always ethically and politically cut-and-dried. While many view the practice of locking out users from a platform based on their geographic location as discriminatory in ways that violate the principles of an open internet, those invested in the financial well-being of musicians in the twenty-first century might also desire music platforms that compensate artists fairly. If Pandora is geoblocked in part because its business model allows for somewhat fairer royalty payment (relative, at least, to a platform like Spotify), there are reasons behind its geoblocking other than ignorance or apathy toward some parts of the world.

Spotify and the Promise of Unbounded Listening

Whatever the reasons for its existence, the sum effect of geoblocking for many listeners is that it imposes material geography on a medium often sold as borderless and immaterial. Of all the major streaming services, Spotify most visibly peddles a ubiquitously accessible listening experience. The platform came about in a moment marked by both excitement and fear about the internet's effects on the spatial reaches of popular music distribution. Reflecting hopes for an ideally borderless internet, users and industries alike (though with vastly different motives) celebrated the fact that music seemed even more mobile and ethereal than ever before.[27] Early writers on digital music and entertainment explored the possibilities of a more readily available stream of music. David Kusek and Gerd Leonhard's 2005 book *The Future of Music* begins with a vision of music consumption set in 2015 wherein music would be "like water: ubiquitous and free flowing."[28] Even earlier, the promises of online music inspired discourses of a "celestial jukebox" that have circulated for the last couple of decades. Popularized by a 1994 book by Paul Goldstein, the celestial jukebox describes an idealized online marketplace or service where listeners can access virtually any song or album they like. As Patrick Burkart and Tom McCourt point out, the metaphor suggests that online music delivery embodies "heavenly attributes, a gift from God."[29] Such promises speak to the contradiction at the heart of geoblocked digital music platforms—they at once promise to reach, connect, and transport listeners across vast spaces while ensuring that music's spatial dimensions are controlled and regulated.

Thus, the invocation of "celestial" points to a common mythology surrounding online music: that it is fundamentally deterritorialized, both in the sense that it is disruptive of dominant organizations of capital and in the more literal sense that it violates or transcends traditional relations of space and place. If digital music platforms remediate radio, they also remediate that medium's familiar tug-of-war between a potentially broad spatial reach and the requirement that this reach be contained. Michele Hilmes points to this tension in early American radio, which promised to connect far-flung geographic spaces while simultaneously defining its audience within national borders.[30] In the context of broadcasting, the immateriality of radio waves has long evoked spatial transgressions both dangerous and liberating. Thomas Streeter has shown how the history of early American broadcasting is marked by states, militaries, and corporations attempting to limit and control radio's inherent "omnidirectionality" in favor of a more easily regulated point-to-point address.[31] As Hilmes suggests, radio's immateriality and possibility for connection across geographic space set conditions for forms of cross-cultural contact considered dangerous by the dominant and powerful.[32] Reanimating battles over the spatial control of sound's omnidirectionality and immateriality, geoblocking seeks to rein in aural cross-border flows that might be dangerous to the record industries' carefully managed distribution routes.

The tensions among the inherent properties of a medium, cultural expectations for its ability to traverse borders, and the wills of those who would keep it from doing so are by now familiar to readers, but they are particularly pronounced in an art form as seemingly unrooted as contemporary music. As John Connell and Chris Gibson argue, music's relationship to place is marked by a key tension between the art form's "fixity" and its "fluidity." Music's fluidity is ontological (music as sound waves), cultural (music as part of traveling people and cultures), and economic (music as fundamental to "the desire of entertainment companies to capture dispersed markets and seek new sources of music").[33] While music as a globally distributed commodity indicates the form's mobility, geoblocking shows how media institutions attempt to keep that mobility controlled. In geoblocking, music's supposedly ontological fluidity butts up against its economic and geographic fixity—a fixity resulting in part from the art form's commodification and incorporation into capitalist distribution. A platform like Spotify embodies this seeming paradox, which trades on a branded musical experience of fluidity in many senses but is actually marked by complex and often disjunctive infrastructures, business arrangements, tiered access, and mechanisms of back-end regulation.[34] Harvey puts it bluntly: "The industry's investment in today's technology is designed in large part to wrench back control via unlimited access after a decade of ceding power to mp3-downloading fans."[35] As a result, the celestial jukebox is actually "a walled garden of closed networks with restricted access and tightly circumscribed activities," in the words of Burkart and McCourt.[36] Although they are writing about control and locked-down platforms in a broader sense, we can think about how regional lockout makes the "walled garden" an even more potent metaphor through its construction of digital barriers.

The realities of streaming platforms' tightly controlled access clash with popular discourses of the agential listener flitting between places while listening to her curated playlists. For better or worse, a platform like Spotify prides itself on understanding and catering to its users with surgical, algorithmic precision. In that context geoblocking is a blunt instrument reminding us that our ability to soundtrack our lives is still shaped by the political economy of the global music industries. If, as streaming platforms seem to promise, music has become as easily accessible as a utility like water or air, containing it within national or regional borders would seem to contradict its naturally ubiquitous state. That these promises are couched within still-prevalent ideas about the internet as inherently globally connective (rather than segmented by geography) only intensify the irritations of geoblocking, as they did for those in the previous chapter who pushed back against geoblocked streaming video. Such arguments are characterized by the frustrations of one Spotify user upset about differential access and pricing between different national markets: "With digitally distributed, geo-IP locked content—you lose that ability to shop across markets. To me, it sends the wrong signals to charge one group of people one price, and another group of people another price for the mostly the same content when it's available on the same global network . . . I guess it just grinds my gears that the price for the same 1s and 0s is higher."[37] Such comments are representative of an oft-repeated argument that the internet's universal usability and global compatibility should supersede geography.

Spotify's nominal ability to provide a free, massive, on-demand collection of popular music means that demand for the platform remains high in many countries where it has not been introduced. This was true in the United States until the platform was released there in 2011. Indeed, until that point, Spotify was the digital entertainment platform invoked most often and most intensely in American public discourse about regional lockout. Long negotiations with the major American record labels kept Spotify out of the United States. As one report from the platform's launch noted, in hyperbolic prose that pointed to Spotify's desirability, "For innumerable music lovers in America, the world changed on July 14."[38] Spotify's arrival was greeted with excitement from American consumers and the tech press alike, and some writers even suggested that the platform could help take down the iTunes Music Store. Indeed, subsequent Nielsen numbers indicated that streaming music would begin to overtake digital downloads, leading Apple to respond with its own streaming platform, Apple Music, in 2015.[39] Opportunities to sign up for Spotify were in high demand after its American introduction, and the platform used corporate partners to help grease the wheels even more by offering sign-up access codes on Coca-Cola and Sprite's websites.[40] The New York Times framed the service's newly American presence as a win for global progress in the form of an inevitable march toward technological advancement, arguing that it represented "a great step forward toward the holy grail: free, legal, song-specific and convenient."[41] Finally, it seemed that the celestial jukebox was in reach for US listeners.

But of course the breathless celebrations over Spotify's introduction to the States tended to ignore the fact that the platform was still unavailable in many countries—a condition further masked by the platform's "everywhere" brand. The company's PR often indicates that Spotify's geoblocked condition is simply a temporary setback, suggesting that its eventual goal was to bring Spotify to the entire world.[42] For instance, Spotify Asia's director has said, simply, "We want to be everywhere." CEO Daniel Ek has stated the company's global goals in terms of content acquisition as well, saying, "We want all the African music, all the Asian music, all the South American music . . . Our goal really is to have all the world's music."[43] Though the company's business model is built increasingly on global expansion, moving into new territories is still expensive.[44] It would therefore be too easy to suggest that simply because one platform begins to expand, the global media environment is moving farther and farther away from geoblocking as standard practice. Statements like Ek's serve to hide the fact that regional restrictions and differences continue to exist even while platforms seek to offer their services to more users.

Spotify's Borders and Boundaries

Such disjunctures are not immediately apparent in Spotify's branded musical experience, which is characteristic of streaming music's "promises of constant, fluid, and mobile access," in the words of Morris and

Powers.[45] As a platform built around an increasingly global brand, Spotify sells what we might call an unbounded experience of listening. This unboundedness is at once highly individualized and yet potentially global. Its individual characteristics come from the ability to create personal playlists, listen on the go via mobile devices, and access tailored music (and advertisements) via tracked data and algorithmic recommendation systems. While this is not in itself unique to Spotify, the company has put forward the most consistent and thorough paratextual brand promoting this unboundedness as a distinct characteristic of online digital music. The "free your music" mantra is as much about freeing it from the grasp of linear radio broadcasting schedules and physical formats like CDs and cassettes as it is about unshackling it from geography. Spotify extrapolates this unboundedness to the experience of traveling through space and time, a now-common trope of mobile listening. One Spotify ad includes a single shot of a man looking wistfully out a bus window and listening to music on his headphones, all while voice-over narration explains that this song is transporting him back to "the place that made you and I us, for a moment." While brief and rather abstract, the ad connotes the idea that music can be at once personal yet transformative—that Spotify has the power to move us figuratively to other places and times.

More to the concerns of this book, Spotify often articulates this experience of unbounded listening in distinctly global terms—as an experience not only unrestrained by geographic borders, but also one that can theoretically help us broaden our horizons as listeners. Through advertisements such as the one that began this chapter, as well as a number of interactive initiatives highlighting the platform's international reach, Spotify's promotional materials and PR rhetoric present the platform's professed ethos of globally expansive and interconnected listening. One example is the 2015 launch of an interactive browser-based map titled "Musical Map: Cities of the World."[46] The map contains clusters of clickable dots representing various cities on the globe, each of which links to a Spotify playlist of the most "distinctively popular" songs in that particular city. Distinctively popular songs are those that people in one city listen to but that listeners in others do not. In a blog post, Spotify ties this product into their broader promotion of cosmopolitan, global experiences: "In our connected world, people everywhere tend to enjoy the

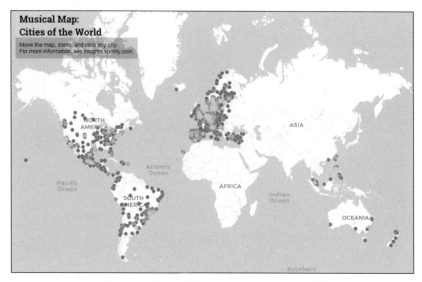

Figure 4.2. Spotify's "Musical Map" inadvertently reveals its geoblocked nature. Screenshot: Spotify, "Musical Map." © OpenStreetMap contributors (CC BY-SA).

same top hits, as we can tell by looking at the top song in each country. But when most travelers visit another place, they don't seek out the same food they eat at home, even if they can find it. We travel to experience what makes a place different, and special, by sampling local specialties." As some trade reports were quick to point out, however, the map perhaps unwittingly pointed to the massive gaps in the platform's availability.[47] A screenshot of the map from 2018 reveals Spotify's unequal access, somewhat undercutting the platform's exhibited mission of cataloging local taste around the world.

Spotify has a habit of accidentally highlighting its geoblocked condition within celebrations of its international reach. A piece of digital art that the company commissioned in 2014 unintentionally captures the contradiction between the platform's brand of global interconnection and the disjointedness caused by geoblocking. Titled "Serendipity" and built from real-time listening data by "media artist in residence" Kyle McDonald, the work visualizes various, instantaneous cross-border relationships created between users of the platform.[48] Whenever two people in different countries click the same track at the same second, the platform points out the locations of the two listeners on a map of the world and plays a snippet of the song. "Serendipity" suggests that these moments are endemic of a broader, cosmopolitan orientation toward the world—one built on connection and shared by the platform and its users. Indeed, the name and general idea of the platform unintentionally evoke Ethan Zuckerman's understanding of serendipity as a fortuitous and surprising intercultural connection via digital media. The press release announcing the platform affirms this: "Although they might not speak the same languages, live in the same climates, or believe the same things, they're playing the same song at the same time. We've always known that music brings people together—and now, we can see that togetherness in real time."[49] "Serendipity" extends the service's "Music for Everyone" brand by showing how Spotify can help users embody a kind of cosmopolitan global engagement. These moments of serendipity show how music might forge transnational connections while also promoting Spotify as a fundamentally global platform.

"Serendipity" bears out its intended purpose only intermittently. Sometimes, the platform visualizes a connection across remarkable stretches of space, such as users in Quezon City and Bogotá listening to the same song. Just as often, however, the platform zooms into two users in the same country and, occasionally, the same city. Although such moments speak to the possibility that music can bind us at local and translocal levels, they also indicate that the transnational connections forged by Spotify are part of a branding strategy as much as they are accurate descriptions of the platform's possibilities. This is underscored by the fact that Spotify is geoblocked in many countries around the world—a condition that "Serendipity" inadvertently highlights. Watching "Serendipity," one begins to see the same handful of territories crop up, and it does not take long to realize that Africa and much of Asia in particular are not included in Spotify's dictum that "this is what it looks like when the world listens together."[50] "The world" becomes shorthand for the handful of territories that are able to connect to the platform.

Spotify further underscored its professed distaste for borders in the summer of 2017 with a transmedia project titled "I'm with the Banned." A protest against President Trump's travel ban against six predominately Muslim countries, "I'm with the Banned" is a playlist and series of videos showcasing musicians from Iran, Sudan, Syria, Libya, Yemen, and Somalia traveling to Toronto in order to collaborate with American

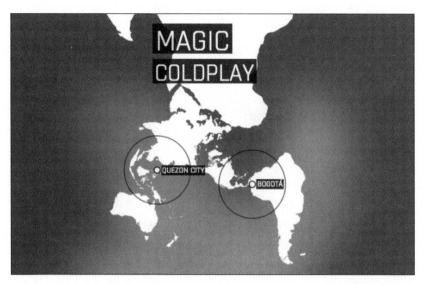

Figure 4.3. Simultaneous listening across the world. Screenshot: McDonald, "Serendipity."

musicians. The videos highlight the kinds of cross-cultural, transborder experiences of travel, collaboration, and empathy that Spotify seeks to associate with music as an art form. In one video, Iranian DJ Kasra V laments his inability to travel freely around the world, explaining, "I tend to fly a lot in my dreams for some reason. Just levitate and fly around. I wish I had that freedom in real life." "I'm with the Banned" aligns this desire for a kind of existential freedom with transnational music experience. It connects music—both making and listening—to an unbounded life. In a video documenting his collaboration with Syrian singer Moh Flow, American rapper Pusha T makes the thesis of this project explicit: "Music is the ultimate connecter of people and it knows no boundaries." Such ideas are underscored in another video by rapper Desiigner, who professes, "Music really has no language." His collaborators, the Somali hip-hop collective Waayaha Cusub, explain that their god made humans "to know each other." Boundaries of geography and culture are erased, here, in favor of common humanity and artistry.

While they do not touch on geoblocking directly, at times the videos make a case for the importance of trans-border media access. Kasra V talks about his experience growing up in Iran, illegally accessing MTV via satellite. Moh Flow points to the importance of American rap as he came of age in Syria. In another video, Sudanese music producer Sufyvn begins his collaboration with R & B singer BJ the Chicago Kid via Skype while stuck in Cairo waiting for a travel visa. Such anecdotes make a case for the power of media to connect across borders, both as a window into another world and as a literal mechanism of cross-cultural connection and collaboration. If geoblocking is not an explicit part of these conversations, the videos nonetheless speak to several of the concerns that hover around it: the cosmopolitan potential of accessing culture from another place, the hurdles that make such access challenging, the implied loss that accompanies an inability to access global media, and the necessity of violating legal and authorized practices in order to gain access. Whether "I'm with the Banned" is a commendable protest against an unjust policy or, as music journalist Liz Pelly puts it, "Spotify's way of cynically deploying woke optics and commodified activism," it is consistent with Spotify's branded experience of seamless, global listening.[51] This should not also suggest that the experiences of people who are marginalized and barred from travel are similar to the relatively mundane practice of bumping into a "This song is not available in your country" message. Rather, the initiative is another way that Spotify promotes its ethos of the importance of transnational cultural interaction. An unspoken irony, then, is that the requisite business practices of the global record industry ensure that policies remain in place to keep people from accessing the very platform promoting these artists.

Even if "Serendipity" and "I'm with the Banned" do not explicitly engage geoblocking, they are part of a broader promotional push by Spotify to conceal its still internationally fragmented availability through signifiers of progressive, cosmopolitan global liberalism. A 2018 *Rolling Stone* piece on Jamaican dancehall music illustrates some of the pitfalls of streaming music's limited geographic availability. Titled "Why Isn't Jamaican Dancehall Bigger in the U.S.?" the article points out that streaming platforms like Spotify and Apple Music should be well suited to the promotion and discovery of international acts.[52] After all, as the article's author, Elias Leight, puts it, such platforms "have a proven record of sidestepping the language barrier when it comes to Spanish and Korean-language songs, and they enable artists to do an end-run around the conservative gatekeepers of terrestrial radio." Leight goes on to point out that if anything, streaming is hurting dancehall due to these platforms' lack of availability in Jamaica and Africa, where the genre enjoys immense popularity. Because Spotify's listener data do not reflect global dancehall fandom, the platform fails to recommend the music to listeners who might not know about the genre but who may enjoy it. This is a problem beyond the level of geography. Pelly has written about the dominance of men on Spotify's playlists, wondering if "streaming is creating a data-driven echo chamber where the most agreed-upon sounds rise to the top, subtly shifting us back toward a more homogenous and overtly masculine pop music culture."[53] This critique can be extrapolated to a broader concern about how limited options and availability reassert global hegemony through streaming.

This is where geoblocking becomes particularly insidious for global culture—not so much in users' lack of access to the platform per se, but in how this lack of access threatens to produce a feedback loop reflecting traditional hierarchies of geographic access. Positing streaming platforms as more cosmopolitan and progressive in their accessibility and tastes ignores their own limitations. Spotify's accidental evocation of Zuckerman's use of the term "serendipity" is particularly ironic, here, as Zuckerman routinely argues that digital platforms should be designed in ways that encourage serendipity, rather than continuing to show us things that we already know and love.[54] In part through their geoblocked nature, Spotify and other streaming platforms do just the opposite— they compile data from a vast yet still limited user base and then sell the ensuing catalog and recommendations as a globally cultivated music library. One consequence of geoblocking may not be a continued fragmentation of global streaming experience, as one might expect, but a reinforcement of dominant musicians and record labels.[55] Spotify pushes against this idea rather explicitly through its aforementioned Musical Map, which purports to emphasize the diversity of music that is popular throughout various locales. But even in doing so, the company acknowledges that a survey of global artist popularity would likely yield rather uniform results. Furthermore, the gaps in the map highlight a platform-consumer relationship that works in tandem to reinforce the favorite products of the global music industry's preferred markets.

If regional lockout serves to make the rich richer through its geob-locked data feedback loop, it masks such processes behind a brand that constantly evokes geography while refusing to pin down any coherent sense of the locative nature of the platform. For example, by making use of imagery regarding both global travel and individual transport, the Spotify branded experience effectively conflates unboundedness in an individual, mobile sense with a broader, cosmopolitan globality. By now, music's experiential and ontological mobility—its ability to be taken on the go—is a familiar one. Mobile devices like MP3 players and iPhones have exacerbated music's mobility in the twenty-first century, but the Sony Walkman (and later, the Discman), boom boxes, portable radios, car stereos, and a host of similar devices have long made listening an essentially nomadic experience.[56] The Walkman in particular helped produce and popularize forms of listening that can move from place to place—what Shuhei Hosokawa calls *musica mobilis*.[57] Thus, mobile music technologies are inflected with economic, technological, industrial, ontological, and experiential dynamics that traverse multiple scales: global, national, transnational, and local. Listeners who attempt to access a streaming platform only to find it geoblocked have an experience that is distinctly national. For those who do have access to the platform and listen to it on their iPhone on a walk or commute, the experience can be at once local (in the space traversed while walking or commuting), national (in that access to these platforms is informed by one's national location), and transnational (in the use of platforms, devices, and perhaps even texts that come out of a variety of transnational industries). These various geographic scales collapse together in Spotify's promotion of a global yet translocal experience that is nonetheless tied tightly to the category of the national.

However, Spotify's conflation of mobility and unrestrained global listening ignores the fact that mobile devices are just as integrated into geolocative systems as other digital media, if not more so. As Florian Sprenger reminds us, because mobile devices are connected to cellular towers and have locative addresses, the same technological infrastructures that enable mobility also enable the consistent tracking of users' locations.[58] In other words, the technological systems that enable an experience of mobility as well as tailored playlists (i.e., back-end surveillance and geolocation) are also employed for the purposes of geoblocking. Intentionally or not, Spotify's global image is produced from a sleight of hand that asks us to ignore the very real reasons digital technologies and the music industry keep the platform geoblocked. This is comparable to Patrick Vonderau's argument that Spotify conceals its zeal for growth and complex technical and financial operations within an "aura of 'Nordic cool' and public benefit around its use of music."[59] Spotify's financial dealings and technical infrastructures, which make the platform unavailable in many parts of the world, are ignored in favor of a cosmopolitan image. The ability to take one's music on the go during a commute and the ability to carry it across a national border are not the same, something that Spotify's branded experience of global listening fails to make clear.

Ultimately, in their simultaneous promotion of an individualized life soundtrack and the possibilities for unbounded living and connection, streaming music platforms attempt to ease concerns about the potentially isolating dimensions of mobile-media cocooning and algorithmic culture as well as the forms of geographic control promoted by geoblocking. In doing so, they mask the mechanisms of control on which streaming platforms are built as well as the ways geoblocking in fact perpetuates a wildly unequal global music industry. Harvey contrasts streaming music's "hyper-personalized" project against radio's earlier project of cultivating imagined communities. In doing so, he quotes Susan Douglas's understanding of broadcasting's charge to bring "diverse and unknown people together as an audience."[60] Spotify seeks to have it both ways—to make the listener feel catered to while asking her to imagine a life of global interconnection via music. However, geoblocking is too tightly integrated into the functional logics of many such platforms for us to ignore it.

"You Know What's Cool? America": Access and Capital

Although Spotify's promotion of a global listening experience and its centrality in discourses of geoblocking in music make it a particularly rich case study, we can extrapolate its lessons to streaming music platforms more generally. While this chapter has emphasized how the branded musical experiences of streaming platforms paper over their ties to familiar, material geography, the previous chapters' lessons on the relationship between geoblocking and geocultural capital are also germane. After all, streaming platforms offer vague promises of universal access but in fact tend to reinforce traditional lines of power and privilege in the global record industry. Digital music's discourses of global accessibility and ubiquity smooth over the actual inequalities of geocultural capital between territories that have differential access to these music platforms. A satirical *TechCrunch* article highlighted how streaming music services illustrate broader, unequal relations of cultural status and value between territories. Posted on April Fools' Day 2011, three months before Spotify announced its US launch, the article reported that Spotify would be ending its European operations in order to launch in the United States. It contained excerpts from a fake email from Ek to European users that stated, "America has always been the most important and lucrative market for web services, and so the decision to close down our European operations to fund a US launch was, frankly, a no-brainer." Another fabricated quote from Napster cofounder and former Facebook president Sean Parker, an early investor in Spotify, states, "Europe isn't cool. You know what's cool? America."[61] By satirizing the often-unquestioned characterization of the United States as a uniquely privileged, lucrative market, the article reveals some truths about regional lockout. Because American audiences have generally enjoyed the privilege that comes with living in a premier media market, US frustrations about geoblocked platforms reflect assumptions that Americans *should* have access to the cornucopia of streaming art and entertainment made available to those living in other parts of the world—an extension of American exceptionalism into the market logics of entertainment media. Therefore, Americans' irritation over Spotify's lack of availability was as much about the geocultural capital that comes with representing the peak of global media access and power as it was a political interest in fair and open digital media.

Spotify's availability reflects relations of economic and (geo)cultural value within certain places. By invoking the notion of "cool," the fake quotation from Parker shows how questions of cultural capital and social value have become wrapped up in geoblocking and transnational access to platforms. The joke that an *entire country* can be cool in fact highlights how a nation's level of media access reflects its perceived value as a social and cultural entity, and not simply an economic one. A *New*

York Times report on the US launch of Spotify likewise underlined how access feeds geocultural capital, suggesting that if you do not know or care about Spotify, "then you're clearly out of touch with the Europeans."[62] Thus, geoblocking illustrates the relevance of geography to the links between music as an art form, expressions of cultural capital, and the ways engagement with music can grow out of certain class positions. These relationships are central to Pierre Bourdieu's foundational work on cultural capital, which focused heavily on musical taste and included the argument that "nothing more clearly affirms one's 'class,' nothing more infallibly classifies, than tastes in music."[63] When the abilities to accumulate knowledge about, and participate in, popular music cultures are closed off due to geographic restrictions, this can affect the degree to which a listener feels like she belongs to the wider conversation about a song, artist, or scene.

The discourses surrounding geoblocking in digital music represent a kind of global public debate over the appropriate relationships among music, technology, regulation, culture, and geography. Over the past fifteen years or so, music has bound listeners not just through the abstractions of cultural capital, taste cultures, and fan communities, but also literally through connections forged via social networks and online fan and torrenting communities. No wonder, then, that even if streaming music platforms are cutting down on illegal downloads and file sharing, for many the easiest way to get around a geoblock is still through informal means. As Patrick Burkart argues, listeners acting in opposition to the corporate controllers of the celestial jukebox "are trying to save a place for music as a zone for reproduction of 'free culture,' identity formation, and broad participation in making music and music scenes."[64] Geoblocking and its circumvention enable us to explore these dynamics across transnational media cultures. If, as I have argued, geoblocking's nation-based contours contradict the popular vision of online music as at once transnationally fluid and individually customizable, differential levels of access have implications for understanding popular music as a form of cross-cultural art. Theoretically, then, circumventing regional lockout can encourage forms of media consumption that seek out artists and genres from different backgrounds. Either way, circumvention is an emerging, increasingly simple aspect of media consumption that enables its own cultures of users sharing tips and resources on how to get around geoblocks. *Locked Out*'s final chapter examines moments when consumers, distributors, and retailers alike have flouted regional lockout, instead consuming and trading media in ways that reject the cultural industries' regional restrictions. Taking region-free DVD use in diasporic and cinephile communities as its case studies, chapter 5 explores the cultural and political-economic significance of region-free media as well as the practices and politics of rejecting regional lockout.

5

Region-Free Media

Collecting and Selling Cultural Status

"Good cinema is culture, but really all kind of knowledge is good and it's important to have access to knowledge." Bootleg DVD salesman Santos Demonios utters these words in a short video by Vice Media's *Motherboard* about the pirate DVD trade in Lima, Peru. Titled "Peru's DVD Pirates Have Exquisite Taste," the report at times reflects *Vice's* customary exoticizing gaze on illegal and surreptitious activities in the Global South, but it also sheds light on how distributors and retailers in certain parts of the world make do when they are cut off from formal media circulation networks. The first words of the video, spoken by Demonios, emphasize the personal, cultural, and economic importance of media access: "One has to adapt to their own economic possibilities. Unfortunately, our economy only allows us to afford piracy. Yes, piracy is illegal, but in a country that's hungry for access to knowledge, which is also a form of development, we have to embrace illegality."[1] There is a lot to unpack in this short statement. For one, Demonios indicates that the state of media distribution networks in a particular place can be a barometer of broader economic circumstances. An intertitle expands on his suggestion that Peruvians can only "afford piracy," telling us that Peru's informal DVD trade stems from a combination of slow internet speeds, high costs of formally distributed DVDs, and a general lack of officially distributed films in the country.

Demonios also stresses a key premise of this book: that media products like DVDs represent cultural resources that people use to attain knowledge and participate in broader conversations about art and popular culture. Thus, informal media networks like this one respond and contribute to cultural conditions as much as economic ones. The rest of the video portrays the business practices of a DVD stand in a Lima shopping mall, where we observe Demonios and two other salesmen burning (assuredly region-free) copies of DVDs and discussing topics like their approach to packaging and their relationship with the local police. In particular, the report highlights the popularity of independent and global art films such as *Blue Is the Warmest Colour* (2013), *The Act of Killing* (2012), and *Uncle Boonmee Who Can Recall His Past Lives* (2010) as well as films by French New Wave directors like Jean-Luc Godard, François Truffaut, and Eric Rohmer, a development the video presents as somewhat surprising (indeed, consider the attempt at irony in the video's title, "Peru's DVD Pirates Have Exquisite Taste"). On the one hand, the video points to some of the overlaps between informal media trades and cinephilia. On the other, the implied incongruity between the informal trade practices of the Global South and global high culture indicates that many in the West see cinephilia as a predominately Western, Anglo-American, or European experience.

The video captures two sides of region-free media that this chapter will explore further: the way region-free DVDs have sustained both informal bootleg economies and global film culture. As I have shown in chapters 2 and 3, media audiences routinely figure out ways to get around regional lockout systems. Exploring these trends, I analyze region-free media use among two broad and overlapping cultural perspectives, each of which embodies a different set of power relations within the global mediascape: diasporic media culture and cinephilia. By showing that region-free media use is not just one thing but rather a heterogeneous series of practices, I argue that the cultural politics of region-free media are more ambivalent than many of its promoters or detractors—whether film critics, copyright activists, consumer rights groups, lawmakers, or media industries—might suggest. Focusing primarily though not exclusively on the use of region-free media forms in the Global North, I begin with an analysis of region code circumvention and region-free DVD use by diasporic video retailers in the United States. Drawing in part on interviews with several owners and employees of diasporic video stores, I show how the circumvention of DVD region codes can represent both a bottom-up challenge to the distribution routes and global space-time relations of dominant media industries as well as a more everyday practice of making cultural resources available to local immigrant populations. When media important to these communities are not released in the United States through formal means, such retailers import and create

EL CHATO
BOOTLEG SELLER
There's some people that can't get access
to these films

Figure 5.1. Bootleggers offer Peruvians access to film. Screenshot: Motherboard, "Peru's DVD Pirates."

region-free DVDs for their consumers. While this research reveals uses of region-free media by the less powerful, the next case study shows how region-free DVD cultures can also reflect an ironic yet common blend of cosmopolitanism and cultural dominance. I illustrate this through the long-standing use of region-free DVD by cinephiles, collectors, and cultists who seek out global film culture. Often, such practices represent an admirable desire to engage the wealth and diversity of global cultural production. At the same time, they can manifest as cultural tourism laced with overtones of masculinized cosmopolitanism and a commoditizing collector's mind-set.

This chapter shows that digital regulation's effects are not always uniform. Even if a particular form of technological regulation has a relatively simple and straightforward impact on the *affordances* of a media technology, the way users take up, understand, interact with, talk about, and circumvent it will reflect a multitude of viewpoints and user practices following different political trajectories. The unauthorized trade and consumption of, say, *The Blue Angel* (1930) or *Floating Weeds* (1959) from the UK's Eureka Entertainment / Masters of Cinema line can function both as an act of cinephilic, completist consumption and as an action that retains some bit of control over distribution routes traditionally shaped by formal media industries. Even more so, the existence of bootleg copies of Senegalese films in a shop in Harlem, New York, operates at least in part as a media "contra-flow" that exists alongside and even in opposition to formal circulation networks.[2] Still, by ending on a note of critique levied at the ways region-free media culture can in fact reinforce dominant cultural power, I argue broadly that we should not *always and necessarily* presume that media practices are politically progressive simply because they seem to oppose powerful industries and copyright regimes. Such practices certainly *can* be resistant or subversive, but often they simply reflect consumerist logics that view access to media products as a benchmark for equitable participation in the global mediascape. And while this chapter primarily explores the use of region-free media to access various kinds of nondominant or niche media, it similarly shows that regional lockout and its circumvention by users exist on a more complex axis of cultural politics than one that would simply posit "lockout = bad, circumvention = good."

If the previous four chapters emphasized cultural industries' regulation of media technologies, this chapter focuses more on how people have responded. In analyzing the meanings of region-free media, I provide sketches of a history of region-free media culture, focusing in particular on the emergence and adoption of region-free DVD players while touching on other circumvention practices. These histories complement earlier analyses of the DVD region code (chapter 1), region-hacking gamers (chapter 2), the use of proxies and VPNs to get past geoblocking restrictions (chapter 3), and the perceptions of digital media's cosmopolitan potential (chapter 4) by illustrating how region-free DVD's popularity resulted in a broader global conversation about regional lockout's economic, regulatory, and cultural effects. DVDs offer an instructive case study of region-free media culture for a couple of reasons. For one, they provide a historical perspective on both region-free media and forms of cultural regulation more broadly. Indeed, DVD was the first medium to provoke widespread public discussions of regional lockout systems, and its relationship to the DVD's CSS encryption meant that it was often incorporated into public discourses about copyright, digital rights management, and the Digital Millennium Copyright Act. Second, I have touched on circumvention practices around other media forms in the previous chapters, and so this chapter affords an opportunity to focus more closely on the cultural politics of one particular region-free medium in a few different cultural and political-economic contexts. As a result, the chapter adds further layers to my argument about the DVD's significance as an institutionalizing force for regional lockout and a forebear for the lockout systems that would come to be installed in streaming platforms even as the world supposedly moved out of an era dominated by "physical" media.

Region-Free Media Cultures

Region-free media refers to any media technology, text, or experience that consciously and intentionally rejects regional lockout systems. It can manifest in multiple ways across a host of media technologies: multi-region DVDs and DVD players; video game consoles that have been hacked to play game discs and cartridges from around the world; and VPN and proxy services that allow users to connect to streaming video and music platforms unavailable in their area. As this indicates, region-free media operate at the levels of both hardware and software (and in the interactions between the two). Furthermore, as I showed in chapter 2, region-free media are not new. Methods of hacking regional lockouts and incompatibilities existed in video game culture as far back as the 1980s, and users have adapted lockout circumvention practices to virtually every media delivery technology that has come into existence since.

Region-free media embody a number of practices revolving around particular technologies that allow users to circumvent regional lockout. The region-free DVD can thus be considered its own kind of format, existing in relation to but still distinct from "region-coded" DVD, with its own set of meanings and protocols. Jonathan Sterne argues that the concept of a "format" "names a set of rules according to which a technology can operate."[3] Although it is an offshoot of the DVD format, region-free DVD operates according to its own set of rules different from those of region-coded DVD. Furthermore, region-free DVD's social and cultural meanings are different from those of region-coded DVD, suggesting an entirely different set of viewing and distribution practices. With this in mind, considering region-free media as not simply a technology but as a cluster of cultural practices offers a fuller illustration of how it shapes media tastes and circulation networks.

Many who engage in or promote region-free media cultures present them as clandestine and subversive antiestablishment practices. This viewpoint is evident in some of the pioneering scholarly work on region-free DVD. In his piece on DVD region codes, for example, Brian Hu sees the use of region-free DVD players as, in part, a form of "fan agency" against Hollywood's distribution routes and technological standardizations.[4] Drawing on Hu's reading, Tessa Dwyer and Ioana Uricaru point out that the practice of hacking region-coded DVD players was key to accessing uncensored and native-language fan subtitles and pirate media in Romania.[5] Without explicitly drawing on it, such framing recalls John Fiske's de Certeauian view of popular culture as "using *their* products for *our* purposes."[6] In this formulation, the power of popular culture comes from how people mobilize it against dominant orders.[7] Extending this to unauthorized media uses (not much of a stretch given that Fiske illustrates his analysis through the example of shoplifting), piracy and lockout circumvention can be read not simply as acquiring a product through different means but as an affront against the systems of markets and power within which that product exists. The interactive affordances of digitally networked technologies, which easily enable piracy and lockout circumvention through proxy servers, seemingly intensify the possibility of making consumption productive.

Thus, with piracy and lockout circumvention, the lack of consideration for traditionally understood global space-time relations is just as potentially transgressive as the theft of a product. Given global cultural industries' reliance on controlled distribution, the space, place, and time of consumption become important for accumulating capital. Whether critical or celebratory, the circumvention of regional restrictions is often rhetorically presented as placeless—as a transgression of geography and the social and consumptive norms that accompany geographical rootedness. One critic of geoblocking notes that "the makers of music videos, TV shows and movies still think nationally . . . but file sharing already knows no borders . . . Technology will roll right over those 'Not available in your country' notices in due course."[8] The material threat to media industries' bottom lines is obvious, but there is a broader, more abstract form of transgression taking place here. If recognition as a subject partly

relies on one's location within a matrix of power and signification informed by geographic structure, lockout circumvention on some level
represents a challenge to these structures. David Morley points out that
placelessness and mobility tend to be pathologized as "geographical deviance" in a world that places individuals and groups in fixed locations
and categories.[9] Writing specifically about the circumvention of regional
restrictions on media, Morley reminds us that "in an era of electronic
communications, conflict is conducted by the invasion not only of geographical but also of virtual territory."[10] Such conflict results in what
Ramon Lobato calls the "proxy wars," or the policies and mechanisms
developed by a platform like Netflix to push back against VPNs and
proxies as means of unauthorized global access.[11] As evidenced in the
BBC iPlayer example from chapter 3, this conflict can take place between users and forces of power, but it can also take place between users
residing in different territories.

A more celebratory take on placelessness and geographical deviance
is apparent in the websites and brand logos of file-sharing, proxy, and
VPN services. Often, these draw on diverse images of global travel: sea-
faring pirates, cosmopolitan globalism, freedom from the shackles of
bondage, clandestine disguise, and even guerilla warfare. Drawing on
the popular image of the "pirate" as a pillager roaming through international waters and unmoored from normative geography, the Pirate Bay
torrent site famously presents an emblem of a pirate ship in which the
Jolly Roger has been replaced by the logo for the 1980s "Home Taping
Is Killing Music" anti-copyright-infringement campaign. The logo for
the proxy database site Xroxy.com was at one time a globe adorned with
several national flags. This not only suggests an image of global communities ignoring corporate-defined borders, it promotes a more open
internet as a window to an engagement with global culture. Adopting a
more antiauthoritarian approach, another proxy site, PublicProxyServ-
ers.com, uses as its slogan "Breaking chains since 2002." The logo for the
VPN service Hide My Ass! puns on its name by presenting a donkey
adorned in a Sam Spade–like trench coat, fedora, and sunglasses. The
logo for the proxy service Proxify likewise incorporates a camouflage
fatigues color scheme.

Nevertheless, many who buy and sell region-free media products do
not do so with the goal of undermining more formal networks of circu-

lation; they simply want to access the media they want to watch or listen to on the consumer end and make some money in meeting that demand on the supply end. On the part of torrent and VPN services, the use of clandestine and subversive imagery is as much a branding strategy as it is a pronouncement of taking up arms against oppressive corporate forces (the informal flip side of Spotify's cosmopolitan global brand discussed in chapter 4). This is not to minimize the political power of region-free media—particularly when it comes to issues of identity, taste, and cultural globalization—but simply to complicate it. Region-free DVD uses among cinephiles and diasporic groups offer more than simplistic David-and-Goliath, consumers-versus-studios stories.

Region-Free DVD

Region-free DVDs and DVD players have been around as long as the DVD itself. In some places, they even preceded the format's launch. One trade report from 1998 notes that region-free players were beginning to show up in London even before the DVD was introduced formally to the UK.[12] By this point, UK and European consumers in particular were used to the headaches that could come with living in a secondary market for global home video, and they were keen to avoid many of these same issues with the introduction of DVD. Given the prevalence of region-free players throughout Europe, and the fact that Hollywood could not use language as a natural barrier against import as easily as it could in other regions, the region became particularly problematic for Hollywood's maintenance of its distribution windows. One estimate from 2000 suggested that 75 percent of DVD players in Europe were region-free.[13] A trade report from the same year suggested that in Europe, region codes were "almost a non-issue" due to the widespread use of region-free players across the continent.[14] Usually, because many major films at this time were emanating from Hollywood, which was still engaging in staggered global release dates, many region-free DVDs or parallel imports manifested as bootlegged Hollywood products entering overseas territories before a film's official release. While region-free discs and players were often sold and adopted to play imported Region One DVDs, there are plenty of examples of region-free media flowing in the other direction. In 2001, for instance, reports surfaced of official

Region Three and bootlegged region-free DVDs of Ang Lee's *Crouch-ing Tiger, Hidden Dragon* making their way to the United States while the film was still in theaters, as the title had been released in Singapore theaters five months before its American debut.[15]

As this indicates, Europe was far from the only region with a high demand for region-free DVD. Many places with less geocultural capi-tal in global film markets found themselves stocked with players and discs to get around regional lockout. If anything, such resources could be more common in spaces that Hollywood did not track as closely as they did their secondary markets. A report from late 1998 notes that the Middle East saw an increased demand for imported European DVDs, and region-free players were beginning to become available to con-sumers.[16] As early as 1999, region-free players could be found easily in Mexico and throughout the rest of Latin America.[17] Soon enough, they became accessible to consumers around the world. One trade report from 1998 noted, "Retailers in [the] Far East already are doctoring Pio-neer players before sale to consumers, while [the] European company Techtronics will modify [a] variety of brands for [a] $65 service fee."[18] North American trades, industry types, and news sources often discur-sively construct region-free DVD players as threatening to industrially sanctioned distribution, and Western press discourse about region-free DVDs and DVD players posits these technologies as bootleg products invading trade routes from far-off regions. Trade and news reports refer to "cheaper DVD players from the Far East," and in 1999 a number of studios stopped adding Spanish-language tracks to Region One DVDs because they feared these discs were making their way to Latin America through unauthorized distribution routes.[19] Here, region-free DVD players stand in for a potentially dangerous, immigrant Other, invad-ing places they do not belong, a common trope in talk about bootleg technology. In chapter 1, I argued that DVD region codes were a system of representation as much as one of regulation because they offered a means by which powerful institutions could represent the rest of the world. The characterization of region-free technologies as emblematic of leaky borders is not just an issue of media economics; it also reflects broader anxieties surrounding border transgression.

Around this time, people began using the internet to access instruc-tions on how to purchase region-free players or hack their players in order to play region-free DVDs.[20] Websites like the now-defunct DVD Utilities Resource Center spread information on hacking, and like-minded message boards figured as spaces where users could circulate knowledge on the various methods of circumventing regional lockout systems.[21] For DVDs, one can buy discs without region codes, purchase a region-free player, or hack a conventional player in order to make it multi-standard. The latter involves a number of different technological fixes that range from physically rewiring the player to simply pressing a combination of buttons on the remote control that result in an overriding of the region coding system. Among other things, this functioned as an opening up of hacking and other unauthorized media practices and competencies to a broader base of consumers, even well before the concept of "lifehacking" made the relative democratization of hacking culture more banal. These extended well beyond the DVD. Although Blu-ray has in some ways loosened regional restrictions (as some studios simply do not bother region-coding their discs), it is in many ways more difficult to circumvent regional locks on Blu-ray players and discs. One Australian writer describes his experience of paying $1,000 for a region-free player before stumbling on a cheaper player that included a firmware disc that let him reset the player for different region codes.[22] Furthermore, as shown in chapter 2, gamers have long undertaken rather involved measures to ensure that cartridges or discs from one part of the world can play on consoles from another.

As these examples indicate, it would be far too easy to suggest that media distribution routes have always followed the contours of regional lockout maps. At the same time, the question of whether region-free media made the region code system dysfunctional is a complex one. Brett Christophers argues that this conclusion is too simplistic: "The studios, surely, would not be investing large quantities of time and money in lobbying for the continued application of region coding if they believed that they were not longer realizing meaningful economic benefits from doing so."[23] This constant push and pull between control and resistance characterized public battles over region-free DVD. In the context of the format's emergence and popularization, cultural commentators and advocacy groups framed region-free media as an issue of consumer rights. Examples abound of popular references to region-free DVD players giving consumers "more choice," and consumer rights groups have long been critical of region codes.[24]

Consumers did not always have to take it on themselves to learn how to hack region-free technologies. Often, they had help from media retail establishments. Although the trade in region-free media has many connections to informal, bootleg media networks, locating region-free players and discs did not prove particularly difficult for people in larger metropolitan areas. While the importance of retailers in region-free media culture is particularly evident in the bootleg production and circulation practices of video stores catering to diasporic groups, more formal retailers and big-box stores (particularly outside the United States) have also had a hand in helping consumers overcome regional lockout. This is because it is often more lucrative for local distributors and retailers to ensure that consumers have the hardware and software they want rather than adhere to the distribution routes of the Hollywood studios. As the *Sydney Morning Herald* reported in the first few years of DVD's existence, "Local DVD retailers say the demand for multi-region DVD players is so high they regularly premodify players to ensure a minimum of delay for consumers."[25] Reports of major chains like Tesco in the UK and Circuit City in the United States selling region-free players were common in the late 1990s and early 2000s.[26] Around this time, Tesco wrote a letter to Warner Home Video president Warren Lieberfarb, unsuccessfully lobbying for the elimination of region codes.[27] Indeed, such retailers have helped users get around regional lockout systems for as long as DVD players have been around. As early as 1998, a report on region-free players in London discusses one shopkeeper who eagerly demonstrates to the writer how to hack certain players to bypass region locks and explains which studio's discs are harder to hack.[28]

Furthermore, the emergence of online media retailers like Amazon, Deep Discount DVD, and region-specific sites like YesAsia made accessing global media even easier. In the early years of DVD, such online retailers were similarly nascent, and the potential riches of borderless online purchasing and the desire to gain greater access to digital media culture through region-free media seemed a perfect match. Indeed, part of the reason manufacturers and retailers began making and selling region-free DVD players was to meet the demands of non-US consumers who ordered Region One DVDs from online retailers.[29] Much of this discourse promoted a vision of digital distribution that Chris Anderson would famously theorize as "the long tail," the idea that online distribution would focus less on big hits and instead help reach niche consumers by eliminating scarcity and making obscure and specialized products more easily available.[30] Here, those served by the long tail were the consumers who would push against Hollywood's will and seek out region-free DVD.

Region-Free DVD in Diaspora

On the whole, a fairly diverse group of consumers make use of region-free media: cinephiles interested in global film; anime fans in East Asia, North America, and elsewhere; gamers using physical and digital hacks to import and play discs and cartridges; ex-pats and people in the military; and ultimately anyone who has the motive and the initiative to access media from across borders.[31] One of the more prominent audience segments for region-free DVD has been immigrant and diasporic communities. The reason for region-free media's popularity among diasporic people is evident enough: they enable viewers to more easily consume media from other territories, such as one's home country. Likewise, burning and converting region-coded DVDs into region-free DVDs and DVD-Rs make the circulation of films and television programs from one's homeland or from another part of the world much easier. The histories of diasporic home video circulation are multiple, heterogeneous, and impossible to catalog in any cohesive manner, but they generally reveal communities building up semiformal and informal distribution and retail infrastructures that circulate films and film culture otherwise ignored or blocked by formal, dominant media distribution routes.

Throughout much of the world, the destination points for many of these region-free imports are the video stores that cater to diasporic people. On one level, these video stores are spaces of niche, narrowcast migrant media culture.[32] On another level, as businesses woven into immigrant communities as well as spaces of neighborhood gathering and discussion, they are part of what Stuart Cunningham calls diasporic "public sphericules," or community-based public spheres sustained in

part through engagement in diasporic media culture. Video stores—
and diasporic media more broadly—can help fulfill public sphericules'
charge to "provide a central site for public communication in globally
dispersed communities, stage communal difference and discord produc-
tively, and work to articulate insider ethno-specific identities—which
are by definition 'multi-national,' even global—to the wider 'host' environments."[33] Because video stores function as nodes in the circulation
of diasporic media, they offer cultural resources that viewers can use as
sites of identity affirmation and negotiation.[34]

As several studies have shown, diasporic video retailers do not trade
only in video. Often, they are more generally focused retail establishments such as grocery stores or electronics and housewares stores that
also sell videos. Dona Kolar-Panov's survey of video stores in various
Australian suburbs showed that while few formal video stores contained
material in languages other than English, other kinds of business establishments like newsstands, delis, and pharmacies contained non-
English-language videos, usually "determined by and directly linked to
the ethnic background of the shop owner."[35] Writing about the Indian-
American diaspora, Aswin Punathambekar points out that a period of
intensified migration in the 1980s saw a boom in family-owned Indian
grocery stores that also sold bootlegged videocassettes of Hindi films.[36]
As Bart Beaty and Rebecca Sullivan show, Asian diaspora communities
were in large part responsible for the proliferation of region-free DVDs
and players as a way to more easily import Pacific Rim cinema to Canada.[37] Writing earlier, Glen Lewis and Chalinee Hirano show in their
study of Thai video stores in Australia that such establishments began
popping up in the 1980s, with grocery store proprietors asking relatives
in Thailand to send recordings of Thai television programs.[38] Together,
these portraits of global diasporic video culture indicate a combination
of formal and informal distribution networks linked to family, national
identity, and transnational distribution routes.

Region-free DVDs move among diaspora communities in ways that
reflect Arjun Appadurai's vision of commodity flow as "a shifting compromise between socially regulated paths and competitively inspired di-
versions."[39] When they diverge from media industries' preferred paths,
they are part of the "shadow economies" of media distribution existing
alongside (and even in place of) more formal distribution and retail in-

frastructures.[40] These operate as crucial points of media access for many around the world, and particularly for those living in and hailing from the Global South. Indeed, trade journals and industry lore about region-free media connected the circulation of region-free DVD players to a broader network of informal commodity trade. In 1999, the US-based trade magazine *Audio Week* reported on a Hong Kong–based electronics company that represented a "one-stop source for ceiling fans, vacuum cleaners, lighting fixtures—and DVD players whose regional code settings can be changed or overridden."[41] *Audio Week*'s occasionally pathologizing invocation of these players' "mysterious origin" characterizes the view that the Global South's media manufacturing and distribution institutions operate outside the domain of accepted, traceable, and knowable media industries. Indeed, beginning in the late 1990s, customs officials in the UK and the United States began to seize shipments of DVD players from Asia. These officials claimed that this had more to do with the players' "lack of compliance with electrical standards" than their lack of regional encoding, but the hardware's ability to violate intellectual property regulations assuredly played a part.[42] Whatever the reason, such seizures indicate an anxiety surrounding the unauthorized import of cultural products.

To understand region-free DVD's specific role in diasporic media access, I observed and interviewed employees and proprietors of diasporic video stores serving a variety of Global Southern diasporic communities in the United States—specifically, in the metro areas of New York City, Detroit, Milwaukee, and Madison, Wisconsin. In general, I found that the impacts and cultural politics of regional lockout and region-free media on diasporic media cultures are a mixed bag. For some, regional lockout is a minor annoyance—ripping and burning DVDs in order to overcome such restrictions is a regular part of the workday. For others, it hardly registers at all, particularly for those stores that receive shipments of DVDs that are already region-free. For still others, however, it affects their consumers' ability to gain access to resources that can figure as an important site of "cultural continuity" or negotiation, in the words of Lewis and Hirano.[43]

Of course, not all diasporas are equal and thus cannot be fully understood through one explanatory or analytical framework. This is to say that the observations here are more a comparative survey of region-free practices than a sustained study of one particular group. This view reveals some differences in diasporic DVD retail practices, but it highlights one thing many of these stores have in common: a predilection toward bootleg DVDs stripped of region codes. The pervasiveness of region-free media in diasporic life illustrates a complicated mixture of the subversive and the everyday. While some have argued that piracy and parallel imports transgress media conglomerates' mechanisms of spatial control, the presence of parallel imported and region-free DVDs in these stores seems far more ordinary.[44] The hard-to-find shelves, bootlegged tapes, and handwritten labels discovered by Lucas Hilderbrand in his own analysis of Korean video stores in Orange County, California, are readily apparent, but these conditions are common realities of media distribution in diaspora communities more than overtly transgressive pirate practices.[45] Part of this reality is a common awareness of regional lockout and how it works. Shelves and DVDs are regularly marked with signs or stickers that either indicate which region the DVDs come from or note their region-free status. A Brighton Beach, Brooklyn, store specializing in Russian goods includes large "PAL" stickers to indicate DVDs that will not work on NTSC players and televisions. One store in the Koreatown neighborhood of Manhattan includes some region-free DVDs, but it also includes many Region Three DVDs, which are labeled as such. These are common sights in stores that offer media products from around the world.

The perceived impact of these regional lockout systems on the customer depends on the individual establishment. While many stores do what they can to instruct customers on what region codes are and how to circumvent them, others simply eschew region-coded DVDs altogether in favor of region-free discs. Whether regional lockout is a headache for such stores seems to be determined by how easily they can rip and burn DVDs, how easy it is for their customers to do so, or whether they can acquire DVDs without region codes. Often, this will depend on which national or regional industry produced them. The manager of an Indian / South Asian DVD shop in the basement of a shopping center in Jackson Heights, Queens, told me when I asked if his DVDs were region-coded, "The DVDs that we have, you can watch it anywhere in the world . . . [region codes] are only for India. If you go to India then you get it in PAL, and the VCD you get it in PAL. The

English original movies that they sell down there where they have the rights in India, everything is in PAL, but Indian movies are not. Indian DVDs are not. They're region-free."[46] Although understandably evasive on where his DVDs come from, his response stresses that not all region-free DVDs are bootlegs. Indeed, some are legitimately produced and formally distributed discs wherein the publisher has opted to use discs without region codes, as in the Indian DVDs he discusses. Some stores were careful to point out that their region-free discs were on the up and up. When I asked an employee of a Milwaukee-based Indian grocery store about region codes, he stressed, "These are all region. I know other places have copies that are pirated, but we don't. Only legal copies."

Still, bootleg practices abound. For many stores, when DVDs do arrive with region codes intact, they find measures to get around them—usually by ripping and burning new copies of the region-coded DVDs. An employee of an African DVD store I visited in Harlem's Le Petit Sénégal neighborhood indicated somewhat vaguely that the store owns a "converter" that can change the region code (presumably, this would simply be a process of ripping and burning the DVDs onto different discs rather than a process of "converting" the hard-coded Regional Playback Control encryption). Indeed, many of these stores are not shy about their methods—a woman sitting outside the above-mentioned Jackson Heights store was actively burning DVDs and printing cover art from a laptop computer. In another indication of the small, one-room store's informal nature, the shop also included an older woman tailoring clothing for sale next to the racks of DVDs.[47] Another Milwaukee store—an Indian grocery store/restaurant that also sold a handful of DVDs—presented its inventory as haphazardly organized stacks of DVD-Rs with handwritten labels in a few small plastic baskets. When asked about region codes, the manager told me, "These are all copies, so they will play on any DVD player. Back when we opened the store, we had to buy a bunch of convertors . . . and we spent $500–$600. And now those are sitting in my garage." Though the specific methods may change, the practice of finding region-code workarounds remains.

The common reminders of regional lockout (as well as its circumvention) speak to the diasporic video store's status as a hybrid space, one existing on a spectrum from formal to informal and reflecting the complex geography of global cultural interaction. Indeed, many stores contain a blend of various national and regional cinemas (like Telugu, Tamil, and Bengali films, for instance, in South Asian video stores, and Senegalese and Nigerian films in a Harlem Senegalese DVD store) alongside bootlegged versions of mainstream American films. Getting around region codes thus helps make the DVD a more fundamentally global medium, in the sense that it enables easier access to a diversity of films from various parts of the world. These transnational dynamics were apparent in discussions with the managers and owners even as they were generally vague about *precisely* where their DVDs originated. Indeed, many of them spoke to both formal and informal networks of transnational commodity distribution. After the Milwaukee employee stressed the legality of the store's product, he proceeded to explain that their DVDs come from wholesalers based in Chicago's Devon Avenue Indian neighborhood who received their shipments from India or elsewhere in South Asia.

This reference to local and translocal distribution, however, reveals the significance of local communities in region-free media culture in addition to transnational ones. Diasporic video stores serve as important sites of gathering for people to gain access to culturally proximal media and cultural resources—resources that would be difficult if not impossible to access without region-free media.[48] Speaking to the idea of diasporic media as part of a "public sphericule," workers reiterated that their customers are mostly members of the diasporic communities in the immediate area. Although they are different in their urban and diasporic character, these establishments have similarities to the small-town American video stores analyzed by Daniel Herbert in his book *Videoland*, in that they "interweave movie culture with a wide variety of local conditions and concerns."[49] By serving particular, localized, and usually ethnically specific populations, diasporic video stores are saturated with and help structure the cinematic tastes and broader cultural matters of the surrounding community. Catering to what James Clifford refers to as the "crucial community 'insides' and regulated traveling 'outsides" of diasporic neighborhoods, their proprietors and employees see themselves as serving a simultaneously local and transnational community.[50] This is especially the case in a place like New York, where the size of the city and the development of diasporic neighborhoods has resulted in the existence of particular ethnic enclaves (e.g., Greeks in Astoria,

South Asians in Jackson Heights, Latinos in East Harlem). As spaces of reterritorialization amid the deterritorializing processes of globalization and migration, these neighborhoods are at once differentiated communities and spaces influenced by global processes.

Because these stores carry hard-to-find films and television programs from around the world, their customers occasionally spread beyond their relative diasporic customer base.[51] Indeed, part of what gives the United States (and particularly large cities like New York) a wealth of geocultural capital in the global entertainment environment is the opportunities it gives to find relatively rare cultural products. One employee of a Japanese book and video store in Midtown Manhattan told me that while the Japanese-American diaspora made up a large part of his customer base, he also regularly sells DVDs to American anime collectors. In Milwaukee, the manager of an Indian grocery store told me, "Some whites come to buy spices or to eat, and they say they're interested in Bollywood," and a manager of an Indian DVD store in Jackson Heights, Queens, similarly said, "I have Spanish and white customers in here as well, watching Indian movies." These dynamics became even more apparent to me in my interviews: in general, interviewees met my questions with less reticence once I expressed knowledge about the directors, films, and genres for sale or rent at these establishments. For example, the employee of the store in Le Petit Sénégal opened up and talked with me quite a bit more once I mentioned the legendary Senegalese director Ousmane Sembène. He seemed to acknowledge my awareness of Senegalese cinema as a genuine interest in the workings of his store and the flows of African film culture rather than rote or suspicious information gathering. As a result, we had a conversation that lasted quite a bit longer than some of my interviews in other stores, and he gave me two (bootlegged, region-free) Sembène DVDs as a parting gift when I left. Similarly, in many stores catering to the Indian-American diaspora, proprietors were more likely to talk to me once it was clear that I understood that "Bollywood" is not synonymous with "Indian cinema." My awareness of other regional cinemas in India and Senegalese directors like Sembène is also indicative of my own privilege and cultural capital, as I have had access to a film and media education that has contributed to my interest in and knowledge about these global film cultures. All this is to say that while diasporic video stores' trade in region-free DVD helps sustain the cultural practices of particular diasporic communities, it also taps into a broader circuit of global film viewing that sees such video stores as sites for the accumulation and trade of cultural capital.

Region-Free Cinephilia and Cosmopolitanism

Throughout the late 1990s and the 2000s, much resistance against DVD region codes articulated two schools of thought. The first is the idea that cinema is a purely *global* art form that should encourage the free flow of films across borders and the appreciation of cinema from other countries. The other, discussed throughout this book, is the notion that the internet and digital media technologies more broadly would open up the world and make this free flow possible. The former is in part an outgrowth of cinephilia, a particular mode of film spectatorship and thought represented by a transnational cluster of like-minded film critics and appreciators. Cinephilia corresponds with a certain approach to taste that encompasses art house and cult movies and comes about in part through a privileged relationship to film. Scholars have pointed out similarities to the "art critical discourse of connoisseurship" and called it "a kind of aristocratic cine-literacy."[52] In other words, cinephilia requires not only the time and financial capital to seek out and watch as many movies as possible, but the cultural capital to appraise and appreciate particular films, directors, and national cinemas. In this vein, it involves a recognition of the "globalness" of cinema as an art form and space of cultural engagement. Thomas Elsaesser points to the transnational routes endemic to the cinephile experience when he writes, "Cinephilia . . . is not simply a love of the cinema. It is always already caught in several kinds of deferral: a detour in place and space, a shift in register and a delay in time."[53] In addition to the temporal deferrals of rediscovery and nostalgia, cinephilia functions as a geocultural and spatial kind of detour—an engagement with emblems of international culture that follow various transnational distribution paths on their way to the audience. In this way, it intersects with what Henry Jenkins has called "pop cosmopolitanism," the cultivation of a kind of global awareness through media and popular culture. While cinephilia and pop cosmopolitanism have different relationships to taste, they both speak to media culture's ability to offer opportunities for intercultural engagement.[54]

For many cinephiles, digital platforms like the DVD promised a democratization of global film culture, something seemingly impeded by region codes.[55] Thus, it was only natural that they would begin to get around this form of DRM. A 1999 editorial from *The Australian* with the demonstrative headline "Studios Divide and Rule to Keep Movie Disc Titles Scarce" makes a case for circumventing regional restrictions on cinephile grounds: "The film studios eventually will have to come to their collective senses and realize that film, the most universal of the arts, should be region-free and truly international. Until then, it gives great satisfaction to thwart them."[56] The editorial points to region-coded DVDs as an impediment to "film junkies" with "catholic" tastes, as the author describes himself. Around the world, critics and cultural commentators with similar preferences extolled the virtues of region-free DVDs and DVD players as a way to access global film culture. *New York Times* critic Manohla Dargis wrote in 2004 that cinephiles had to take on some agency in the face of a homogeneous cultural market and "become their own cultural gatekeepers, to reach beyond the multiplex and chain video store. You have to seek—sometimes quite resourcefully—in order to find."[57] As she explains, part of that resourceful engagement involves finding and purchasing region-free DVD players. Throughout the 2000s, cinephilia-minded film critics in the United States like Jonathan Rosenbaum, J. Hoberman, and Dave Kehr regularly promoted region-free media, and Rosenbaum in particular has long been one of the United States' premier champions of region-free film cultures. His long-running *Cinema Scope* column "Global Discoveries on DVD" acted as a consumer report of differently encoded DVDs for cinephiles who owned region-free players. In his initial installment of the column he writes, "The word is still getting out about the riches that are currently available to cinephiles owning DVD players that play discs from all the territories."[58] With the flourishing of film criticism on blogs and the development of social media platforms that could connect viewers and critics from different parts of the world, knowledge about different global film movements as well as ways of accessing and appraising films from these movements (including through region-free DVD) circulated among this loose community.[59]

This mode of region-free consumption often involves an auteurist mode of cinephilia, wherein many who hunt down region-free

DVDs collect international art films and the works of certain directors. Region-free DVD is essential to these completists: not only because of the wealth of films that have not been released in various markets around the world, but also because North America's premier distributor of high-quality DVDs of classic and global art films—the Criterion Collection—encodes its DVDs and Blu-rays as Region One and Region A, respectively. In fact, the Criterion Collection remains steadfast in region-coding its Blu-rays, even as other distributors have eschewed region codes. The reasons for this are that Criterion sees its market as North America specifically and does not own the international home video distribution rights for many of the films in its collection (hence its now-defunct streaming VOD service, FilmStruck, also being made available only in the United States). Because Criterion serves cinephiles primarily—what Barbara Klinger calls a "true upper-crust niche market"—the line's region coding has become a topic of debate and discussion among its fans.[60] As a response to Criterion's region codes, some users bristle at what seems to be a contradiction between the line's celebration of films, directors, and cinemas from all over the world and its propensity to lock down its products for the North American market. As one blogger puts it: "There's something fundamentally wrong with The Criterion Collection ending up as an exclusively American endeavour, because the series has always prided itself on recognising global contributions to cinema. The films are selected from around the world, reflecting different eras and perspectives, and they represent the whole world. These films are an encapsulated example of world-wide cinema at its very best, so it's hypocritical to restrict access like this."[61] The author goes on to invoke the commonly held idea that digital distribution technologies should forge easier connections across geographic borders and that technologies like region codes betray these possibilities. He argues that Criterion would do well to follow the "general trend . . . towards a region-free world, which is great from a conceptual point of view—the free market and the global village in action, the notion of a global film community becoming closer to a reality."[62] This kind of rhetoric, which marries the free-market tech utopia of the Californian Ideology with a vision of cinephilia as a transnational community, takes up region-free media as essential to film culture reaching its full potential of cosmopolitan globalism in a digital age.[63]

If Hollywood would not rethink its commitment to region codes, then local video stores took up the charge of selling region-free film culture to consumers. In addition to the diasporic stores described above, establishments like Scarecrow Video in Seattle, Washington, and I Luv Video in Austin, Texas, serve the aforementioned cultist and cinephile groups with their shelves stocked with obscure cinematic texts in a variety of different region-coded and region-free conditions. This exemplifies the relatively high geocultural capital of the United States as well as particular cities within it: they are places where people can access a range of different films from around the world, some of them rare or impossible to find outside of informal economies. Indeed, these sorts of stores are often located closer to the metropolitan centers of cities rather than the ethnic enclave neighborhoods that (as in the case of many of the neighborhoods visited in New York) often develop in the peripheries of urban areas. Such locations better exemplify what Herbert calls "video capitals," or well-known, often independently owned video stores that carry a wide variety of videos and "exhibit a highly detailed, comparatively sophisticated understanding of movie history and aesthetics" in part through their cinephile employees and detailed, knowledgeable methods of categorizing their titles.[64]

Although cosmopolitan cinephilia has generally been centered in major metropolitan areas, DVD opened up the possibilities of global film viewing to cinephiles who did not live near repertory theaters or art houses—a trend exacerbated by the relatively easy accessibility of region-free players. This is evident in a letter to the cinephile-oriented magazine *Film Comment* by a reader from Grand Rapids, Michigan, who writes, "I continue to be grateful and impressed for/by the ever-increasing accessibility of undistributed and neglected films on DVD. With a region-free player, people who live in cities without major festivals can catch up with major films a lot faster than they were able to before."[65] Similarly, Joan Hawkins argues in her mid-2000s work on art horror that the "mainstreaming of exploitation [film]" was taking place not in art house theaters but "at the level of DVD sales and stock" because it is easier for farther-flung fans to gain access to obscure media that way.[66] In this context, region-free players are often appealing to fans of particular global film and media movements, and distributors and retailers who address these fans ensure that such consumers will be able to watch region-coded DVDs. As Hawkins points out, various boutique DVD dealers like Facets Multimedia, Luminous Film and Video Wurks, and Nicheflix (now defunct) regularly stock and distribute DVDs from all regions and point their customers toward sites where they can purchase region-free players.

While region-free players were not particularly difficult to find (or produce by hacking a region-coded machine), awareness of global film culture and technological acumen were necessary to know that DVDs were region-coded in the first place, much less that region-free players existed. Although some might point to the possibilities of DVD for the democratization of media culture, region-free DVD represents a space where people in particular taste cultures share obscure knowledge that may be inaccessible to outsiders. The subcultural capital of region-free media culture manifests as insider knowledge expressed through an awareness of not only particular directors and filmmaking communities, but also the political economics and cultural geography of global media circulation and one's place within it.[67] By eschewing dominant tastes, cinephilic region-free DVD culture often positions itself as a refusal of the industrial (read: Hollywood) logics imposed by region codes. Here, a distaste for Hollywood mass culture blends with a like-minded rejection of corporate industry practices. In a published letter from 2003 that also speaks to the cinephilic and auteurist inclinations of region-free culture, Rosenbaum says: "It's pretty easy to buy a tristandard VCR in Europe, but to get one in Chicago I had to order it from New York—a media equipment outlet that Jim Jarmusch sent me the catalogue for. It's much easier to find DVD players in the US that can accommodate all the territories. Of course, this drives the Jack Valentis of the world nuts, because the rights to certain films are supposed to be territorialized along with their access—which is presumably why I had to buy my DVD of *Johnny Guitar* in Paris."[68] Rosenbaum's writing reflects a cinephile's orientation to film through not only the reference to Nicholas Ray's 1954 cult classic *Johnny Guitar* but also in his espoused friendship with indie director Jarmusch. It marries a film-loving mind-set to a vision of critics and independent filmmakers traversing the world, angering the arbiters of Hollywood's intellectual property. This taps into a broader understanding of unauthorized media access as a violation of Hollywood hegemony, which is also apparent in the hacker and pirate cultures that occasionally

Figure 5.2. Kim Dotcom mocks Hollywood. Screenshot: Dotcom, "MPAA."

overlap cinephilia communities. Kim Dotcom, the eccentric founder of the file-hosting platforms Megaupload and Mega, crystallized this argument in a tweet mocking the Motion Picture Association of America (the Hollywood studios' trade group and lobbying arm, of which Jack Valenti, mentioned by Rosenbaum, was president from 1966 to 2004).[69] Dotcom frames regional lockout as an injustice against consumers that had foolishly been put in place due to the misconceived priorities of Hollywood's primary governing body. In response, he presents measures undertaken to circumvent regional lockout—even file sharing and piracy—as natural responses to an unjust system.

Gendering Region-Free DVD

Region-free media thus serves as an unlikely meeting point for diasporic groups, cultist popular culture fans, globally oriented cinephiles, and libertarian digital freedom advocates. As a result, its heterogeneity highlights power dynamics more complex than simple resistance. For one thing, many (though by no means all) cinephiles looking for region-free media hail from North America and Europe. Indeed, while it carries romantic overtones, cinephilia remains in tension between cosmopolitan engagement in global cultures (a zeal for global difference that Ethan Zuckerman calls "xenophilia") and a commodifying impulse that sees international films and filmmakers as collectibles.[70] This orientation to global media culture comes from a place of privilege, made easier if one lives in an area of the world with a significant amount of geocultural capital. Indeed, geocultural capital is symbolized in part by the degree to which people have access to media culture from across borders.

Other related dimensions of cultural power are at play here. In particular, it will not surprise anyone who read chapter 2 that region-free media culture shows up in media practices that are often aligned with masculinity. Namely, region-free media is gendered as an extension of often-masculinized cultures of cinephile film criticism.[71] This moves beyond the traditional trope of travel-as-masculine and into the question of how cosmopolitans treat and comprehend other cultures. As Anna Tsing has argued, many nominally cosmopolitan projects in fact "enlarge the hegemonies of Northern centers even as they incorporate peripheries."[72] One of these hegemonies is that of dominant masculinity, and self-described cosmopolitans can incorporate peripheries in ways that flatten and minimize fine-grained cultural specificities and Orientalize the global Other. Although the two forms of informal trade are very different in obvious ways, we can nevertheless find an analogue to this gendering of global travel and consumption in Felicity Schaeffer-Grabiel's work on the cyberbride industry. Here, Schaeffer-Grabiel observes a particular "transnational masculinity" that does not rely on a simplistic white-Other binary but rather tries on a kind of colonialism presented in the guise of "corporate multiculturalism."[73] It goes without saying that even the most commoditizing DVD collector mind-set is not in the same league as cyberbride purchasing vis-à-vis the issue of human exploitation. However, region-free media culture occasionally embodies similarly contradictory ideals of colonial knowledge/control and cosmopolitan multiculturalism. Indeed, such dynamics are apparent in how the diasporic storeowners I interviewed talk about the white consumers who enter the stores looking for Bollywood films to purchase along with their spices.

Region-free media's blend of global consumption and technical mastery reflects two phenomena often represented in masculine terms:

global travel/consumption and control of digital technologies. In the transnational distribution networks of region-free media technologies, as well as the accompanying knowledge-sharing networks surrounding technological "how-tos" and hacks for lockout circumvention, the body of the consumer, hacker, or instructor is often gendered male. Part of this builds on a long-standing home video culture that, as Ann Gray has shown, is gendered along lines of masculine control over the viewing space and experience.[74] Years later, these same expressions of dominance manifest in talk about region-free DVD players as crucial to a high-quality home theater. Indeed, the ability to bypass regional lockout systems embodies these twin masculine ideals of mastery over technology and the ability to maintain control over time and space. Barbara Klinger refers to this as a mode of "contemporary high-end film collecting" that expresses a "white male technocratic ethos" from which women and people of color are often excluded.[75] Because region-free DVD and Blu-ray players actually go *above and beyond* the usual affordances of the media equipment found in the average home, they are the perfect adornments for the top-of-the-line home theaters that help constitute a certain mode of contemporary Western masculinity.

Bookending chapter 1's argument that region codes were systems of representation that expressed global inequalities, we can consider how advertisements, message board chatter, and other forms of discourse represent region-free DVD's normative user. These often invoke the "man cave"—that is, a domestic space such as a garage, den, or home theater where no women are allowed—as an appropriate space for one's region-free player, indicating that such technology belongs in a men-only space. Indeed, references to man caves pop up on websites and message boards devoted to cult film viewing that also regularly promote region-free DVD use. One typical poster on the message board Geekzone includes as his signature a list of the technology he keeps in his "man cave" (including a region-free Blu-ray player) and another post on the AV forum VideoHelp asks about hacking a region-coded DVD player that is also piece of *Star Wars* merchandise: "I already have several region free DVD players—but it's not about being able to play my R4 DVDs . . . it's about being able to play my R4 sci-fi dvd's in my 'Man Cave' on my R2-D2 DVD projector."[76] Across a number of message boards and blogs relating to film fandom and AV technology, similar examples abound of a relationship between region-free home video technologies and man cave home theater configurations. In the eyes of the men that want and build them, man caves and their AV setups serve as sanctuaries from a domestic space marked by femininity.[77]

In the context of region-free media, man caves (and gendered viewing more broadly) often align with cultist tastes.[78] Although the oppositional stance of cultism might imply an upheaval of the traditional cinephile's canon, it in fact overlaps with it. After all, the auteurism of the 1950s and 1960s that helped spur on the kind of cinephilia described in the above section was an ancestor of cultism.[79] The relationship between this axis of auteurism/cultism/cinephilia and a kind of masculinized engagement with region-free media is exemplified by a YouTube unboxing video for a region-free 3D Blu-ray player by a user who, incidentally, also hosts a livestreamed online video program called *The Sausage Factory*, billed as a "movie discussion show, featuring a group of opinionated guys who watch WAY too many movies."[80] The video incorporates several signifiers of masculine cultist film fandom: the host makes a show of unboxing the player with his "trusty Joker knife," a switchblade modeled after the knife used by the Joker in Christopher Nolan's 2008 film *The Dark Knight*, then explains that he purchased the player specifically to watch region-coded discs from Arrow Video, a UK-based distributor that specializes in cult and horror films. He also connects this fandom to transnational film-sharing networks, showing off the player's playback of a Scandinavian Blu-ray of Tobe Hooper's 1974 horror classic *The Texas Chainsaw Massacre* that he received from a friend in Sweden. Region-free culture, here, manifests as masculinist totems of fandom and boasts of technological acumen and knowledge of global film movements.

Region-free media, however, is not exclusive to this kind of cultist, auteurist, cinephilia. It also exists in contemporary television fandoms—and occasionally those that focus their energies on "quality" television and new media platforms such as Hulu and Netflix. In an example that expresses a somewhat different relationship to media taste, an Australian blog called *The Real Man's Guide to Absolutely Everything* published a post titled "How to Bypass Geo-Blocking in Australia." Instructing the reader on how to set up a home theater PC and use VPN services to circumvent geoblocks, the article is illustrated with a blood-dripped image of Kevin Spacey as *House of Cards'* Frank Underwood, an archetypical male antihero (and a picture suffused with toxic masculinity even before Spacey became an avatar of Hollywood's culture of sexual abuse). In aligning the presumed male reader (this is *The Real Man's Guide*, after all) with a male protagonist known for illegal and surreptitious acts, the article promotes the subversive thrill of hacking technological regulation. This aligns the circumvention of geoblocking and the promotion of platforms like Netflix with what Michael Newman and Elana Levine have called the discursive "legitimation" of television as a higher art form. Key to this is not only a vaunting of "complex," masculinity-driven narratives but also an articulation of television and interactive digital technologies which promote a "masculinization of television as a newly active experience of mediated leisure" that contrasts against the medium's feminized history.[81] The rest of the article bears out the masculine address, invoking the man cave (if not by name) with references to setting up a home theater in the "lounge room" and a suggestion that one can also use his home theater PC to access the gaming platform Steam or watch pornography.[82] Along with the clearly masculinized invocation of porn, mentioning Steam as a potential component of the man cave recalls the gendered dimension of hardcore gamer culture discussed in chapter 2.

It is no wonder that many of the most visible protests against region coding emerge from these masculinized spaces. In global power networks that, quite simply, do not value the voices of women, people of color, and diasporic populations as much, issues that affect those who hold global power and capital are more likely to be taken up as causes for concern. This is why public debates over regional lockout and geoblocking tend to focus on the problem of not accessing major streaming platforms in a country like Australia rather than the need to ensure that immigrant viewers are less disadvantaged in the global media marketplace. For one, in the eyes of many, the former issue is harder to criticize and dismiss than the informal economies of the latter, which are more easily pathologized and dismissed as "piracy." In addition to the traditional motivators of xenophobia and ethnocentrism, though, this is the case because those who hold more cultural power (i.e., Western white men) are perceived as being able to affect change through their wallets. When so much of the discourse about reforming regional lockout exists at the level of consumers' rights, economic and market-based incentives for reform suppress those based on eliminating *cultural* discrimination. That is, consumers' rights groups and anti-copyright activists are more likely to gain the attention of major regulators and industrial players by appealing to problems they can relate to more easily, such as lacking access to a major platform like Netflix rather than a particular Nollywood video. When criticisms of industry and regulatory practices appeal only to the most powerful, the discursive terrain of regional lockout and its circumvention becomes doubly discriminatory. It reflects the valuation of certain kinds of consumption and circumvention practices over others and ensures that even regional lockout circumvention will align with cultural power.

Still, if this chapter has been critical of how region-free media have at times been incorporated into masculinized forms of media practice, I want to end by emphasizing how regional lockout circumvention negotiates and rejects the wills of dominant media-industrial power. There is a distinction between the ways region-free DVD cultures can be presented in terms that would presume a Western, masculine user and the actual, everyday experiences of lockout circumvention, which circulate among more diverse groups of media users. The dominant gendered representations of media and technology use do not always align with who actually uses media and how they use it (indeed, this is part of what can make these discourses so damaging to broader participation in media culture). In other words, I want to avoid reifying the trope of the young, white, Western, male, tech-head cinephile as the only figure that engages in region-free media. For one, the first half of this chapter cataloged region-free media use by communities who do not represent dominant global powers. However, there are other examples that more clearly contradict the masculine tenor of much of what I have described in this section. For instance, in a study of Japanese women viewing the Korean serial drama *Winter Sonata*, Yoshitaka Mōri points out that most of them "use media technology adeptly to gather information." Such media technologies include online streaming services, language translators, and region-free DVD players.[83] Lawrence Eng points out that *otaku* culture—long marked by regional circumvention practices—contains many women who buck the media industries' preferred demographics.[84] Christine Becker has also remarked that unauthorized access to the BBC iPlayer, discussed in chapter 3, is a common practice among fans of *Sherlock*, a predominantly female group of viewers.[85] One could add non-UK-based fans of British soaps like *EastEnders* to the mix, and on and on. Just because many of the viewing subcultures involved in circumvention have centered the experiences and wishes of men does not mean that the actual practices of circumvention are not more inclusive.

Long-deferred hopes for regional lockout's disappearance likewise emanate from diverse groups of people. As the conclusion for *Locked Out* shows, calls for the end of geoblocking arise from a variety of global sites, even if they ultimately represent dreams of a truly borderless internet that likely will not—and cannot—exist. Regional lockout animates a desire in users for a more open media environment, a desire often echoed—cynically or not—by tech companies promoting their own visions of an open worldwide marketplace. Thus, discussions about the end of geoblocking represent a complex blend of desires for pop-cosmopolitan consumption, free-trade global capitalism, and tech-libertarian digital freedom. Where these negotiations can become particularly progressive is through the promotion of media practices and literacies that value engagement with media from other parts of the world. Thus, the book ends with a brief exploration of the "end of geoblocking" discourse as well as how media research and education might take up region-free media in order to promote a broader diversity of global media.

Conclusion

The End of Geoblocking? or, Region-Free Media Literacy

As I was putting the finishing touches on this book, I spent some down-time listening to the *New York Times Popcast*. On one episode of the pop-music news and discussion podcast, the assembled panelists were discussing the implications of musicians keeping certain songs off Spotify and other streaming music platforms. Although my aim was to pull away from the manuscript for a bit, the discussion kept circling back to some of the larger concerns I have been working through in this book. Toward the end of the podcast, host and *Times* music critic Jon Caramanica goes on a mini-rant:

> I think the internet has spoiled us in a way, right? Like, we believe that we are entitled to a complete jukebox of all things; we believe that we are entitled to permanence . . . We believe that these are . . . the kind of God-given rights that the internet has given to us. And then we get a little bit haughty and testy, and we're like, "Oh, that thing's not on the internet anymore?" But the internet is equally as unreliable as any prior form of content distribution, whether it was print, or whether it was an LP, or an 8-track. The internet has holes, the internet is controlled . . . there are legal concerns, there are all these things that are brought to bear on what remains and what doesn't remain . . . Why do we expect the internet to be better?[1]

Caramanica is not talking about geoblocking or regional lockout here, but he captures a question that has bubbled under the surface of much of this book. Why should we expect the internet to be a space of unfettered access when it is just as subject to regulations and material constraints as other media? Extrapolating this to regional lockout, we might ask why the internet would somehow be free from the spatial concerns that have shaped centuries of media before its arrival. Geography has been an inescapable reality throughout the history of media access, and the last few decades of digital dominance are no different. To think that digital media unbind us from regulated access is to buy into the tech and entertainment industries' breathless hype.

Rather, I have argued throughout this book that regional lockout both reflects and shapes the world's geocultural divisions. It does so in its effects on digital technologies' affordances and capabilities, the distribution routes that media take around the world, and the ways media reinforce cultural capital and cultural differences at broad, transnational scales. Central to this claim is the idea that media function as a kind of cultural resource that people use for various reasons—to be entertained or comforted, to dissect and analyze, to negotiate their identities, to learn something about the world and the people in it, and so on. As a result, unequal distribution of these cultural resources can correspond with inequalities of cultural capital between broadly scaled geographic territories such as nations or regions—a condition that I have called geocultural capital. This argument has enabled an assessment of regional lockout that does not assume uniform global effects. After all, as Cameran Ashraf and Luis Felipe Alvarez León remind us, characterizing the internet as naturally open and geoblocking as a restriction on it presupposes a "binary open/closed model" that fails to recognize the internet for what it is: a heterogeneous set of networks and experiences functioning along a variety of different territorial logics.[2]

That the internet is a cluster of different practices and networks is apparent in the many different stakes and perspectives global institutions bring to bear on regional lockout. Consumers, consumer rights groups, regulators, and even media industry figures regularly pronounce that regional lockout is—or should be—dying. A spate of anti-geoblocking protests and pronouncements from the 2010s that we might call the "end of geoblocking" discourses illustrate the gap between a differentiated internet and one free of geographic regulation. Many of these discourses have emerged from initiatives like Europe's Digital Single Market proposal explored in chapter 3, though their broader context is a series of global demonstrations on the importance of internet freedom (e.g., activism in favor of net neutrality, against private-sector and state censorship, and so forth). Coming from a variety of sources and perspectives, the "end of geoblocking" discourses blur the line between utopian hopes for an open, publicly oriented digital commons, a celestial jukebox where we can access anything at any time, and the internet as a potential landscape for borderless exchange and free-market capitalism. Such complexities are underscored by the fact that figures as different as European Pirate Party members and Netflix CEO Reed Hastings have both called for and celebrated the end of geoblocking, though to significantly different ends. While the Pirate Party has levied its critiques from a platform fighting for an open and free commons, information privacy, and intellectual property reform, Hastings's CES keynote address (discussed in chapter 3) viewed geoblocking as an outmoded barrier to Netflix's ambitions of global television dominance.[3] Ultimately, there is a distinction between anti-geoblocking protests from people who hold out hope for a freer digital landscape and those from commercial entities who see a borderless internet as a possible space to expand their domain.

Whether prematurely pronouncing regional lockout's death or calling for its swift end, the "end of geoblocking" discourses posit that the time has come to abolish the practice. However, such calls tend to treat geoblocking as a historical blip—an extended accident of media industries trying to integrate digital technologies into existing distribution practices and intellectual property rules rather than simply the newest manifestation of long-standing business models based on market segmentation and windowing. Such rhetoric sees the industrial abandonment of geoblocking as part of a natural evolution into an idealized, globally open mediascape rather than the more banal reality that it is an expedient practice of media industries attempting to enter into new global markets. Finally, they smooth over the fact that regional hiccups are in fact produced through a variety of means: poor infrastructure, national content regulations, variable pricing in different territories, and digital entertainment companies' hesitance to expand into new markets too quickly. Such issues point to an even broader palette of interruptions and regulations that we might include under a more expansive rubric of regional lockout. Though such examples are beyond the scope of this book's focus on digital entertainment distribution, some are discussed in the various essays in Ramon Lobato and James Meese's volume *Geoblocking and Global Video Culture*. The book compiles a series of pieces from around the world—and in spaces not covered at length in this book, including China, Turkey, Malaysia, Iran, Cuba, and more—that illustrate how geoblocking operates throughout the Global South in ways both similar to and distinct from practices explored here.[4] The heterogeneity of geoblocking means that its elimination is more a utopian ideal than a realistically attainable goal.

If regional lockout is thus woven into a complex, variegated global media environment, this book has also shown that it would be overly simplistic to characterize it as always repressive in nature (and, correspondingly, that pushing back against it is necessarily a form of counter-hegemonic resistance). It often is, and its roots in capitalist spatial management highlight its role as a mechanism of power. However, a more nuanced view of regional lockout can likewise help us tease out complexities and ambivalences in everyday media life. For one, I have shown how it might make more sense to think of regional lockout as productive of the shape of global media culture—for better and worse—than as a purely restrictive mechanism. In chapter 2, I illustrated how hardcore gamer culture arose in part out of a regionally restricted medium. Furthermore, the previous chapter showed that the nominally more open environment of region-free media can, in fact, produce other marginalizing impulses. In the last chapter, for instance, I was critical of how region-free DVD at times corresponds with the commodifying impulses of predominately masculine, Western collector cultures—media users who, in David Morley's words, "are celebrating not so much a politics of difference as indulging their own sense of the picturesque."[5]

Even in offering this critique, though, Morley acknowledges the possibility that media might engender a cosmopolitanism geared toward accepting and appreciating difference.[6] Region-free media can quite literally set conditions for this kind of openness by enabling users to engage media culture from other parts of the world—hence its particular social value as a cultural resource. This book thus ends by underlining the premise that media can still encourage substantial forms of cosmopolitanism marked by an interest in diversity, empathy with people from across borders and cultures, and shared global cultural citizenship. In her writing on ethnicity and diasporic television, Marie Gillespie lays out the stakes here: "The very coexistence of culturally diverse media is a cultural resource. It engenders a developed consciousness of difference and a cosmopolitan stance. It encourages young people to compare, contrast, and criticize the cultural and social forms represented to them by their parents, by significant others present in their daily lives and by significant others onscreen."[7] Although not always used in this way, region-free media make it easier for consumers to experience the cosmopolitanism-via-film that Charles Acland calls "felt internationalism."[8] Acland is writing about Canadian film audiences primarily, but across a variety of media contexts—Canadian filmgoers, Venezuelan gamers, Swedish Spotify listeners—felt internationalism is bound by a sense that we are participating in something that stretches beyond our own, graspable experience.

Whatever terminology and framework one prefers—Acland's felt internationalism, Gillespie's consciousness of diversity, Henry Jenkins's pop cosmopolitanism—each suggests that foreign media hold possibilities for encountering and appreciating difference. This can serve as a reminder for media educators that a cosmopolitan perspective can be encouraged in the classroom—something that Jenkins discusses explicitly at the end of his essay on pop cosmopolitanism.[9] Here, region-free media become useful for students and teachers alike looking to access media culture from abroad. A 2001 *Washington Post* story about DVD region codes illustrates this by telling the tale of a foreign-language student at Cornell who purchased a region-free DVD player in order to watch Russian films. Later, the article quotes an Atlanta-based electronics retailer who lists language students as one of the three major markets for region-free DVD players (the other two being the populations discussed in the previous chapter: "immigrants who want to watch movies from their home countries" and "foreign-film enthusiasts").[10] Indeed, scholars and practitioners from a variety of educational disciplines and levels have written about the analytical and practical problems that DVD region codes bring to their own work. For instance, Peter Ecke and Matthew Kayahara have each pointed to some of the issues that DVD region codes raise for foreign language and translation studies specifically, with Kayahara explaining that "regions which do not have sizable markets of a given language group will not have translations in that language released in that region." As a result, "it makes it rather difficult . . . for an audiovisual translation theorist in Canada to study, say, the Czech translation of *The End of the Affair*, since that subtitle track is available only on the region 2 DVD, and Canada is in region 1."[11] One consequence of regional lockout, then, is that it can foreclose opportunities for students and users to develop knowledge and competency steeped in awareness and appreciation of foreign media.

This is a problem for film and media researchers and teachers, particularly those who adopt a transnational emphasis in their classrooms or in their research. Furthermore, consider how regional lockout affects the media libraries and archives that offer researchers, teachers, and students access to global media culture. As Jason Puckett summarizes from a librarian's perspective, DRM "creates intentional and artificial information usage barriers. In doing so, it compromises libraries' mission of providing free access to information."[12] Such concerns extend from DRM in physical media to online geoblocking. We might envision, for instance, a professor in Mexico City teaching about the global distribution of telenovelas yet unable to access Hulu's library of Spanish-language programs. In an essay on YouTube and pedagogical media practice, Ted Hovet discusses the potential for students to use the platform to recontextualize and make sense of film clips.[13] However, certain channels are geoblocked around the world, again limiting student access. Additionally, regional lockout affects more than just the library of content available to educators. For educators teaching courses on new media, algorithmic culture, digital platforms, or the materiality of media, these platforms' interfaces may be off-limits due to geoblocking. Of course, showing American students the effects of regional lockout firsthand can itself be instructive in communicating the disconnections that still exist in our nominally connected world. It offers a space for students to reflect on the private-sector and state-based forces that shape media access.

Still, media educators should have the choice to circumvent regional lockout systems in order to access media from across region-locked borders or illustrate the conditions and experiences of media consumption from other parts of the world. In some cases, US media educators are protected legally by exemptions from the DMCA's anti-circumvention rules (as stated by the Copyright Office and the Library of Congress). The fair use guidelines published by the Society for Cinema and Media Studies, the largest film and media studies scholarly organization, inform us that these exemptions allow media educators (though not students) to bypass DRM on media owned by a departmental library.[14] While these guidelines do not discuss region-coded media in particular, it seems that the anti-circumvention exemption would enable media educators to bypass regional lockout in particular instances. Given the ambiguities that still exist, however, region codes and geoblocking may require scholars to engage in legally murky terms of service–violating circumvention practices in order to access material for teaching and research. In her writing on geoblocking and the BBC iPlayer, media studies professor Christine Becker discusses the ensuing frustrations not just for fans but also for educators. In doing so, she echoes a common refrain of media users frustrated by regional lockout: "As someone who researches and teaches British TV, I would happily pay the license fee if given the opportunity to do so."[15] If legal (or at least industrially authorized) options are not available, we may have to make do through alternative means. Although not writing about educators per se, Lucas Hilderbrand helps make this case when he argues that bootlegging is an ethical decision, one that helps preserve and open up access to media.[16] We may not want to break the law, but a mandate to make global culture available to students overrides the need to preserve media industries' distribution routes.

Hilderbrand's invocation of ethics points to the broader stakes of regional lockout and its circumvention. If media offer opportunities for cross-cultural connection, this book has pointed to conditions of digital technologies that defeat such possibilities. In his book *Media and Morality*, Roger Silverstone helps us to understand the consequences of this defeat and where we—as consumers, scholars, activists, and practitioners—might go from here. Drawing on the work of Hannah Arendt, he characterizes our broader media environment as a "mediapolis," a public "space of media appearance" where "contemporary political life increasingly finds its place . . . and where the materiality of the world is constructed through (principally) electronically communicated public speech and action."[17] Crucially, he sees the mediapolis as a moral space marked by "judgments of inclusion and exclusion."[18] Ideally, the global public space of the media would present the world's inhabitants, cultures, and art forms to us in ways that enable an appreciation of this plurality—that bring about the kinds of cosmopolitan perspectives described above. Usually, it fails at this.

Pointing toward a solution, Silverstone proposes that the best way to build a globally inclusive mediapolis is through the development of media literacies that emphasize an ethical commitment to diversity and global citizenship. As he suggests, such media literacies are antithetical to forms of regulation that follow commercial and market logics. This contrast, between cross-cultural connection and commerce-driven regulation, exists at the heart of regional lockout. While numerous institutions have turned to regulation as a way of ensuring that our media operate in certain capacities, Silverstone argues that regulatory regimes based in competitive market logics are insufficient to create the conditions under which the mediapolis can shape a more just, inclusive world. Even some of the commercial and regulatory initiatives against regional lockout discussed throughout this book (Netflix's "Everywhere" campaign, the EU's Digital Single Market) privilege commercial enterprise over cultural pluralism. If entrenched powers see media commerce and regulation as ways of serving corporate bottom lines or state-based regulatory systems rather than methods of encouraging media diversity, then regional lockout will exist at odds with media systems built on an ethics of difference.

This is where the ethical questions of circumventing regional lockout come back into the conversation. If, as Silverstone argues, viewers and regulators alike have a moral obligation to interrogate and experience media as a space of global appearance, the conditions required to fulfill these obligations are often out of reach because of dominant regulatory regimes. Therefore, circumventing these mechanisms can involve a particular ethical stance in relation to the technology. Anti-DRM activists and hackers—including members of the anti-geoblocking Pirate Party described above—subscribe to what Hector Postigo calls a "hacker ethic."[19] Postigo quotes a hacker credo first articulated in 1984 by journalist Steven Levy illustrating that this ethic is marked not only by transparency and free information, but also the importance of accessing "anything that might teach you about the way the world works."[20] Even if this quotation does not respond directly to regional lockout or even DRM, it presages not only the similar questions of ethics that come up in discussions of regional lockout's circumvention, but also the stakes of circumvention as a way of learning about the world that surrounds us. Indeed, one scholarly analysis of the ethics of internet users posting the DeCSS decryption code (which circumvents the DVD's CSS encryption) argues that we need to keep in mind the users' political motives and geographic location: "DeCSS posters from nations without anti-circumvention laws, or with laws that arguably permit non-commercial DeCSS posting, may consider themselves 'global citizens' resisting larger transnational institutions or legal trends rather than national-level laws and legal rulings."[21] Circumvention, here, raises the question of whether we orient ourselves through the media as national or global citizens. Through an alignment among global citizenship, cosmopolitanism, and the practice of hacking and circumventing regional lockout systems, we can envision possibilities for technically unauthorized but ethically and politically progressive media practices.

In striking out against regional lockout, activists and educators can and should move beyond a line of argument that sees lockout's elimination as merely one part of a broader movement toward internet freedom and openness. While this can be a good, productive mode of attack, it has the potential to be incorporated into tech-corporate ideals of an open internet as a space for the expansion of capital. Rather, anti-regional-lockout activism and region-free media education should start from a place that recognizes media as resources we use to open ourselves up to global difference. Looking ahead, this will become particularly important in a world where media are at once becoming more mobile but where global intercultural connections are increasingly threatened by the walls, borders, and barricades of reactionary nationalism. Arguments based in libertarian, individualist notions of freedom or abstract infrastructural openness are insufficient on this front. Anti-lockout activism must be steeped in a consciousness and appreciation of difference rather than the market-driven branding strategies of "media everywhere" illustrated at times in this book. In short, a critique of regional lockout requires pushing for media systems that allow us to appreciate global cultural production in all its diversity.

ACKNOWLEDGMENTS

Acknowledgments in scholarly books tend to begin by thanking one's professional network before ending on a more personal note of gratitude for family and friends. In my case, the two are so intertwined that I must begin by thanking Kit Hughes, my partner in life and work. Over a decade that has seen five states, four universities, and two cats, we have built quite a life. Many of this book's arguments have been shaped through discussions we have had during hikes, meals, and commutes. I thank her for her support, guidance, and love.

I am also forever indebted to Jonathan Gray. As my mentor at the University of Wisconsin–Madison, he urged me to read widely and think deeply. He is a model researcher and teacher, and his valuable lessons and friendship will continue to guide me. Others have shaped this book, deepening its arguments and honing its focus. Aswin Punathambekar steered the way in transforming this project into a book manuscript. I have also benefited from the patience and generosity of NYU Press. In particular, Lisha Nadkarni has been a steadfast supporter of this project, and I thank her for her comments and guidance. Thanks are also due to Nina Huntemann for early advice and to Adrienne Shaw.

The research for this book began in the Department of Communication Arts at the University of Wisconsin–Madison. Derek Johnson, Michele Hilmes, Jeremy Morris, Eric Hoyt, Lori Kido Lopez, Mary Beltrán, Jeff Smith, and J. J. Murphy taught me how to conceptualize a large-scale research project. I look back on my time in Madison as among the best years of my life, and I want to thank all my Wisconsin colleagues. Special thanks to Myles McNutt, Sarah Murray, Alyx Vesey, Brandon Colvin, and Nora Stone for their friendship. Thanks also to Andrew Bottomley, Christopher Cwynar, Evan Davis, Brian Fauteux, Kyra Hunting, Josh Jackson, Danny Kimball, Caroline Leader, Derek Long, Wan-Jun Lu, Amanda McQueen, Jenny Oyallon-Koloski, Nora Patterson, Matt

Sienkiewicz, Jen Smith, and too many more to name. I will forever relish the feeling of camaraderie developed during post-colloquium Thursdays and afternoons on the Memorial Union Terrace.

The Communication Studies Department at Colorado State University has been an ideal setting for *Locked Out*'s development. My chair, Greg Dickinson, has built an encouraging and stimulating scholarly environment. Nick Marx has been a great pal and guide to Fort Collins. Eric Aoki's friendship has sustained me. Allison Prasch has not only been a terrific friend and colleague, but she organized a departmental writing retreat that helped get me to the finish line on this book. Katie Knobloch and Meara Faw graciously let me overstay my welcome at parties. Hye Seung Chung and Scott Diffrient have been helpful mentors in the department's Media and Visual Culture area. Thanks, too, to Usama Alshaibi, Kari Vasby Anderson, Carl Burgchardt, Martín Carcasson, Tom Dunn, Katie Gibson, Julia Khrebtan-Hörhager, Elinor Light, Ziyu Long, Elizabeth Parks, and Elizabeth Williams. Abby Shupe, John Pippen, and Peter Erickson have been ideal companions in exploring Fort Collins and the Front Range. Thanks also to Gloria Blumanhourst, Dawn McConkey, Nancy Schindele, and Eliza Wagner-Kinyon for making my job easier.

Although I was only at Miami University for one year, I learned a great deal there about teaching and research at the faculty level. Thanks to Ron Becker, Jennifer Malkowski, Kate Mason, Katie Day Good, Rosemary Pennington, Mack Hagood, Lindsay Schakenbach Regele, Richard Campbell, Howard Kleiman, Lisa McLaughlin, David Sholle, and Kathleen German for offering support and friendship in Oxford and Cincinnati. Going back in time, I owe so much to Jennifer Fay and Justus Nieland, who inspired me to follow the path to media professorhood while I was an undergraduate at Michigan State University. They indulged my interests while instilling in me a sense of discipline, and I would not be where I am without them. I was fortunate enough to begin my graduate career at the University of Texas at Austin, where I nurtured my cinephilia while exploring additional avenues of inquiry. Janet Staiger and Tom Schatz offered invaluable mentorship early in my graduate education. Charles Ramírez Berg, Mary Celeste Kearney, and Michael Kackman helped shape my research and teaching. Also in Austin, Peter Alilunas, Bo Baker, Alex Cho, Donovan

Gentry, Leigh Goldstein, Candice Haddad, and Tiff Henning accompanied me to the Hole in the Wall and the Alamo Drafthouse when I needed to decompress.

Beyond my various professional homes, I have been fortunate to receive the advice of many friends and colleagues. Ramon Lobato, especially, has been generous with his time and helped me better comprehend the many dimensions of media distribution. Courtney Brannon Donoghue, Michael Curtin, Joshua Gleich, David Gurney, Eric Harvey, Timothy Havens, Nicole Hentrich, Daniel Herbert, Aynne Kokas, Elana Levine, Casey McCormick, Annemarie Navar-Gill, Michael Newman, Megan Sapnar Ankerson, Phil Scepanski, Mark Stewart, Ethan Thompson, Serra Tinic, and Chuck Tryon have helped me make sense of this project or given moral support. Larry and Phyllis generously provided lodging in New York while I conducted research there. In its earlier phase, *Locked Out* benefited from a Mellon-Wisconsin Dissertation Fellowship. I also thank the book manuscript's reviewers for their helpful comments on earlier drafts. Also, I would like to note that portions of chapter 1 were published as "The DVD Region Code System: Standardizing Home Video's Disjunctive Global Flows," *International Journal of Cultural Studies* 19 (March 2016): 225–40.

Friends and family provided much-needed breaks and uplift during the writing process. So many need to be named, and profuse apologies to anyone I have neglected to mention. Thanks to Erik and Tiff, Carrie, Chi Chi, Matthew, Laura K., Laura B., Andrew, Steph and Mike, Carl and Justin, Stephanie K., Dwight, Jill, Kyle, and Tim. I also thank my family. Listing them all would add considerably to the NYU Press printing budget, so I will just mention a few. Jan and Greg Hughes have provided love and hospitality, and they have introduced me to the many quirks of local Pennsylvania culture. Morgan Jones and Eileen John offer an aspirational model of how to be intellectual yet unpretentious. Doug Baldwin and the late, great Kathy Baldwin exemplify the kind of Zen cosmopolitanism that I try to bring to my life and work. Roy and Stephanie Elkins kept me fed and sustained during my years in Madison and beyond. Granny's pride and kindness has kept me grounded.

My brother, Alex; his wife, Vicki; and my nephew, Xavi have been a godsend to my sanity, checking in with necessary and heartwarming

FaceTime chats. My sister, Allison, continues to make me laugh harder and more regularly than anyone else I know. This book is in part about opening up access to what the world has to offer, so I end by thanking my parents, Susan Jones Elkins and Robert Elkins, who did that for me. I dedicate this book to them.

NOTES

INTRODUCTION

1 BEUC, "Imagine This Happening to You."

2 European Commission, "Digital Single Market."

3 Jeffrey Himpele has shown how this happens in his study of film exhibition in La Paz, Bolivia, concluding that "the location of cinemas, the genre of films they show, their price and the timing (or delay) of their debuts correspond and separate social and cultural differences among film and video audiences." Tessa Dwyer and Ioana Uricaru point out that in communist Romania, "access to VCRs or VHS tapes became a status symbol that could translate directly into either economic or social power." See Himpele, "Film Distribution as Media," 53; Dwyer and Uricaru, "Slashings and Subtitles," 48.

4 I draw on Raymond Williams's definition of incorporation as a process where emergent and potentially threatening cultural practices are eventually subsumed into dominant social and economic orders. See Williams, *Marxism and Literature*, 126.

5 Vaidhyanathan, *Copyrights and Copywrongs*, 177.

6 Lessig, *Code Version 2.0*, 5.

7 Gillespie, *Wired Shut*, 226.

8 Livingstone and Das, "End of Audiences?" 110. See also Hall, "Encoding/Decoding."

9 Gillespie, *Wired Shut*, 101–2.

10 As a result, global internet filtering and censorship like the kinds analyzed by the OpenNet Initiative are related but tangential to the focus of this project. For one, they focus primarily on state-based internet filtering, surveillance, and distributed denial-of-service (DDoS) attacks, whereas my own study investigates forms of regulation developed by transnational entertainment industries (though certainly with the help of governmental regulation). In addition, they train their attention on the internet specifically, whereas my study represents a broader historical analysis of various forms of digital control dating back to the media industries' transitions to digital delivery technologies in the 1980s and 1990s. See Deibert et al., *Access Denied*; Deibert et al., *Access Controlled*; Deibert et al., *Access Contested*.

11 Consider this oft-cited passage from political economist Nicholas Garnham: "It is cultural distribution, not cultural production, that is the key locus of power and profit." Garnham, *Capitalism and Communication*, 162. See also Wasko, *How Hollywood Works*, 59.

12 In this way, they are similar to the undersea internet cables Nicole Starosielski has written about. See Starosielski, *Undersea Network*.

13 Iordanova, "Digital Disruption," 23.

14 Tsing, *Friction*, 6. This also requires thinking about frictions and disjunctures in media access and availability. In the realm of digital media studies, Elizabeth Ellcessor has argued that some of the more celebratory strains of media scholarship "take access for granted," basing concepts like use, collaboration, and participatory culture on the premise that one has access to a technology or technological practice in the first place. And while she is writing primarily about digital media access for people with disabilities, we might think about how these concerns can be adapted to questions of access based on geographic location. See Ellcessor, *Restricted Access*, 5.

15 Havens, *Black Television Travels*, 2.

16 Couldry, *Place of Media Power*, 16.

17 By the term "geocultural," I refer to the ways geography and cultural identity are interlinked in definitions of self and community, particularly in a globalized media landscape. Although I use the word somewhat differently, here, I take inspiration from scholars of global media like Jean Chalaby and Joseph Straubhaar, who write about the importance of geocultural regions in global media markets. Like their uses, mine reflects how the geographical and the cultural are intertwined in the meanings and definitions of places. See Straubhaar, *World Television*; Chalaby, "Towards an Understanding of Media Transnationalism."

18 Sterne, "MP3 as Cultural Artifact," 826. See also the work of John Fiske, who reminds us that "all commodities have cultural as well as functional values." Fiske, *Understanding Popular Culture*, 27.

19 This "circuit of culture" model is proposed and explored in depth in Du Gay et al., *Doing Cultural Studies*. The authors build on an earlier circuit model proposed in Johnson, "What Is Cultural Studies Anyway?" See also a development of the model to the concerns of media studies in D'Acci, "Cultural Studies, Television Studies."

20 Bielby and Harrington, *Global TV*, 145–47.

21 As a result, the book also heeds Alisa Perren's recent call to "attend to the cultural" in studying media distribution. See Perren, "Rethinking Distribution," 170–71.

22 I use Timothy Havens's concept of industry lore, which refers to "institutionalized discourses" and conventional wisdom within media industries. In the context of global television distribution, Havens says that industry lore "is a way of talking and thinking about audiences and programming that permits television insiders to imagine connections between audience members and television programming from around the world." See Havens, *Black Television Travels*, 4.

23 Reda, "I Hate Geoblocking!"

24 Warner, "Is Netflix Chill?"

25 Bourdieu, "Forms of Capital"; Bourdieu, *Distinction*. Recently, a group of scholars writing about Bourdieu provided a clear definition of cultural capital: "The advantage derived from the possession of specific kinds of cultural resource." Bennett et al., *Culture, Class, Distinction*, 3. Scholars like John Fiske and Henry Jenkins have long considered media a kind of cultural resource. See Fiske, *Understanding Popular Culture*, 28; Jenkins, "Why Fiske Still Matters," xxvi.

26 As a theory that describes how we see places themselves as embodying capital, the concept of geocultural capital is inspired by Tim Cresswell's argument that place is a means by which we make classifications and draw borders of difference. See Cresswell, *In Place / Out of Place*, 152–55.

27 Bourdieu, "Forms of Capital," 245. In the context of the accessibility and distribution of information, Nigel Thrift has shown that literature and media access over the last several centuries contributed to an uneven distribution of knowledge. See Thrift, *Spatial Formations*, 108.

28 Vincent Pouliot and Frédéric Mérand describe something akin to geocultural capital in their application of Bourdieu to international relations, arguing that the world is shaped by a "hierarchy of states, whereby some have much greater stocks of economic capital, others military capital, and others cultural capital (akin to what we sometimes call 'soft power')." However, "soft power" is still somewhat imprecise as a way to define cultural capital (and, by extension, geocultural capital), as it incorporates Bourdieuian concepts of social and cultural status into an understanding of global relations primarily through a lens of power. Pouliot and Mérand, "Bourdieu's Concepts," 37. On soft power, see Nye, *Soft Power*.

29 Bourdieu, "Forms of Capital," 245.

30 Bourdieu, *Distinction*, 124. Indeed, at one point he emphasizes that cinemas showing avant-garde films and theaters showing films "overtly designed to entertain" will tend to be found in different places (267). See also the work of Ghassan Hage, whose theories of "national cultural capital" and "cosmopolitan capital" offer geographically inflected adaptations of Bourdieu's concept. The former refers to kinds of language, behavior, dress, taste, accent, and other "valued characteristics" that people deploy and embody which cause them to be seen by others as a legitimate member of a nation. The latter refers to one's expressed interest in, knowledge of, and ability to cross borders and revel in diversity. See Hage, *White Nation*.

31 Ong, *Flexible Citizenship*, 92; Johnson, *Heartland TV*, 6.

32 Curtin, "Media Capital."

33 Herbert, *Videoland*, 86–87.

34 Silverstone, *Media and Morality*, 18.

35 Consalvo, *Atari to Zelda*.

36 Dyer-Witheford and de Peuter, *Games of Empire*.

37 Consalvo, *Cheating*, 3–5.

38 Goldstein, *Copyright's Highway*.

CHAPTER 1. DVD REGION CODES

1 Gruenwedel, "Obama Gives Brown DVD Swag"; Walker, "Brown Is Frustrated."

2 Another example: the *Montreal Gazette* newspaper reported in 2002 that someone in the Quebec Consumer Protection Office was dismayed to find that the DVDs he bought in France were unplayable in a Canadian DVD player. See Perusse, "Why DVD Releases Don't Travel Well."

3 Walker, "Brown Is Frustrated."

4 My characterization of the global flows of entertainment as "disjunctive" takes inspiration from Arjun Appadurai's analysis of global flows or "scapes," wherein he asserts that those scapes are fractal and disjunctive in nature. See Appadurai, *Modernity at Large*.

5 Sebok, "Convergent Hollywood." Central to Sebok's argument is that the DVD developed through the convergence of three industries: filmed entertainment, consumer electronics, and computing.

6 Tryon, *On-Demand Culture*, 18; Benzon, "Bootleg Paratextuality," 89.

7 For more on the cultural composition of so-called early adopters, see Boddy, *New Media and Popular Imagination*; Cubitt, *Timeshift*, 9; Jenkins, *Convergence Culture*, 23; Newman and Levine, *Legitimating Television*.

8 See, for instance, Lobato, *Shadow Economies of Cinema*; Lobato and Thomas, *Informal Media Economy*; Mattelart, "Audio-Visual Piracy"; Starosielski, "Things and Movies"; Wang, *Framing Piracy*. Writing in 2007, Michael Curtin notes that pirated DVDs and Video CDs constituted over 90 percent of mainland China's home video market. See Curtin, *Playing to the World's Biggest Audience*, 248–49.

9 Bordwell, *Pandora's Digital Box*, 40; Wang, *Framing Piracy*; Curtin, *Playing to the World's Biggest Audience*, 80–84; Gray, "Mobility through Piracy," 99–113; McDonald, *Video and DVD Industries*, 101–5; Larkin, *Signal and Noise*.

10 Silverstone, *Media and Morality*, 18.

11 Silverstone, 19.

12 While the region code is not technically a form of content encryption in that it does not scramble content or require a decryption key to access it, the mandated agreement between the software's flag and the hardware's region serves as a form of content protection that to the end user functions similarly. See Taylor, Johnson, and Crawford, *DVD Demystified*, 5–20.

13 Yu, "Region Codes and the Territorial Mess," 193; DVD CCA, "About Us."

14 Taylor, Johnson, and Crawford, *DVD Demystified*, 5–20; Yu, "Region Codes and the Territorial Mess," 193.

15 Balio, "Major Presence," 58–60.

16 McDonald, *Video and DVD Industries*, 1–2.

17 See Gomery, "Hollywood Studio System," 120. Specifically, Gomery discusses the studios' "run-zone-clearance" system of theatrical distribution, which David Bordwell summarizes thus: "A run was the period during which a film was screened in theatres. The first-run showing, usually at a well-appointed downtown cinema,

gave city viewers the first chance to see the movie. The second-run shows, in neighborhood theatres and small towns, took place later, at lower ticket prices. Zones established the territory in which any title could play exclusively. Clearances were the intervals of time separating the runs, typically a matter of weeks or months." Bordwell, "Women and Children First."

18 Wasser, *Veni, Vidi, Video*.

19 The fear of parallel imports was a major reason China and Southeast Asia were placed in their own distinct regions. Because of their bountiful informal DVD trades (i.e., what cultural industries and regulators call piracy), distributors could supposedly more easily control these spaces as DVD markets and ensure that pirated Region Four and Six DVDs did not show up in other places. Of course, in China's case, that country's unique and specific censorship practices also factored in. Remaining its own region would allow the country to more easily regulate the content of its DVDs. Yu, "Region Codes and the Territorial Mess," 215.

20 Ulin, *Business of Media Distribution*, 5.

21 In a study of the economics of global film and television that appeared around the same time as the public availability of the DVD, Colin Hoskins, Stuart McFadyen, and Adam Finn note that in order for market segmentation practices to engender the conditions that allow price discrimination to take place, "it must be possible for the seller to separate markets and keep them separate." See Hoskins, McFadyen, and Finn, *Global Television and Film*, 69.

22 Taylor, "DVD Frequently Asked Questions."

23 See Wang and Zhu, "Mapping Film Piracy in China," 107–8, in which they note, "The VCD development has proved to be one of the most serious and unexpected challenges to the major studios and those transnational makers of electronic hardware that hold, determine, and monopolize video and audio entertainment formats and standards . . . the unexpected rebirth of the VCD in Asia has not only re-drawn the film distribution maps, both legitimate and illegitimate, but also redefined the power relations among various global as well as local players by reversing the flow of global video technology format and standardization."

24 See, for example, Brookey and Westerfelhaus, "Hiding Homoeroticism in Plain View"; Kompare, "Publishing Flow"; Klinger, *Beyond the Multiplex*; Gray, *Show Sold Separately*; Tryon, *Reinventing Cinema*.

25 "Regional Code Circumvention"; Andrews, "DVD Is Taking Off."

26 For thorough histories of these events, see Sebok, "Convergent Hollywood"; Taylor, Johnson, and Crawford, *DVD Demystified*; Wasser, "Ancillary Markets"; Dai, *Digital Revolution and Governance*, 230–37.

27 Herman and McChesney, *Global Media*; Dai, *Digital Revolution and Governance*, 221.

28 Taylor, Johnson, and Crawford, *DVD Demystified*, 5.22.

29 Yu, "Region Codes and the Territorial Mess," 196. As evidence of this, DVD companies that abjure region coding tend to offer boutique titles or material from industries with international distribution routes that don't require the same

digital borders. For example, region-free company DVD International's first titles were *Babes on the Beach* and the home theater calibration disc *Video Essentials*. The same company also released the interactive "multipath film" *I'm Your Man* in 1998. See "Veteran Laserdisc Distributor"; Sporich, "'Multipath DVD Movies."

30 Perusse, "Why DVD Releases Don't Travel Well."

31 Taylor, Johnson, and Crawford, *DVD Demystified*, 2–3.

32 "Philips, Sony Go Solo."

33 "Philips, Sony Go Solo"; Wasser, "Ancillary Markets," 126.

34 "DVD Borders Sought."

35 Homer, "Digital Video Discs."

36 Apar, "DVD Leaves Laser Dealers in Doubt." The author invokes a familiar system of global media incompatibility: the different technical standards for analog color television around the world: The United States' National Television Standards Committee (NTSC) system, the UK and Europe's Phase Alternating Line (PAL) standard, and Séquintiel Couleur à Mémoire (SECAM), used throughout France, Russia, Eastern Europe, Asia, and Africa. Televisions and videocassette players functioning under one of the three different standards are not interoperable with technologies from another standard. DVD Forum chairman Koje Hase claimed in 2000 that region codes were no different from television "being regionalized with NTSC" and computers in different parts of the world shipping with different keyboards. However, this comparison obscures as much as it explains, as the DVD region code system is a different technology created with different motives. As an intentionally installed form of DRM, the region code operates along a much different logic than *incompatible* technical standards, but the elision of these two different systems served to legitimize the region code system by articulating it to the well-established and by that point de rigueur analog television system. See Cole, "DVD Forum's Chairman," 37.

37 Taylor, Johnson, and Crawford, *DVD Demystified*, 11–12.

38 Brass, "Cohen Admits Fall Launch."

39 Parker, "DVD at the Brussels Forum," 11.

40 Stalter and Homer, "DVD."

41 "Another Hurdle Cleared."

42 Stalter, "Sony, WB Set DVD Date," 150.

43 Homer, "Digital Video Discs ," 14; Arnold, "Oscar Noms Boon."

44 Sweeting, "Digital Boom Shatters Distrib Windows."

45 Andrews, "DVD Regional Coding Not Working," 99.

46 "Problems Found with *The Patriot* DVD"; "RCE Fails to Halt Play."

47 Sweeting, "Big Blue Kicks Codes."

48 Whereas DVD split the world into six regions, Blu-ray discs are coded for three different regions (A, B, and C). Furthermore, the Blu-ray region code system is more lenient toward distributors and manufacturers. In other words, it is not a prerequisite to the studios licensing their content to home video distributors. Still, Blu-ray won its own format war against the rival HD DVD in part because

the latter did not include region codes in its technological specifications. During the period when both formats existed at the same time, release dates for the same film would occasionally differ for each format so that the studios could exploit different markets before releasing a region-free version. For example, when New Line released *Hairspray* on Blu-ray and HD DVD, the studio put the Blu-ray version out in November 2007 but held the HD DVD version until early 2008. See Magiera and Clark, "New Line Goes High-Def."

49 Sterne, *MP3*, 8.

50 Lessig, *Code Version 2.0.*

51 Kilker, "Shaping Convergence Media," 24.

52 Virginia Haufler defines global governance as a form of regulation wherein corporations "reach collective decisions about transnational problems with or without government participation." She notes that the 1990s saw increased initiative by multinational corporations across a number of industries to regulate their own operations with as little state interference as possible. Haufler, *Public Role*, 1. See also Mueller, *Networks and States*.

53 Sterne, *MP3*, 135; Bordwell, *Pandora's Digital Box*, 70.

54 Morley and Robins, *Spaces of Identity*; Sterne, *MP3*, 24.

55 Brass, "With DVD Specs Due."

56 Sweeting, "Exemption Contempt."

57 Havens, *Global Television Marketplace*. Xiudian Dai points out that the DVD's creation took place through processes of "business networking involving a large number of companies, in the name of promoting global standardization." Dai, *Digital Revolution and Governance*, 222.

58 "Doubts Grow for DVD Players."

59 Brass, "Cohen Admits Fall Launch."

60 Vonderau, "Beyond Piracy," 114.

61 Vonderau, 112.

62 As Rob Stone argues about region codes, "Region 1 dominates by the mere fact of being called 1, in the same way that a westerner's inclination to read from the top and left to right grants the USA pre-eminent status on a map of a round world that truly has no objective 'up' and could arguably be turned any which way." Stone, "Notes from Region 2," 9.

63 Krygier and Wood, "Ce N'est Pas Le Monde," 198, 202. Krygier and Wood disagree with the notion that maps are forms of representation, but they define representation as a duplication or replication of the world and its spaces. Rather, I adopt a cultural studies–inflected understanding of representation as not a simple replication but as a proposition in its own right. John Fiske's discussion of Gerardus Mercator's sixteenth-century projection of the globe is illuminating here. The Mercator map distorted geographic space and privileged Europe by artificially inflating its size relative to other continents in order to ease global travel and trade. As Fiske points out, this strengthened colonial power both by operating as a "superb technology for capitalism" and by representing Europe as quite literally

a larger global presence than it was. Fiske, *Power Plays Power Works*, 154. See also David Harvey's call for greater focus on how particular institutions create geographic knowledge as well as John Pickles's argument that maps "shape our understanding of the world, and how they code that world"; in "[coding] subjects and [producing] identities," the contours of the region-code map perpetuate the valuation and devaluation of certain places *and* people. See Pickles, *History of Spaces*, 12; Harvey, *Spaces of Capital*, 209.

64 Said, *Orientalism*, 5. Here, Said employs a Foucauldian view of epistemic power. In *Discipline and Punish*, Michel Foucault writes about how the arrangement of spaces, and the distribution, hierarchical ordering, and control of people within those spaces, are forms of power. See Foucault, *Discipline and Punish*, 205. Likewise, Charles Acland refers to Hollywood's distribution maps as "a product of ideological agendas and political will." Acland, *Screen Traffic*, 141.

65 Pickles, *History of Spaces*, 12.

66 "DVD Summit 2," 13.

67 Tsing, *Friction*, 57. Cristina Venegas has called for closer emphasis on how media industries "construct regionality out of an assortment of sociopolitical circumstances and economic conditions." See Venegas, "Thinking Regionally," 122.

68 On industry lore, see Havens, *Black Television Travels*, 3. On trade storytelling, see Caldwell, *Production Culture*, 34.

69 "Europe Probes Role of Region Codes." The inclusion of the United States and Canada in one region reflects the quasi-imperial industry practice of including Canadian box office numbers in the United States' "domestic" box office total. See Acland, *Screen Traffic*; Hoskins, McFadyen, and Finn, *Global Television and Film*, 60.

70 "Europe Probes Role of Region Codes."

71 "Europe Probes Role of Region Codes."

72 Region codes often became a sort of shorthand for regional or national cultural difference in popular journalistic discourse. For example, in a rather strange essay by *Sydney Morning Herald* columnist Richard Glover about a visit to Mexico's Teotihuacan, the columnist points out that his Mexican tour guide calls himself a "zone-4 Johnny Depp." The tour guide, aligned with Region Four on the DVD region code map, stands in as a copy of a Hollywood product from a different part of the world, with the implication that the Mexican Depp is Othered as a bootleg of the more authentic, highly valued Hollywood product. See Glover, "Nudes Bring Dickie Knee Back."

73 Booth, "Product Test Report"; italics in original.

74 Stalter and Homer, "DVD."

75 "Disney DVDs Carry Dual-Regional Coding."

76 Borrowman, "ELAC Bounces Back."

77 Rowe, "Globalization, Regionalization, and Australianization," 51.

78 Dunt, Gans, and King, "Economic Consequences," 37.

79 Saarinen, "DVDs."

80 See, for example, Weatherall, "Locked In," 21.

81 Sweeting, "Price to Be Paid"; Sweeting, "Nations Search for a Hidden Code."

82 "Australians to Battle PlayStation."

83 "Allan Fels Leads Investigation."

84 Sweeting, "French Fried." As a result of this, the Blu-ray Disc Association, the consortium responsible for developing the format, initially considered designating Australia and New Zealand region-free in their (voluntary) region code system, though they were eventually included in Region B with Europe, Africa, and much of the Middle East.

85 Malcolm, "How the Trans-Pacific Partnership Threatens."

86 "U.S. 'the Enemy.'"

87 Malcolm, "Final Leaked TPP Text."

88 Masnick, "With the U.S. Out."

89 Bennett and Carter, "Introduction," 2.

90 Bennett and Carter, 2.

91 Dunt, Gans, and King, "Economic Consequences," 36n12.

CHAPTER 2. CONSOLE GAMES

1 Adelman, "@Cheesemeister3k." "SNES" here refers to the company's earlier, region-locked home console, the Super Nintendo Entertainment System (called Super Famicom in Japan).

2 Sheffield, "Brick Wall."

3 Adelman, "Happy to announce."

4 Gamers and game publications have built lists of Atari games and the different international TV formats on which they will work. See "Atari 2600 Format Conversions."

5 Consalvo, "Console Video Games," 122.

6 O'Hagan and Mangiron, *Game Localization*, 232–33.

7 Dyer-Witheford and de Peuter, *Games of Empire*.

8 Consalvo, *Cheating*.

9 While an in-depth look at online, PC, and mobile games is beyond the scope of this chapter's focus on console gaming, it is worth mentioning that such games have not been subject to the exact same regional restrictions as console games—which is not to say they are not geoblocked. CD-ROMs and PC-DVDs were generally not region-locked, but mobile game availability is often contingent on the user's geographic location. Furthermore, although this is not an issue of regional lockout per se, the user experience of online and PC games that require an internet connection depend on broadband quality and accessibility, which varies greatly around the world. The availability of fast broadband speeds in South Korea, for instance, has helped sustain a particularly robust online gaming culture. This is an instance where differences in gaming capital and geocultural capital come about not through the intentional lockout of certain territories by the industry, but through the presence of internet infrastructures. See Jin, *Korea's Online Gaming Empire*.

10 Kerr, *Business and Culture of Digital Games*, 55.

11 Aslinger, "Make Room for the Wii," 212.

12 O'Donnell, "North American Game Industry," 101–3.

13 Zackariasson and Wilson, "Introduction," 3.

14 Ulin, *Business of Media Distribution*, 30.

15 Kerr, *Business and Culture of Digital Games*, 55.

16 Egenfeldt-Nielsen et al., *Understanding Video Games*, 14; O'Donnell, "This Is Not a Software Industry," 24–25; Edwards, "Economics of Game Publishing."

17 Ip and Jacobs, "Territorial Lockout," 511.

18 Consalvo, "Console Video Games," 131.

19 Consalvo, 131.

20 Alexander, "Report."

21 Montfort and Bogost, *Racing the Beam*, 153n3.

22 Carless, *Gaming Hacks*, 191.

23 Altice, *I Am Error*, 91; O'Donnell, "Production Protection," 59. Of course, this example highlights one difference between regional lockout in the game industry and the home video industry: whereas DVD region codes were put in place primarily by the Hollywood studios (i.e., the creators of texts and content) at the expense of hardware and software manufacturers, the development of lockout mechanisms in the console game industry was led by the *hardware* manufacturers at the expense of game developers and publishers. In other words, both industries' implementation of lockout systems pitted manufacturers of technology and producers of texts against each other, but the power dynamics were quite different in each field.

24 Kline, Dyer-Witheford, and de Peuter, *Digital Play*, 109.

25 O'Hagan and Mangiron, *Game Localization*, 51.

26 Kline, Dyer-Witheford, and de Peuter, *Digital Play*, 111–12.

27 Kline, Dyer-Witheford, and de Peuter, 136.

28 Carless, *Gaming Hacks*, 194.

29 Carless, 194–95; Elusive, "Guide."

30 Carless, 194.

31 Dyer-Witheford and de Peuter, *Games of Empire*, 74.

32 Aside from its metaphorical usefulness, theorists have taken up de/reterritorialization as an explanation for what John Tomlinson has referred to as the "weakening ties of culture to place" due in part to media technologies' capacity for global connection. See Tomlinson, *Globalization and Culture*, 29.

33 O'Hagan and Mangiron, *Game Localization*, 55.

34 As consoles became increasingly powerful and, through the logics of convergence, adopted more and more functions, popular narratives suggested that these technologies should have moved well past the compatibility issues familiar to consumer electronics. However, as Ian Bogost reminds us, "a spectre of incompatibility still hangs over consoles" despite these desires. See Bogost, "Xbox One."

35 On "trusted systems" see Gillespie, *Wired Shut*, 9. On "tethered appliances" see Zittrain, *Future of the Internet*, 104.

36 Gibson, "No Region Locking for PS3?"

37 Nix, "GDC 06."

38 Bramwell, "Wii Upholds Cube Region Lock"; Kietzmann, "Wii Not Even Remotely Region-Free."

39 Plunkett, "Meet the First Ever Region-Locked PS3 Game."

40 Good, "*Persona 4 Arena*."

41 Rockstar Games, "Grand Theft Auto V"

42 For example, see "Region-Free Xbox 360 Games."

43 O'Hagan and Mangiron, *Game Localization*, 114.

44 Ip and Jacobs, "Territorial Lockout," 515.

45 Carless, *Gaming Hacks*, 191.

46 Schreier, "Xbox One Needs to Connect."

47 Stuart, "Xbox One Region Lock."

48 Pearson, "21 Launch Countries."

49 Yoshida, "And yes"; Krupa, "PlayStation 4 Is Region-Free."

50 Stuart, "Xbox One DRM Restrictions Dropped."

51 Phillips, "Nintendo Blames Region-Locking"; George, "Nintendo's President Discusses Region Locking."

52 Link_Is_My_Homie, "Region Locked."

53 Whitehead, "Talking Point."

54 Olivarez-Giles, "Nintendo Defends Wii U Region Locking"; "Top Posts in Miiverse Community."

55 Cheesemeister, "Let's Convince Nintendo."

56 Stevens, "Stop Region Blocking."

57 As Charles Bernstein reminds us, read-only memory "is out of sight only to control more efficiently." Bernstein, "Play It Again, Pac-Man," 166.

58 Ashcraft, "Should Digital Games Be Region Locked?"

59 Ashcraft.

60 Consalvo, "Unintended Travel."

61 Edwards, "Performing a Permanent Famicom to NES Game Conversion."

62 "NES Cart Converters."

63 Bhaduri, "Gaming"; Burke, "Future in a Vault of Plastic," 99.

64 Payne, "Connected Viewing, Connected Capital," 188.

65 Carless, *Gaming Hacks*, 192.

66 Consalvo, *Cheating*, 183.

67 Jenkins, "Modded Xbox 360s Blocked."

68 "The Myths of Modding."

69 Dyer-Witheford and de Peuter, *Games of Empire*, 86.

70 Consalvo, *Cheating*, 85. Many scholars have stressed that rules are part of what makes a game a unique and particular form of social experience. They are crucial

to the procedural rhetoric that Ian Bogost argues is central to games; Alexander Galloway begins his book on games by calling them "[activities] defined by rules." See Bogost, *Persuasive Games*; Galloway, *Gaming*, 1. For more on the importance of rules to games, see Crawford, *Video Gamers*, 68–70.

71 Consalvo, *Cheating*, 7.

72 Dymek, "Video Games," 38–39.

73 Carless, *Gaming Hacks*, 190.

74 Whitehead, "Talking Point"; italics in original.

75 Dyer-Witheford and de Peuter, *Games of Empire*, 81; italics in original. On video games and gender, see Cassell and Jenkins, *From Barbie to Mortal Kombat*; Kafai et al., *Beyond Barbie and Mortal Kombat*; Nakamura, "Don't Hate the Player, Hate the Game"; Shaw, "On Not Becoming Gamers"; Fisher, "Sexy, Dangerous—and Ignored"; Chess, *Ready Player Two*.

76 Jordan, *Hacking*, 124–26.

77 O'Donnell, "North American Game Industry," 110.

78 Kirkpatrick, *Computer Games and the Social Imaginary*, 81–91.

79 Dyer-Witheford and de Peuter, *Games of Empire*, 86.

80 Morley, *Home Territories*, 68. See also Freeman, "Is Local."

81 Dyer-Witheford and de Peuter, *Games of Empire*, 84–85.

82 Dyer-Witheford and de Peuter, xv.

83 Link_Is_My_Homie, "Region Locked."

84 Rashy, "Arab Gamer Episode 3."

85 Ito, "Japanese Media Mixes"; Ito, Okabe, and Tsuji, *Fandom Unbound*.

86 Ito, "Japanese Media Mixes," 51–52.

87 Bowling, "Beginner's Guide."

88 Iwabuchi, *Recentering Globalization*, 27.

89 Consalvo, *Atari to Zelda*, 33.

CHAPTER 3. VIDEO ON DEMAND

1 Netflix, "Netflix CES 2016 Keynote."

2 Lobato, *Netflix Nations*.

3 On the disconnect between popular notions of television's ubiquity and the reality of uneven access, see Stewart, "Myth of Televisual Ubiquity."

4 Lobato, *Netflix Nations*.

5 Morley and Robins, *Spaces of Identity*, 11–12.

6 Kompare, "Cult Streaming"; Tryon, *On-Demand Culture*; Dixon, *Streaming*; Iordanova, "Digital Disruption."

7 For more on the practices and technologies of geoblocking, see Lobato, "New Video Geography."

8 Ashraf and León, "Logics and Territorialities of Geoblocking," 42; Deibert et al., *Access Contested*, 17.

9 Even a recent legal analysis of geoblocking suggests that "though physical borders—and sometimes difficult to surmount digital borders—still exist, the

reality is that most things can be obtained online." See Burnett, "Geographically Restricted Streaming Content," 463.

10 Dalley, "Navigating Online Geoblocking."

11 Ng, "Finding a New Future."

12 Galvin, "What Is . . . Geoblocking?"

13 Tryon, *On-Demand Culture*, 41.

14 Urquhart and Wagman, "This Content Is Not Available," 125.

15 Lobato, "Politics of Digital Distribution."

16 Stewart, "Myth of Televisual Ubiquity," 702.

17 Turner, "Content Unlimited." See also Lobato and Meese, "Australia."

18 "Committee Seeks IT Pricing Equity."

19 As Deb Verhoeven points out, the Australian film industry has often positioned itself against a perceived American commercial culture—here, manifesting as conglomerate Hollywood. See Verhoeven, "Film, Video, DVD, and Online Delivery," 153–54.

20 Lobato and Meese, "Australia."

21 O'Donnell, "Sky Beware," 10.

22 Fellenbaum, "Slingshot Users in New Zealand."

23 As Marketa Trimble has pointed out, this out-of-court settlement has kept the legality of circumvention in a gray area. See Trimble, "Geoblocking, Technical Standards, and the Law," 60.

24 Healey, "New Zealand ISP's 'Global Mode.'"

25 Lobato and Meese have argued that politicians opportunistically used geoblocking as a way to blend populist, nationalist rhetoric with free-market ideologies. See Lobato and Meese, "Australia," 122–23.

26 Duckett, "'Australia Tax' Is Real."

27 "Committee Seeks IT Pricing Equity."

28 Cartwright, "Arrested Development."

29 "Choice's Letter to Netflix."

30 Cartwright, "Arrested Development."

31 Silverstone, *Media and Morality*, 18.

32 Here, I focus mainly on the iPlayer's television programming, as its radio programs are not subject to many of the same geographic restrictions as its television broadcasts.

33 Lawler, "BBC Brings Global iPlayer"; "BBC Global iPlayer to Close."

34 Hern, "BBC iPlayer's US Rollout Blocked."

35 Lotz, *Portals*.

36 Gillespie, "Politics of Platforms," 348.

37 Govil, "Thinking Nationally," 138.

38 Hall, "Which Public, Whose Service?" quoted in Morley and Robins, *Spaces of Identity*, 196.

39 Bennett et al., *Multiplatforming Public Service Broadcasting*, 18.

40 Bennett et al., 24. See also Miller, *Something Completely Different*; Becker, "From High Culture to Hip Culture"; Steemers, *Selling Television*.

41 Klosowski, "How an American Can Stream."

42 Pash, "How to Access."

43 Nederkorn, "I'm an American."

44 Pash, "How to Access"; italics added.

45 Pash.

46 Pash.

47 Such comments also illustrate the distinct relationship among American and British viewers and broadcasting industries—one based, as Michele Hilmes has shown, on a long-standing, complex history of both mutual influence and strategic opposition. See Hilmes, *Network Nations*.

48 For more on the BBC as a national public utility, see Scannell and Cardiff, *Social History of British Broadcasting*.

49 Jackson, "BBC iPlayer Users Will Have to Pay."

50 Kemp, "BBC Director General Tony Hall."

51 Newman, "Free TV."

52 Sorrel, "BBC Launches Subscription-Based."

53 "E.U. Wants iPlayer Access."

54 Fiveash, "Netflix Abroad Set for Showtime."

55 Science|Business, "EU Vice-President Ansip."

56 European Commission, "Geo-Blocking."

57 "Europe Probes Role of Region Codes"; Goldstein, "International Quarrel with Codes."

58 European Parliament, "Written Questions."

59 "Priority."

60 Schmidt, "Why Europe Needs a Digital Single Market"; Barbrook and Cameron, "Californian Ideology."

61 Roxborough, "Can Europe Set Up a Digital Single Market?"; Roxborough, "What's behind a Europe Plan."

62 Baker, "Netflix, Amazon Given Quotas."

63 Stone, "Notes from Region 2," 10.

64 Morley, *Home Territories*, 259.

65 Uricchio, "We Europeans?" 12.

CHAPTER 4. DIGITAL MUSIC

1 SpotifyVideoChannel, "Spotify."

2 Morris and Powers, "Control, Curation and Musical Experience," 107.

3 Morris and Powers, 107.

4 Harvey, "Station to Station."

5 Hesmondhalgh, *Cultural Industries*, 250; Rogers, *Death and Life*, 70.

6 International Federation of the Phonographic Industry, *Global Music Report*, 6.

7 Negus, "Corporate Strategies," 23.

8 Burnett, *Global Jukebox*, 27.

9 Negus, "Corporate Strategies," 25.

10 Pohlmann, *Compact Disc Handbook*, 11; Philips Research, "History of the CD."
11 Morris, *Selling Digital Music*, 74.
12 Garofalo, "I Want My MP3," 88.
13 Kernfeld, *Pop Song Piracy*, 180.
14 Kernfeld, 181.
15 Indeed, contrast this with the case of the DVD's CSS and region code technical standards, analyzed in chapter 1. On the MP3 and media globalization, see Sterne, *MP3*, 24.
16 Reports on Spotify have shown that the cost of music licensing—which grows as the platform moves into new markets—has been an impediment to the still-unprofitable company's ability to make money. See Mak, "What Spotify's Lack of Profits May Mean."
17 Rand, "Cost of Spotify Premium."
18 Burkart and McCourt, *Digital Music Wars*, 32–33.
19 See, for example, Pogue, "Online Music, Unshackled."
20 Hong, "As Spotify Passes One Year in Asia"; Steimle, "Spotify Plans to Own."
21 Fagenson, "Spotify Eyes Latin America."
22 Harvey, "Station to Station"; Walker, "Song Decoders."
23 Sherman, "Pandora Touts 200 Million Listeners."
24 Harvey, "Station to Station." This is due to a regulatory distinction between public performance (e.g., on terrestrial radio and in public spaces) and digital public performance (e.g., on satellite and internet radio stations like SiriusXM and Pandora). The former pays out royalties to publishers and songwriters where the latter pays out royalties to labels and performing artists.
25 Rushton, "Listing Values Loss-Making Site"; Peoples, "Business Matters."
26 Resnikoff, "Europeans Have No Idea."
27 Connell and Gibson, *Sound Tracks*, 44; Lacey, "Listening in the Digital Age."
28 Kusek and Leonhard, *Future of Music*, 3. See also Kassabian, *Ubiquitous Listening*. Several writers have also pointed out that the metaphor of "the cloud" likewise invokes a condition of immateriality that ignores the physical infrastructures that keep digital media running. See Holt and Vonderau, "Where the Internet Lives," 82; Morris, *Selling Digital Music*, 168.
29 Burkart and McCourt, *Digital Music Wars*, 4; Goldstein, *Copyright's Highway*.
30 Hilmes, *Radio Voices*, 13–14.
31 Streeter, *Selling the Air*, 61.
32 Hilmes, *Radio Voices*, 15.
33 Connell and Gibson, *Sound Tracks*, 9–10.
34 Vonderau, "Spotify Effect"; Morris and Powers, "Control, Curation and Musical Experience."
35 Harvey, "Station to Station."
36 Burkart and McCourt, *Digital Music Wars*, 5.
37 adfhogan, "Re: Cost of Spotify Premium."
38 Smith, "Web Services Grow."

39 Hamilton, "Spotify Smooths Exit"; O'Malley Greenburg, "Nielsen's Mid-Year Report."

40 McWilliams, "Singing Coke's Praises Evolves."

41 Pogue, "Online Music, Unshackled."

42 "Spotify Begins Rollout."

43 Hong, "As Spotify Passes One Year in Asia"; "Spotify Sets Sights."

44 Marsden, "One Giant Jukebox."

45 Morris and Powers, "Control, Curation and Musical Experience," 111.

46 Spotify, "Musical Map."

47 Roettgers, "Spotify Puts the World's Music."

48 Van Buskirk, "Serendipity Visualizes Simultaneous Listening"; McDonald, *Serendipity.*

49 Zuckerman, "Homophily, Serendipity, Xenophilia"; Van Buskirk.

50 Van Buskirk.

51 Pelly, "Problem with Muzak."

52 Leight, "Why Isn't Jamaican Dancehall Bigger."

53 Pelly, "Discover Weakly."

54 Zuckerman, *Digital Cosmopolitans.*

55 David Hesmondhalgh's 1996 writing, where he expresses skepticism about the argument that global music markets were becoming increasingly fragmented, feels prescient here. As he pointed out, "It seems likely that the globalization and horizontal integration of the cultural industries has emphasized the central importance of a small number of major acts." See Hesmondhalgh, "Flexibility, Post-Fordism," 483.

56 Berland, "Locating Listening," 133.

57 Hosokawa, "Walkman Effect," 166.

58 Sprenger, "Network Is Not the Territory," 4.

59 Vonderau, "Spotify Effect," 4.

60 Douglas, *Listening In,* quoted in Harvey, "Station to Station." On streaming music's approaches toward defining and constructing the "individual," see Prey, "Nothing Personal."

61 Carr, "Spotify Announces US Launch"; Peoples, "Business Matters."

62 Pogue, "Online Music, Unshackled."

63 Bourdieu, *Distinction,* 10.

64 Burkart, *Music and Cyberliberties,* 2. See also Lessig, *Free Culture.*

CHAPTER 5. REGION-FREE MEDIA

1 Motherboard, "Peru's DVD Pirates."

2 Thussu, "Mapping Global Media Flow and Contra-Flow."

3 Sterne, *MP3,* 7.

4 Hu, "Closed Borders and Open Secrets."

5 Dwyer and Uricaru, "Slashings and Subtitles," 50.

6 Fiske, *Understanding Popular Culture,* 36.

7 Fiske, 39.

8 Foley, "*Doctor Who* Knows No Borders."

9 Morley, *Home Territories*, 33.

10 Morley, 103.

11 Lobato, *Netflix Nations*.

12 "Region-Free DVD Deck Sales."

13 "DVD Regionalization Strategy in Tatters."

14 "Issues Remain for Euro Market."

15 Rivero, "Lee's Tiger on the Loose."

16 Frost, "Middle East Sees 20% IT Growth."

17 "Use of Spanish DVD Tracks."

18 "Regional Code Circumvention More Prevalent in Europe."

19 Powell, "Remote Regions"; "Use of Spanish DVD Tracks."

20 "Internet Offers Detailed 'How-To.'"

21 Creed, "Internet Update."

22 Clarke, "Break Down Blu-ray Borders."

23 Christophers, *Envisioning Media Power*, 149.

24 Miles, "Click Here for Easy Wish Fulfillment"; "Mod Chips Now Legal"; Australian Competition and Consumer Commission, "Consumers in Dark."

25 Borrowman, "All the World's a Stage."

26 "Microsoft Launches X-Box."

27 Cole, "DVD Forum's Chairman."

28 "Region-Free DVD Deck Sales."

29 "John Barker's Gaithersburg Address."

30 Anderson, *Long Tail*.

31 Luh, "Breaking Down DVD Borders."

32 For more on this, see Naficy, "Narrowcasting in Diaspora."

33 Cunningham, "Popular Media as Public 'Sphericules,'" 133.

34 See, for instance, Gillespie, *Television, Ethnicity, and Cultural Change*; Naficy, *Making of Exile Cultures*; Punathambekar, "Bollywood in the Indian-American Diaspora"; Kim, "Diasporic Nationalism and the Media."

35 Kolar-Panov, "Video and the Macedonians," 111.

36 Punathambekar, "Bollywood in the Indian-American Diaspora," 154–55.

37 Beaty and Sullivan, *Canadian Television Today*, 123.

38 Lewis and Hirano, "Mi Arai Mai Mai Mai?" 199–200.

39 Appadurai, *Future as Cultural Fact*, 22.

40 Lobato, *Shadow Economies of Cinema*.

41 "Chinese Code-Free DVD Maker."

42 "Hardware Notes."

43 Lewis and Hirano, "Mi Arai Mai Mai Mai?" 185.

44 As mentioned elsewhere in this book, Ramon Lobato points out that informal media economies are, in fact, "everyday, banal phenomena." Lobato, *Shadow Economies of Cinema*, 48–49. See also Wang, *Framing Piracy*, 185.

45 Hilderbrand, *Inherent Vice*, 27–32.

46 In order to preserve confidentiality, references to interviews will include the city and/or neighborhood and type of establishment but will not include the names of people or establishments.

47 Here, a gendered split was apparent in the kind of labor undertaken in these stores, wherein the more traditionally feminized domains of garment production and design contrasted with the male manager's more active role as the DVD salesperson and point of interaction for consumers (as well as an interviewer like myself). While the man running the store took phone calls and spoke to me as the official representative of the establishment, the women working at the store undertook more mundane tasks and gendered forms of work. Such labor divisions recall arguments from Youna Kim and Ien Ang that diasporic existence should not be idealized and that scholarship on such modes of existence should emphasize marginalization, alienation, and gendered discrimination. See Kim, "Diasporic Nationalism and the Media"; and Ang, *On Not Speaking Chinese.*

48 At the same time, a dynamic seems to be taking shape that reflects broader shifts in media consumption. Many of my interviewees indicated that DVD sales have slumped (and in some places completely fallen off) due to the availability of video streaming platforms which are not beholden to the region code system. They suggested that consumers were increasingly forsaking DVD for platforms like YouTube and online pirated file sharing. This has the possibility of disarticulating diasporic media experience from a particular locality (by making the local video store less essential as a community outpost for cultural engagement). For more on this dynamic, see Elkins, "Changing Scales of Diasporic Media Retail."

49 Herbert, *Videoland*, 123.

50 Clifford, "Traveling Cultures," 108.

51 Bart Beaty and Rebecca Sullivan point out that non-Asian cinephiles regularly flock to Asian markets to pick up cheap bootlegs of Hong Kong action films, for example. See Beaty and Sullivan, *Canadian Television Today*, 123.

52 Keathley, *Cinephilia and History*, 15; Klinger, "DVD Cinephile," 23.

53 Elsaesser, "Cinephilia," 30.

54 Jenkins, "Pop Cosmopolitanism." See also Mia Consalvo's discussion of cosmopolitanism among video game consumers who have used the medium to connect with Japanese culture. Consalvo, *Atari to Zelda.*

55 For more on this, see Klinger, "DVD Cinephile," 25–26.

56 Clarke, "Studios Divide and Rule."

57 Dargis, "21st Century Cinephile."

58 Rosenbaum, "Global Discoveries on DVD."

59 Elsaesser describes this as a "post-auteur, post-theory cinephilia that has embraced the new technologies, that flourishes on the internet and finds its *jouissance* in an often undisguised and unapologetic fetishism of the technical prowess

of the digital video disc, its sound and its image and the tactile sensations now associated with both." Elsaesser, "Cinephilia," 36. For more on this, see Tryon, *Reinventing Cinema.*

60 Klinger, "DVD Cinephile," 27.

61 Darren, "Criterion Criteria."

62 Darren.

63 On the Californian Ideology, see Barbrook and Cameron, "Californian Ideology."

64 Herbert, *Videoland*, 86. See also Curtin, "Media Capital."

65 "Readers' Comments."

66 Hawkins, "Culture Wars."

67 On "subcultural capital," see Thornton, *Club Cultures.*

68 Rosenbaum and Martin, *Movie Mutations*, 185.

69 Dotcom, "MPAA."

70 Zuckerman, "Homophily, Serendipity, Xenophilia." Similarly, Henry Jenkins talks about how "pop cosmopolitans," or people who engage international culture through popular culture, "[walk] a thin line between dilettantism and connoisseurship, between orientalist fantasies and a desire to honestly connect and understand an alien culture, between assertion of mastery and surrender to cultural difference." See Jenkins, "Pop Cosmopolitanism," 127.

71 As David Morley argues, "The figure of the cosmopolitan, like that of the *flaneur*, is clearly masculine, and is often a symbolic figure of the West and its sophistications marked out against a backward other." Morley, *Home Territories*, 231.

72 Tsing, "Global Situation," 343–44.

73 Schaeffer-Grabiel, "Planet-Love.com," 337.

74 Gray, *Video Playtime.*

75 Klinger, *Beyond the Multiplex*, 89.

76 Rollux, message board post.

77 As Mimi White reminds us, the man cave trope is a response to the idea that "houses in general, and the varied domestic activities and habits they contain, are redolent with femininity." White, "Gender Territories," 240. See also the work of James Kendrick, who discovers that for many men "the creation of a home theater environment within the domestic space is a way of reworking the gendered nature of television and its association with everydayness into a masculine domain of control." Kendrick, "Aspect Ratios and Joe Six-Packs," 65.

78 Here I use Greg Taylor's definition of cultism, which "identifies and refuses 'mass' taste by developing a resistant cult taste for more obscure and less clearly commodified cultural objects." See Taylor, *Artists in the Audience*, 15.

79 Wollen, "Auteur Theory," 72.

80 Pizowell, "Unboxing OREI Region Free 3D Blu-ray Player."

81 Newman and Levine, *Legitimating Television*, 132.

82 "How to Bypass Geo-Blocking in Australia."

83 Mōri, "*Winter Sonata* and Cultural Practices," 134.

84 Eng, "Strategies of Engagement," 100.

85 Becker, "Access Is Elementary."

CONCLUSION

1 "Can Guns N' Roses."

2 Ashraf and León, "Logics and Territorialities," 52.

3 For more on the Pirate Party, see Burkart, *Pirate Politics*.

4 Lobato and Meese, *Geoblocking and Global Video Culture*.

5 Morley, *Home Territories*, 235.

6 Morley, 23. Here, he draws on Wilson, "New Cosmopolitanism," 355.

7 Gillespie, *Television, Ethnicity, and Cultural Change*, 206. On cultures of cosmopolitanism, see the work of philosopher Kwame Anthony Appiah. He argues that cosmopolitanism requires both "obligations that stretch beyond those to whom we are related by the ties of kith and kind, or even the more formal ties of a shared citizenship" as well as the need to "take seriously the value not just of human lives but of particular human lives, which means taking an interest in the practices and beliefs that lend them significance." Ethan Zuckerman responds to Appiah's summary by quipping, "My taste for sushi and my fondness for Afropop are insufficient to make me a cosmopolitan." In other words, to be truly cosmopolitan, consumer culture cannot simply be branded as superficially "global" without an appreciation of difference grounded in ethical obligations toward shared humanity. See Appiah, *Cosmopolitanism*, xv; Zuckerman, *Digital Cosmopolitans*, 24.

8 Acland, *Screen Traffic*, 44.

9 Jenkins, "Pop Cosmopolitanism," 133–36.

10 Luh, "Breaking Down DVD Borders."

11 Kayahara, "Digital Revolution."; Ecke, "Coping with the DVD Dilemma."

12 Puckett, "Digital Rights Management," 11.

13 Hovet, "YouTube and Archives."

14 "The Society for Cinema and Media Studies' Statement," 160.

15 Becker, "Access Is Elementary."

16 Hilderbrand, *Inherent Vice*, 5.

17 Silverstone, *Media and Morality*, 31.

18 Silverstone, 54.

19 Postigo, *Digital Rights Movement*, 116.

20 Levy, *Hackers, 23*, quoted in Postigo, 116.

21 Eschenfelder, Howard, and Desai, "Ethics of DeCSS Posting."

BIBLIOGRAPHY

Acland, Charles R. *Screen Traffic: Movies, Multiplexes, and Global Culture.* Durham, NC: Duke University Press, 2003.

Adelman, Dan (@Dan_Adelman). "@Cheesemeister3k @gypsyOtoko @lite_agent @EndRegionLock I too used to live in Japan. Had 2 SNESs—one Japanese, one US. I feel your pain." Twitter, September 10, 2013, 8:09 p.m. http://twitter.com/dan_adelman/status/377630034342596608.

———. "Happy to announce I reached an arrangement w/ @NintendoAmerica whereby I can tweet again. Arrangement includes my not working there anymore." Twitter, August 4, 2014, 5:06 a.m. http://twitter.com/Dan_Adelman/status/496265936283140096.

adfhogan. "Re: Cost of Spotify Premium for Different Countries in Relation to USD." Spotify Help, September 30, 2012. http://community.spotify.com.

Alexander, Leigh. "Report: Nintendo Warns of UK Xmas DSi Shortages." *Gamasutra*, March 3, 2009. www.gamasutra.com.

"Allan Fels Leads Investigation into Digital Videodisk Prices." *Video Store*, April 20, 2003.

Altice, Nathan. *I Am Error: The Nintendo Family Computer / Entertainment System Platform.* Cambridge, MA: MIT Press, 2015.

Anderson, Chris. *The Long Tail: Why the Future of Business Is Selling Less of More.* New York: Hyperion, 2006.

Andrews, Sam. "DVD Is Taking Off in Europe, but Issues Hinder Full Growth." *Billboard*, May 1, 1999.

———. "DVD Regional Coding Not Working: Suppliers Seek Solutions to Protect Theatrical Release in Europe." *Billboard*, November 18, 2000.

Ang, Ien. *On Not Speaking Chinese: Living between Asia and the West.* London: Routledge, 2001.

"Another Hurdle Cleared as Agreement Is Reached on DVD Regional Coding System." *Video Store*, September 29, 1996.

Apar, Bruce. "DVD Leaves Laser Dealers in Doubt." *Video Business*, May 31, 1996.

Appadurai, Arjun. *The Future as Cultural Fact: Essays on the Global Condition.* London: Verso, 2013.

———. *Modernity at Large: Cultural Dimensions of Globalization.* Minneapolis: University of Minnesota Press, 1996.

Appiah, Kwame Anthony. *Cosmopolitanism: Ethics in a World of Strangers.* New York: Norton, 2006.

Arnold, Thomas K. "Oscar Noms Boon to Columbia TriStar International Division." *Video Store*, February 25, 2001.

Ashcraft, Brian. "Should Digital Games Be Region Locked?" *Kotaku*, August 14, 2009. http://kotaku.com.

Ashraf, Cameran, and Luis Felipe Alvarez León. "The Logics and Territorialities of Geoblocking." In *Geoblocking and Global Video Culture*, edited by Ramon Lobato and James Meese, 42–53. Amsterdam: Institute of Network Cultures, 2016.

Aslinger, Ben. "Make Room for the Wii: Game Consoles and the Construction of Space." In *A Companion to New Media Dynamics*, edited by John Hartley, Jean Burgess, and Axel Bruns, 209–18. Malden, MA: Wiley-Blackwell, 2013.

"Atari 2600 TV Format Conversions." *AtariAge*. http://atariage.com.

Australian Competition and Consumer Commission. "Consumers in Dark about DVD Imports." Press release, December 21, 2000. www.accc.gov.au.

"Australians to Battle PlayStation and DVD Regional Coding." *Consumer Electronics*, February 18, 2002.

Baker, Jennifer. "Netflix, Amazon Given Quotas for EU-Produced Video, Face New Tax." *Ars Technica*, May 25, 2016. http://arstechnica.com.

Balio, Tino. "'A Major Presence in All of the World's Important Markets': The Globalization of Hollywood in the 1990s." In *Contemporary Hollywood Cinema*, edited by Steve Neale and Murray Smith, 58–73. London: Routledge, 1998.

Barbrook, Richard, and Andy Cameron. "The Californian Ideology." *Science as Culture* 6, no. 1 (1996): 44–72.

"BBC Global iPlayer to Close in June." *BBC News*, May 13, 2015. www.bbc.com.

Beaty, Bart, and Rebecca Sullivan. *Canadian Television Today*. Calgary: University of Calgary Press, 2006.

Becker, Christine. "Access Is Elementary: Crossing Television's Distribution Borders." *Flow*, January 13, 2014. http://flowtv.org.

———. "From High Culture to Hip Culture: Transforming the BBC into BBC America." In *Anglo-American Media Interactions, 1850–2000*, edited by Joel H. Weiner and Mark Hampton, 275–94. New York: Palgrave Macmillan, 2007.

Bennett, James, Niki Strange, Paul Kerr, and Andrea Medrado, *Multiplatforming Public Service Broadcasting: The Economic and Cultural Role of UK Digital and TV Independents*. London: University of London Press, 2012.

Bennett, Tony, and David Carter. "Introduction." In *Culture in Australia: Policies, Publics, and Programs*, edited by Tony Bennett and David Carter, 1–10. Cambridge, UK: Cambridge University Press, 2001.

Bennett, Tony, Mike Savage, Elizabeth Silva, Alan Warde, Modesto Gayo-Cal, and David Wright. *Culture, Class, Distinction*. New York: Routledge, 2009.

Benzon, Paul. "Bootleg Paratextuality and Digital Temporality: Towards an Alternate Present of the DVD." *Narrative* 21, no. 1 (2013): 88–104.

Berland, Jody. "Locating Listening: Technological Space, Popular Music, Canadian Mediations." *Cultural Studies* 2 (1988): 343–58.

Bernstein, Charles. "Play It Again, Pac-Man." In *The Medium of the Video Game*, edited by Mark J. P. Wolf, 155–68. Austin: University of Texas Press, 2001.

BEUC—The European Consumer Organisation. "Imagine This Happening to You While Shopping (Hidden Camera)." YouTube video, 2:31. April 4, 2016. http://www.youtube.com/watch?v=WbiacSD13qk.

Bhaduri, Saugata. "Gaming [draft] [#digitalkeywords]." *Culture Digitally: Examining Contemporary Cultural Production*, June 5, 2014. http://culturedigitally.org.

Bielby Denise D., and C. Lee Harrington. *Global TV: Exporting Television and Culture in the World Market*. New York: New York University Press, 2008.

Boddy, William. *New Media and Popular Imagination: Launching Radio, Television, and Digital Media in the United States*. Oxford, UK: Oxford University Press, 2004.

Bogost, Ian. *Persuasive Games: The Expressive Power of Videogames*. Cambridge, MA: MIT Press, 2007.

———. "Xbox One and the Endless, Hopeless Dream of Convergence." *Edge*, May 30, 2014. www.edge-online.com.

Booth, Stephen A. "Product Test Report: Marantz DVD Player." *Popular Electronics* 16, no. 9 (1999): 17–19.

Bordwell, David. *Pandora's Digital Box: Films, Files, and the Future of Movies*. Madison, WI: Irvington Way Institute Press, 2012.

———. "Women and Children First." *Observations on Film Art*, October 22, 2008. www.davidbordwell.net.

Borrowman, Greg. "All the World's a Stage." *Sydney Morning Herald*, January 31, 2000.

———. "ELAC Bounces Back." *Sydney Morning Herald*, October 27, 1997.

Bourdieu, Pierre. *Distinction: A Social Critique of the Judgement of Taste*. Translated by Richard Nice. Cambridge, MA: Harvard University Press, 1984.

———. "The Forms of Capital." In *Handbook of Theory and Research for the Sociology of Education*, edited by John G. Richardson, 241–58. New York: Greenwood, 1986.

Bowling, Steve. "A Beginner's Guide to Importing Games." *Talk amongst Yourselves*, January 31, 2014. http://tay.kotaku.com.

Bramwell, Tom. "Wii Upholds Cube Region Lock." *Eurogamer*, October 3, 2006. www.eurogamer.net.

Brass, Kevin. "Cohen Admits Fall Launch of DVD Is 'Dicey.'" *Video Store*, July 7, 1996.

———. "With DVD Specs Due in 30 Days, Backers Still Eye a Fall Launch." *Video Store*, March 24, 1996.

Brookey, Robert Alan, and Robert Westerfelhaus. "Hiding Homoeroticism in Plain View: The *Fight Club* DVD as Digital Closet." *Critical Studies in Media Communication* 19, no. 1 (2002): 21–43.

Burkart, Patrick. *Music and Cyberliberties*. Middletown, CT: Wesleyan University Press, 2010.

———. *Pirate Politics: The New Information Policy Contests*. Cambridge, MA: MIT Press, 2014.

Burkart, Patrick, and Tom McCourt. *Digital Music Wars: Ownership and Control of the Celestial Jukebox*. Lanham, MD: Rowman and Littlefield, 2006.

Burke, Roland. "The Future in a Vault of Plastic: Physical Geolocking in the Era of the 16-Bit Video Game Cartridge." In *Geoblocking and Global Video Culture*, edited by Ramon Lobato and James Meese, 94–105. Amsterdam: Institute of Network Cultures, 2016.

Burnett, Jerusha. "Geographically Restricted Streaming Content and Evasion of Geolocation: The Applicability of the Copyright Anticircumvention Rules." *Michigan Telecommunications and Technology Law Review* 19 (2012): 461–88.

Burnett, Robert. *The Global Jukebox: The International Music Industry*. London: Routledge, 1996.

Caldwell, John Thornton. *Production Culture: Industrial Reflexivity and Critical Practice in Film and Television*. Durham, NC: Duke University Press, 2009.

"Can Guns N' Roses, or Any Artist, Erase an Unflattering Moment?" *New York Times Popcast*, August 4, 2018. www.nytimes.com.

Carless, Simon. *Gaming Hacks: 100 Industrial-Strength Tips and Tools*. Sebastopol, CA: O'Reilly, 2005.

Carr, Paul. "Spotify Announces US Launch; Closing European Service to Fund It." *TechCrunch*, April 1, 2011. http://techcrunch.com.

Cartwright, Madison. "Arrested Development, Netflix, and Geoblocking." *Choice*, May 30, 2013. www.choice.com.au.

Cassell, Justine, and Henry Jenkins, eds. *From Barbie to Mortal Kombat: Gender and Computer Games*. Cambridge, MA: MIT Press, 1998.

Chalaby, Jean K. "Towards an Understanding of Media Transnationalism." In *Transnational Television Worldwide: Towards a New Media Order*, edited by Jean K. Chalaby, 1–13. London: I. B. Tauris, 2005.

Cheesemeister. "Let's Convince Nintendo to Go Region-Free!" NeoGaf, June 12, 2013. www.neogaf.com.

Chess, Shira. *Ready Player Two: Women Gamers and Designed Identity*. Minneapolis: University of Minnesota Press, 2017.

"Chinese Code-Free DVD Maker Testing Waters Here." *Audio Week*, February 22, 1999.

"Choice's Letter to Netflix." Facebook, May 27, 2013. www.facebook.com.

Christophers, Brett. *Envisioning Media Power: On Capital and Geographies of Television*. Lanham, MD: Lexington Books, 2009.

Clarke, Anthony. "Break Down Blu-ray Borders." *The Age* (Melbourne), September 27, 2012.

———. "Studios Divide and Rule to Keep Movie Disc Titles Scarce." *The Australian*, January 1, 1999.

Clifford, James. "Traveling Cultures." In *Cultural Studies*, edited by Lawrence Grossberg, Cary Nelson, and Paula Treichler, 96–116. London: Routledge, 1991.

Cole, George. "DVD Forum's Chairman Speaks Out." *One to One*, April 2000.

"Committee Seeks IT Pricing Equity." Australian Associated Press Newswire, July 29, 2013.

Connell, John, and Chris Gibson. *Sound Tracks: Popular Music, Identity, and Place*. London: Routledge, 2003.

Consalvo, Mia. *Atari to Zelda: Japan's Videogames in Global Contexts*. Cambridge, MA: MIT Press, 2016.

——. *Cheating: Gaining Advantage in Videogames*. Cambridge, MA: MIT Press, 2007.

——. "Console Video Games and Global Corporations: Creating a Hybrid Culture." *New Media and Society* 8, no. 1 (2006): 117–31.

——. "Unintended Travel: ROM Hackers and Fan Translations of Japanese Video Games." In *Gaming Globally: Production, Play, and Place*, edited by Nina B. Huntemann and Ben Aslinger, 119–38. New York: Palgrave Macmillan, 2013.

Couldry, Nick. *The Place of Media Power: Pilgrims and Witnesses of the Media Age*. London: Routledge, 2000.

Crawford, Garry. *Video Gamers*. London: Routledge, 2012.

Creed, Adam. "Internet Update." *Newsbytes*, October 1, 1999.

Cresswell, Tim. *In Place / Out of Place: Geography, Ideology, and Transgression*. Minneapolis: University of Minnesota Press, 1996.

Cubitt, Sean. *Timeshift: On Video Culture*. London: Routledge, 1991.

Cunningham, Stuart. "Popular Media as Public 'Sphericules' for Diasporic Communities." *International Journal of Cultural Studies* 4 (2001): 131–47.

Curtin, Michael. "Media Capital: Towards the Study of Spatial Flows." *International Journal of Cultural Studies* 6, no. 2 (2003): 202–28.

——. *Playing to the World's Biggest Audience: The Globalization of Chinese Film and TV*. Berkeley: University of California Press, 2007.

D'Acci, Julie. "Cultural Studies, Television Studies, and the Crisis in the Humanities." In *Television after TV: Essays on a Medium in Transition*, edited by Lynn Spigel and Jan Olsson, 418–46. Durham, NC: Duke University Press, 2004.

Dai, Xiudian. *The Digital Revolution and Governance*. Aldershot, UK: Ashgate, 2000.

Dalley, Elise. "Navigating Online Geoblocking." *Choice*, May 29, 2013. www.choice.com.au.

Dargis, Manohla. "The 21st Century Cinephile." *New York Times*, November 14, 2004.

Darren. "The Criterion Criteria: Why Are Criterion Blu Rays Region Coded?" *The movie blog*, November 3, 2011. http://themovieblog.com.

Deibert, Ronald, John Palfrey, Rafal Rohozinski, and Jonathan Zittrain, eds. *Access Contested: Security, Identity, and Resistance in Asian Cyberspace*. Cambridge, MA: MIT Press, 2012.

——. *Access Controlled: The Shaping of Power, Rights, and Rule in Cyberspace*. Cambridge, MA: MIT Press, 2010.

——. *Access Denied: The Practice and Policy of Global Internet Filtering* Cambridge, MA: MIT Press, 2008.

"Disney DVDs Carry Dual-Regional Coding." *Video Business*, November 29, 1999.

Dixon, Wheeler Winston. *Streaming: Movies, Media, and Instant Access*. Lexington: University Press of Kentucky, 2013.

Dotcom, Kim (@KimDotcom). "MPAA: Don't be a pirate / You: OK I'll pay! / MPAA: Not available in your country / You: How can I get it? / MPAA: You can't / You:

Idiots! *pirating." Twitter, January 4, 2015, 9:34 a.m. http://twitter.com/KimDotcom/status/551748513961242625.

"Doubts Grow for DVD Players and Discs This Fall." *Daily Record*, July 2, 1996.

Douglas, Susan J. *Listening In: Radio and the American Imagination*. Minneapolis: University of Minnesota Press, 1999.

Duckett, Chris. "The 'Australia Tax' Is Real: Geoblocking to Stop." *ZDNet*, July 29, 2013. www.zdnet.com.

Du Gay, Paul, Stuart Hall, Linda Janes, Hugh Mackay, and Keith Negus. *Doing Cultural Studies: The Story of the Sony Walkman*. Thousand Oaks, CA: Sage, 1997.

Dunt, Emily, Joshua S. Gans, and Stephen P. King. "The Economic Consequences of DVD Regional Restrictions." *Economic Papers* 21, no. 1 (2002): 32–45.

"DVD Borders Sought: Gray Market in New Discs Feared." *Video Business*, March 1, 1996.

DVD CCA. "About Us." www.dvdcca.org.

"DVD Regionalization Strategy in Tatters." *Inside Multimedia*, April 10, 2000.

"DVD Summit 2." *One to One*, May 1999.

Dwyer, Tessa, and Ioana Uricaru. "Slashings and Subtitles: Romanian Media Piracy, Censorship, and Translation." *Velvet Light Trap* 63 (2009): 45–57.

Dyer-Witheford, Nick, and Greig de Peuter. *Games of Empire: Global Capitalism and Video Games*. Minneapolis: University of Minnesota Press, 2009.

Dymek, Mikolaj. "Video Games: A Subcultural Industry." In *The Video Game Industry: Formation, Present State, and Future*, edited by Peter Zackariasson and Timothy L. Wilson, 34–56. New York: Routledge, 2012.

Ecke, Peter. "Coping with the DVD Dilemma: Region Codes and Copy Protection." *Teaching German* 38, no. 1 (2005): 89–93.

Edwards, Benj. "Performing a Permanent Famicom to NES Game Conversion." *Vintage Computing and Gaming*, December 5, 2005. www.vintagecomputing.com.

Edwards, Ralph. "The Economics of Game Publishing." *IGN*, May 5, 2006. www.ign.com.

Egenfeldt-Nielsen, Simon Nielsen, Jonas Heide Smith, and Susana Pajares Tosca. *Understanding Video Games: The Essential Introduction*. New York: Routledge, 2013.

Elkins, Evan. "The Changing Scales of Diasporic Media Retail." In *Point of Sale: Analyzing Media Retail*, edited by Derek Johnson and Daniel Herbert. New Brunswick, NJ: Rutgers University Press, forthcoming.

Ellcessor, Elizabeth. *Restricted Access: Media, Disability, and the Politics of Participation*. New York: New York University Press, 2016.

Elsaesser, Thomas. "Cinephilia; or, The Uses of Disenchantment." In *Cinephilia: Movies, Love, and Memory*, edited by Marijke de Valck and Malte Hagener, 27–44. Amsterdam: Amsterdam University Press, 2005.

Elusive. "Guide: Importing Gaming on Your Mega Drive / Genesis." *Sega 16 Forum*, April 3, 2010. www.sega-16.com.

Eng, Lawrence. "Strategies of Engagement: Discovering, Defining, and Describing Otaku Culture in the United States." In *Fandom Unbound: Otaku Culture in a Connected World*, edited by Mizuko Ito, Daisuke Okabe, and Izumi Tsuji, 85–104. New Haven, CT: Yale University Press, 2012.

Eschenfelder, Kristin R., Robert Glenn Howard, and Anuj C. Desai. "The Ethics of DeCSS Posting: Towards Assessing the Morality of the Internet Posting of DVD Copyright Circumvention Software." *Information Research* 11, no. 4 (2006): www.informationr.net.

"E.U. Wants iPlayer Access Extended across Europe." *BBC News*, May 6, 2015. www.bbc.com.

"Europe Probes Role of Region Codes in DVD Pricing." *Consumer Electronics*, June 18, 2001.

European Commission. "Commission Makes an Important Step toward a Digital Single Market." May 25, 2016. http://ec.europa.eu.

———. "A Digital Single Market for Europe." YouTube video, 1:32. May 7, 2015. http://www.youtube.com/watch?v=ORGNoRLo8oc.

———. "Geo-Blocking." March 6, 2016. http://ec.europa.eu.

European Parliament. "Written Questions by Members of the European Parliament and Their Answers Given by a European Union Institution OJ C 254E." September 4, 2013. http://eur-lex.europa.eu.

Fagenson, Zachary. "Spotify Eyes Latin America Where Growth on Pace with Parts of Europe." Reuters, May 5, 2015. www.reuters.com.

Fellenbaum, Alzbeta. "Slingshot Users in New Zealand Now Able to Bypass Geoblocking." *Screen Digest*, July 2, 2013. www.screendigest.com.

Fisher, Howard D. "Sexy, Dangerous—and Ignored: An In-Depth Review of the Representation of Women in Select Video Game Magazines." *Games and Culture* 10 (2015): 551–70.

Fiske, John. *Power Plays Power Works*. 2nd ed. New York: Routledge, 2016.

———. *Understanding Popular Culture*. Boston: Unwin Hyman, 1989.

Fiveash, Kelly. "Netflix Abroad Set for Showtime after EU Strikes a 'Portability' Deal." *Ars Technica UK*, February 8, 2017. http://arstechnica.co.uk.

Foley, Stephen. "*Doctor Who* Knows No Borders." *The Independent*, April 3, 2010.

Foucault, Michel. *Discipline and Punish: The Birth of the Prison*. Translated by Alan Sheridan. New York: Vintage, 1977.

Fox-Brewster, Thomas. "The Netflix VPN Can Be Bypassed: Here's How It Can Be Done Responsibly." *Forbes*, June 29, 2016. www.forbes.com.

Frank, Allegra. "Our Biggest Nintendo Switch Questions." *Polygon*, October 24, 2016. www.polygon.com.

Freeman, Carla. "Is Local: Global as Feminine: Masculine? Rethinking the Gender of Globalization." *Signs* 26 (2001): 1007–37.

Fritz, Ben. "Apple Expands Cure." *Daily Variety*, June 16, 2004.

Frost, Tim. "Middle East Sees 20% IT Growth." *One to One*, December 1, 1998.

"Full List of Territories Where Spotify Is Available." Spotify Support. http://support.spotify.com.

Galloway, Alexander R. *Gaming: Essays on Algorithmic Culture*. Minneapolis: University of Minnesota Press, 2010.

Galvin, Nick. "What Is . . . Geoblocking?" *Sydney Morning Herald*, May 29, 2011.

Garnham, Nicholas. *Capitalism and Communication: Global Culture and the Economics of Information*. London: Sage, 1990.

Garofalo, Reebee. "I Want My MP3: Who Owns Internet Music?" In *Popular Music: Critical Concepts in Media and Cultural Studies, Volume II*, edited by Simon Frith, 87–104. London: Routledge, 2004.

"'Geoblocking' Sites Is a Business Issue." *Toronto Star*, July 5, 2010.

George, Richard. "Nintendo's President Discusses Region Locking." *IGN*, July 3, 2013. www.ign.com.

"Get Your Music on Spotify." Spotify Artists. www.spotifyartists.com.

Gibson, Ellie. "No Region Locking for PS3?" *Eurogamer*, November 9, 2005. www.eurogamer.net.

Gillespie, Marie. *Television, Ethnicity, and Cultural Change*. London: Routledge, 1995.

Gillespie, Tarleton. "The Politics of Platforms." *New Media and Society* 12, no. 3 (2010): 347–64.

———. *Wired Shut: Copyright and the Shape of Digital Culture*. Cambridge, MA: MIT Press, 2010.

Glover, Richard. "Nudes Bring Dickie Knee Back from Depps of Despair." *Sydney Morning Herald*, June 30, 2012.

Goldstein, Paul. *Copyright's Highway: From Gutenberg to the Celestial Jukebox*. New York: Hill and Wang, 1994.

Goldstein, Seth. "International Quarrel with Codes Could Affect US Plans." *Video Store*, June 24, 2001.

Gomery, Douglas. "The Hollywood Studio System, 1930–49." In *Hollywood: Critical Concepts in Media and Cultural Studies, Vol. 1*, edited by Tom Schatz, 107–28. London: Routledge, 2004.

Good, Owen. "*Persona 4 Arena* Is Region-Locked Because the Dollar Is Weak against the Yen." *Kotaku*, July 7, 2012. http://kotaku.com.

Govil, Nitin. "Thinking Nationally: Domicile, Distinction, and Dysfunction in Global Media Exchange." In *Media Industries: History, Theory, and Method*, edited by Jennifer Holt and Alisa Perren, 132–43. Malden, MA: Wiley-Blackwell: 2009.

Gray, Ann. *Video Playtime: The Gendering of a Leisure Technology*. London: Routledge, 1992.

Gray, Jonathan. "Mobility through Piracy; or, How Steven Seagal Got to Malawi." *Popular Communication* 9 (2011): 99–113.

———. *Show Sold Separately: Promos, Spoilers, and Other Media Paratexts*. New York: New York University Press, 2010.

Gruenwedel, Erik. "Obama Gives Brown DVD Swag, British Tabloids Fume." *Home Media Magazine*, March 9, 2009. www.homemediamagazine.com.

Hage, Ghassan. *White Nation: Fantasies of White Supremacy in a Multicultural Society*. New York: Routledge, 2000.

Hall, Stuart. "Encoding/Decoding." In *Culture, Media, Language*, edited by Stuart Hall, Dorothy Hobson, Andrew Lowe, and Paul Willis, 128–38. London: Hutchinson, 1980.

———. "Which Public, Whose Service?" In *All Our Futures: The Changing Role and Purpose of the BBC*, edited by Wilf Stevenson, 23–38. London: British Film Institute, 1993.

Hamilton, Ian. "Spotify Smooths Exit from iTunes." *Orange County Register*, July 20, 2011.

"Hardware Notes." *Consumer Multimedia Report*, July 12, 1999.

Harvey, David. *Spaces of Capital: Towards a Critical Geography*. New York: Routledge, 2001.

Harvey, Eric. "Station to Station: The Past, Present, and Future of Streaming Music." *Pitchfork*, April 16, 2014. http://pitchfork.com.

Haufler, Virginia. *A Public Role for the Private Sector: Industry Self-Regulation in a Global Economy*. Washington, DC: Carnegie Endowment for International Peace, 2001.

Havens, Timothy. *Black Television Travels: African American Media around the Globe*. New York: New York University Press, 2013.

———. *Global Television Marketplace*. London: British Film Institute, 2006.

Hawkins, Joan. "Culture Wars: Some New Trends in Art Horror." *Jump Cut* 51 (2009): www.ejumpcut.org.

Healey, Nic. "New Zealand ISP's 'Global Mode' Gives Users Access to Netflix and More." *CNET*, July 7, 2014. www.cnet.com.

Herbert, Daniel. *Videoland: Movie Culture at the American Video Store*. Berkeley: University of California Press, 2014.

Herman, Edward S., and Robert W. McChesney. *The Global Media: The New Missionaries of Global Capitalism*. New York: Continuum, 1997.

Hern, Alex. "BBC iPlayer's US Rollout Blocked by Cable Networks." *New Statesman*, June 19, 2012. www.newstatesman.com.

Hesmondhalgh, David. *The Cultural Industries*. 3rd ed. London: Sage, 2012.

———. "Flexibility, Post-Fordism, and the Music Industries." *Media, Culture & Society* 18 (1996): 469–88.

Hilderbrand, Lucas. *Inherent Vice: Bootleg Histories of Video and Copyright*. Durham, NC: Duke University Press, 2009.

Hilmes, Michele. *Network Nations: A Transnational History of British and American Broadcasting*. New York: Routledge, 2012.

———. *Radio Voices: American Broadcasting, 1922–1952*. Minneapolis: University of Minnesota Press, 1997.

Himpele, Jeffrey D. "Film Distribution as Media: Mapping Difference in the Bolivian Cinemascape." *Visual Anthropology Review* 12, no. 1 (1996): 47–66.

Holt, Jennifer, and Patrick Vonderau. "'Where the Internet Lives': Data Centers as Cloud Infrastructure." In *Signal Traffic: Critical Studies of Media Infrastructures*, edited by Lisa Parks and Nicole Starosielski, 71–93. Urbana: University of Illinois Press, 2015.

Homer, Steve. "Digital Video Discs Are the Next Big Thing, but Don't Expect to Find One under the Tree This Christmas." *The Independent* (London), October 28, 1996.

Hong, Keylene. "As Spotify Passes One Year in Asia, Piracy Is Still Its Number One Challenge." *The Next Web*, July 21, 2014. http://thenextweb.com.

Hoskins, Colin, Stuart McFadyen, and Adam Finn. *Global Television and Film: An Introduction to the Economics of the Business*. Oxford, UK: Oxford University Press, 1997.

Hosokawa, Shuhei. "The Walkman Effect." *Popular Music* 4 (1984): 165–80.

Hovet, Ted. "YouTube and Archives in Educational Environments. *Spreadable Media*. http://spreadablemedia.org.

"How to Bypass Geo-Blocking in Australia." *The Real Man's Guide to Absolutely Everything*. www.realmansguide.com.au.

Hu, Brian. "Closed Borders and Open Secrets: Regional Lockout, the Film Industry, and Code-Free DVD Players." *Mediascape*, 2006. http://www.tft.ucla.edu.

Hunter, Dan. "Harper's Competition Review Is Good News for Netflix Consumers." *The Conversation*, September 26, 2014. http://theconversation.com.

International Federation of the Phonographic Industry. *Global Music Report 2018: Annual State of the Industry*. London: International Federation of the Phonograph Industry, 2018.

"Internet Offers Detailed 'How-To' for Region Code Crackers." *DVD Report*, July 27, 1998.

Iordanova, Dina. "Digital Disruption: Technological Innovation and Global Film Circulation." In *Digital Disruption: Cinema Moves On-Line*, edited by Dina Iordanova and Stuart Cunningham, 1–31. St. Andrews, UK: St. Andrews Film Studies, 2012.

Ip, Barry, and Gabriel Jacobs. "Territorial Lockout: An International Issue in the Videogame Industry." *European Business Review* 16, no. 5 (2004): 511–21.

"Issues Remain for Euro Market." *DVD Report*, June 5, 2000.

Ito, Mizuko. "Japanese Media Mixes and Amateur Cultural Exchange." In *Digital Generations: Children, Young People, and the New Media*, edited by David Buckingham and Rebekah Willett, 49–66. New York: Routledge, 2006.

Ito, Mizuko, Daisuke Okabe, and Izumi Tsuji, eds. *Fandom Unbound: Otaku Culture in a Connected World*. New Haven, CT: Yale University Press, 2012.

Iwabuchi, Koichi. *Recentering Globalization: Popular Culture and Japanese Transnationalism*. Durham, NC: Duke University Press, 2002.

Jackson, Jasper. "BBC iPlayer Users Will Have to Pay TV Licence Fee from 1 September." *The Guardian*, August 1, 2016.

Jenkins, David. "Modded Xbox 360s Blocked from Xbox Live." *Gamasutra*, May 18, 2007. www.gamasutra.com.

Jenkins, Henry. *Convergence Culture: Where Old and New Media Collide*. New York: New York University Press, 2006.

———. "Pop Cosmopolitanism: Mapping Cultural Flows in an Age of Media Convergence." In *Globalization: Culture and Education in the New Millennium*, edited by Marcelo M. Suárez-Orozco and Desirée Baolian Qin-Hilliard, 114–40. Berkeley: University of California Press, 2004.

———. "Why Fiske Still Matters." Preface to *Understanding Popular Culture*, 2nd ed., by John Fiske, xvi–xxxviii. New York: Routledge, 2010.

Jin, Dal Yong. *Korea's Online Gaming Empire*. Cambridge, MA: MIT Press, 2010.

"John Barker's Gaithersburg Address." *Inside Multimedia*, April 10, 2000.

Johnson, Richard. "What Is Cultural Studies Anyway?" *Social Text* 16 (1986): 38–80.

Johnson, Victoria E. *Heartland TV: Prime Time Television and the Struggle for U.S. Identity*. New York: New York University Press, 2008.

Jordan, Tim. *Hacking: Digital Media and Technological Determinism*. Cambridge, UK: Polity, 2008.

Kafai, Yasmin B., Carrie Heeter, Jill Denner, and Jennifer Y. Sun, eds. *Beyond Barbie and Mortal Kombat: New Perspectives on Gender and Gaming*. Cambridge, MA: MIT Press, 2008.

Kassabian, Anahid. *Ubiquitous Listening: Affect, Attention, and Distributed Subjectivity*. Berkeley: University of California Press, 2013.

Kayahara, Matthew. "The Digital Revolution: DVD Technology and the Possibilities for Audiovisual Translation Studies." *Journal of Specialised Translation* 3 (2005): www.jostrans.org.

Keathley, Christian. *Cinephilia and History; or, The Wind in the Trees*. Bloomington: Indiana University Press, 2006.

Kemp, Stuart. "BBC Director General Tony Hall Aims to Create a More 'Bespoke' Broadcaster." *Hollywood Reporter*, October 8, 2013. www.hollywoodreporter.com.

Kendrick, James. "Aspect Ratios and Joe Six-Packs: Home Theater Enthusiasts' Battle to Legitimize the DVD Experience." *Velvet Light Trap* 56 (2005): 58–70.

Kernfeld, Barry. *Pop Song Piracy: Disobedient Music Distribution since 1929*. Chicago: University of Chicago Press, 2011.

Kerr, Aphra. *The Business and Culture of Digital Games: Gamework/Gameplay*. London: Sage, 2006.

Kietzmann, Ludwig. "Wii Not Even Remotely Region-Free." *Joystiq*, September 15, 2006. www.joystiq.com.

Kilker, Julian Albert. "Shaping Convergence Media: 'Meta-Control' and the Domestication of DVD and Web Technologies." *Convergence* 9, no. 3 (2003): 20–39.

Kim, Youna. "Diasporic Nationalism and the Media: Asian Women on the Move." *International Journal of Cultural Studies* 14, no. 2 (2011): 133–51.

Kirkpatrick, Graeme. *Computer Games and the Social Imaginary*. Cambridge, UK: Polity, 2013.

Kline, Stephen, Nick Dyer-Witheford, and Greig de Peuter. *Digital Play: The Interaction of Technology, Culture, and Marketing*. Montreal: McGill-Queen's University Press, 2003.

Klinger, Barbara. *Beyond the Multiplex: Cinema, New Technologies, and the Home*. Berkeley: University of California Press, 2006.

———. "The DVD Cinephile: Viewing Heritages and Home Film Cultures." In *Film and Television after DVD*, edited by James Bennett and Tom Brown, 19–44. New York: Routledge, 2008.

Klosowski, Thorin. "How an American Can Stream the BBC's Olympics Coverage and Overcome #NBCFail." *Lifehacker*, July 31, 2012. http://lifehacker.com.

Kolar-Panov, Dona. "Video and the Macedonians in Australia." In *The Media of Diaspora*, edited by Karim H. Karim, 105–18. London: Routledge, 2003.

Kompare, Derek. "Cult Streaming: Warner Archive Instant." *Flow*, December 16, 2013. http://flowtv.org.

———. "Publishing Flow: DVD Box Sets and the Reconception of Television." *Television and New Media* 7, no. 4 (2006): 335–60.

Kraidy, Marwan. *Hybridity: The Cultural Logic of Globalization*. Philadelphia: Temple University Press, 2005.

Krupa, Daniel. "PlayStation 4 Is Region-Free." *IGN*, June 11, 2013. www.ign.com.

Krygier, John, and Denis Wood. "Ce N'est Pas Le Monde (This Is Not the World)." In *Rethinking Maps: New Frontiers in Cartographic Theory*, edited by Martin Dodge, Rob Kitchen, and Chris Perkins, 189–219. New York: Routledge, 2009.

Kusek, David, and Gerd Leonhard. *The Future of Music: Manifesto for the Digital Music Revolution*. Boston: Berklee Press, 2005.

Lacey, Kate. "Listening in the Digital Age." In *Radio's New Wave: Global Sound in the Digital Era*, edited by Jason Loviglio and Michele Hilmes, 9–23. New York: Routledge, 2013.

Larkin, Brian. *Signal and Noise: Media, Infrastructure, and Urban Culture in Nigeria*. Durham, NC: Duke University Press, 2008.

Lawler, Richard. "BBC Brings Global iPlayer iPad App to Canada, One Step Closer to the US." *Engadget*, December 1, 2011. www.engadget.com.

Leight, Elias. "Why Isn't Jamaican Dancehall Bigger in the U.S.?" *Rolling Stone*, August 3, 2018.

Lessig, Lawrence. *Code Version 2.0*. New York: Basic Books, 2006.

———. *Free Culture: How Big Media Uses Technology and the Law to Lock Down Culture and Control Creativity*. New York: Penguin, 2004.

Levy, Steven. *Hackers: Heroes of the Computer Revolution*. New York: Penguin, 1984.

Lewis, Glen, and Chalinee Hirano. "Mi Arai Mai Mai Mai? Thai-Australian Video Ways." In *Floating Lives: The Media and Asian Diasporas*, edited by Stuart Cunningham and John Sinclair, 185–216. Lanham, MD: Rowman and Littlefield, 2001.

Link_Is_My_Homie. "Region Locked: An Unwanted Relic from Gaming's Past." *IGN*, July 7, 2011. www.ign.com.

Livingstone, Sonia and Ranjana Das. "The End of Audiences?" In *A Companion to New Media Dynamics*, edited by John Hartley, Jean Burgess, and Axel Bruns, 104–21. Malden, MA: Blackwell, 2013.

Lobato, Ramon. *Netflix Nations: The Geography of Digital Distribution*. New York: New York University Press, 2019.

———. "The New Video Geography." In *Geoblocking and Global Video Culture*, edited by Ramon Lobato and James Meese, 10–22. Amsterdam: Institute of Network Cultures, 2016.

———. "The Politics of Digital Distribution: Exclusionary Structures in Online Cinema." *Studies in Australasian Cinema* 3, no. 2 (2009): 167–78.

———. *Shadow Economies of Cinema: Mapping Informal Film Distribution.* London: Palgrave Macmillan, 2012.

Lobato, Ramon, and James Meese. "Australia: Circumvention Goes Mainstream." In *Geoblocking and Global Video Culture*, edited by Ramon Lobato and James Meese, 120–29. Amsterdam: Institute of Network Cultures, 2016.

Lobato, Ramon, and James Meese, eds. *Geoblocking and Global Video Culture.* Amsterdam: Institute of Network Cultures, 2016.

Lobato, Ramon, and Julian Thomas. *The Informal Media Economy.* Cambridge, UK: Polity, 2015.

Lotz, Amanda D. *Portals: A Treatise on Internet-Distributed Television.* Ann Arbor, MI: Maize Books, 2017.

Luh, James C. "Breaking Down DVD Borders." *Washington Post*, June 1, 2001.

Magiera, Marcy, and Samantha Clark. "New Line Goes High-Def with Hairspray." *Video Business*, September 17, 2007.

Mak, Aaron. "What Spotify's Lack of Profits May Mean for Its IPO." *Slate*, April 3, 2018. www.slate.com.

Malcolm, Jeremy. "The Final Leaked TPP Text Is All That We Feared." *Electronic Frontier Foundation*, October 9, 2015. www.eff.org.

———. "How the Trans-Pacific Partnership Threatens Online Rights and Freedoms." *Digital News Asia*, March 15, 2013. www.digitalnewsasia.com.

Marsden, Rhodri. "One Giant Jukebox." *Independent Extra*, November 26, 2008.

Masnick, Mike. "With the U.S. Out, Canada Gets Copyright Out of TPP and Moves Closer to Agreement." *TechDirt*, November 13, 2017. www.techdirt.com.

Mattelart, Tristan. "Audio-Visual Piracy: Towards a Study of the Underground Networks of Cultural Globalization." *Global Media and Communication* 5, no. 3 (2009): 308–26.

McDonald, Kyle. *Serendipity.* 2015. http://kylemcdonald.net.

McDonald, Paul. *Video and DVD Industries.* London: British Film Institute, 2007.

McWilliams, Jeremiah. "Singing Coke's Praises Evolves." *Atlanta Journal-Constitution*, August 7, 2011.

"Microsoft Launches X-Box." *DVD Report*, March 20, 2000.

Miles, Stuart. "Click Here for Easy Wish Fulfillment." *The Times* (London), December 13, 1999.

Miller, Jeffrey S. *Something Completely Different: British Television and American Culture.* Minneapolis: University of Minnesota Press, 2000.

"Mod Chips Now Legal." *Australian PC User*, December 1, 2005.

Montfort, Nick, and Ian Bogost, *Racing the Beam: The Atari Video Computer System.* Cambridge, MA: MIT Press, 2009.

Mōri, Yoshitaka. "*Winter Sonata* and Cultural Practices of Active Fans in Japan: Considering Middle-Aged Women as Cultural Agents." In *East Asian Pop Culture:*

Analyzing the Korean Wave, edited by Beng Huat Chua and Koichi Iwabuchi, 127–42. Hong Kong: Hong Kong University Press, 2008.

Morley, David. *Home Territories: Media, Mobility, and Identity.* London: Routledge, 2000.

Morley, David, and Kevin Robins. *Spaces of Identity: Global Media, Electronic Landscapes, and Cultural Boundaries.* London: Routledge, 1995.

Morris, Jeremy Wade. *Selling Digital Music, Formatting Culture.* Berkeley: University of California Press, 2015.

Morris, Jeremy Wade, and Devon Powers. "Control, Curation and Musical Experience in Streaming Music Services." *Creative Industries Journal* 8, no. 2 (2015): 106–22.

Motherboard. "Peru's DVD Pirates Have Exquisite Taste." YouTube video, 6:01. March 26, 2014. http://www.youtube.com/watch?v=NNrGA6UqXS4.

Mueller, Milton L. *Networks and States: The Global Politics of Internet Governance.* Cambridge, MA: MIT Press, 2010.

"The Myths of Modding: Exploring the Dangers of Playing Online Games." *Xbox Nation,* July 1, 2004.

Naficy, Hamid. *The Making of Exile Cultures: Iranian Television in Los Angeles.* Minneapolis: University of Minnesota Press, 1993.

———. "Narrowcasting in Diaspora: Iranian Television in Los Angeles." In *Planet TV: A Global Television Reader,* edited by Lisa Parks and Shanti Kumar, 376–401. New York: New York University Press, 2003.

Nakamura, Lisa. "Don't Hate the Player, Hate the Game: The Racialization of Labor in *World of Warcraft.*" *Critical Studies in Media Communication.* 26, no. 2 (2009): 128–44.

Nederkorn, Colin. "I'm an American and I Want to Watch the Olympics. What Do I Do?" http://iamnotaprogrammer.com.

Negus, Keith. "The Corporate Strategies of the Major Record Labels and the International Imperative." In *Global Repertoires: Popular Music within and beyond the Transnational Music Industry,* edited by Andreas Gebesmair and Alfred Smudits, 21–31. Aldershot, UK: Ashgate, 2001.

"NES Cart Converters." *Famicom World.* http://famicomworld.com.

Netflix. "Netflix CES 2016 Keynote | Reed Hastings, Ted Sarandos—Full Length." YouTube video, 48:04. January 13, 2016. http://www.youtube.com/watch?v=n-FFfzhtZhg.

Newman, Michael Z. "Free TV: File Sharing and the Value of Television." *Television and New Media* 13, no. 6 (2012): 463–79.

Newman, Michael Z., and Elana Levine. *Legitimating Television: Media Convergence and Cultural Status.* New York: Routledge, 2012.

Ng, Joan. "Finding a New Future." *The Edge Singapore,* June 10, 2013.

Nix, Marc. "GDC 06: Region-Free PS3." *IGN,* March 22, 2006. www.ign.com.

Nye Jr., Joseph S. *Soft Power: The Means to Success in World Politics.* New York: Public Affairs, 2004.

O'Donnell, Casey. "The North American Game Industry." In *The Video Game Industry: Formation, Present State, and Future*, edited by Peter Zackariasson and Timothy L. Wilson, 99–115. New York: Routledge, 2012.

———. "Production Protection to Copy(right) Protection: From the 10NES to DVDs." *IEEE Annals in the History of Computing* 31, no. 3 (2009): 54–63.

———. "This Is Not a Software Industry." In *The Video Game Industry: Formation, Present State, and Future*, edited by Peter Zackariasson and Timothy L. Wilson, 17–33. New York: Routledge, 2012.

O'Donnell, Mike. "Sky Beware, Sunset May Be Coming." *Dominion Post* (Wellington), June 29, 2013.

O'Hagan, Minako, and Carmen Mangiron. *Game Localization: Translating for the Global Digital Entertainment Industry*. Amsterdam: John Benjamins Publishing Company, 2013.

Olivarez-Giles, Nathan. "Nintendo Defends Wii U Region Locking after Xbox One Reversal." *The Verge*, July 6, 2013. www.theverge.com.

O'Malley Greenburg, Zack. "Nielsen's Mid-Year Report Reveals Demise of the Digital Download." *Forbes*, July 7, 2014. www.forbes.com.

Ong, Aihwa. *Flexible Citizenship: The Cultural Logics of Transnationality*. Durham, NC: Duke University Press, 1999.

Parker, Dana J. "DVD at the Brussels Forum: Five Months Later and Major Issues Still Unresolved." *CD-ROM Professional* 9, no. 12 (December 1996): 11–12.

Pash, Adam. "How to Access the BBC iPlayer (and TV Like Doctor Who) from Outside the U.K." *Lifehacker*, March 29, 2010. http://lifehacker.com.

Payne, Matthew Thomas. "Connected Viewing, Connected Capital: Fostering Gameplay across Screens." In *Connected Viewing: Selling, Streaming, and Sharing Media in the Digital Era*, edited by Jennifer Holt and Kevin Sanson, 183–201. New York: Routledge, 2014.

Pearson, Dan. "21 Launch Countries Listed for Xbox One." *Game Industry International*, June 14, 2013. www.gamesindustry.biz.

Pelly, Liz. "Discover Weakly." *The Baffler*, June 4, 2018. http://thebaffler.com.

———. "The Problem with Muzak." *The Baffler* 37 (December 2017): http://thebaffler.com.

Peoples, Glenn. "Business Matters: April Fool's (Jay-Z, Beyoncé Buy EMI) and Not (Live Nation's WMG Bid Impacts Stocks)." *Billboard*, April 1, 2011.

Perren, Alisa. "Rethinking Distribution for the Future of Media Industry Studies." *Cinema Journal* 52, no. 3 (2013): 165–71.

Perusse, Bernard. "Why DVD Releases Don't Travel Well." *Montreal Gazette*, March 21, 2002.

Philips Research. "The History of the CD: The Beginning." Philips. www.research.philips.com.

"Philips, Sony Go Solo with DVD Patent Licenses." *Video Store*, August 11, 1996.

Phillips, Tom. "Nintendo Blames Region-Locking on Local Cultural Differences and Legal Restrictions." *Eurogamer*, July 4, 2013. www.eurogamer.net.

Pickles, John. *A History of Spaces: Cartographic Reason, Mapping, and the Geo-Coded World*. New York: Routledge, 2004.

Pizowell. "Unboxing OREI Region Free 3D Blu-ray Player." YouTube video, 6:33. September 10, 2013. http://www.youtube.com/watch?v=revziuw61sM.

Plunkett, Luke. "Meet the First Ever Region-Locked PS3 Game." *Kotaku*, July 6, 2012. http://kotaku.com.

Pogue, David. "Online Music, Unshackled." *New York Times*, July 27, 2011.

Pohlmann, Ken C. *The Compact Disc Handbook*. 2nd ed. Madison, WI: A-R Editions, 1992.

Postigo, Hector. *The Digital Rights Movement: The Role of Technology in Subverting Digital Copyright*. Cambridge, MA: MIT Press, 2012.

Pouliot, Vincent, and Frédéric Mérand. "Bourdieu's Concepts." In *Bourdieu in International Relations*, edited by Rebecca Adler-Nissen, 24–44. London: Routledge, 2013.

Powell, Nigel. "Remote Regions." *The Times* (London), December 4, 2005.

Prey, Robert. "Nothing Personal: Algorithmic Individuation on Music Streaming Platforms." *Media, Culture & Society* 40, no. 7 (2017): 1–15.

"Priority: Digital Single Market." European Commission, http://ec.europa.eu.

"Problems Found with *The Patriot* DVD." *Consumer Electronics*, November 6, 2000.

Puckett, Jason. "Digital Rights Management as Information Access Barrier." *Progressive Librarian* 34–35 (2010): 11–24.

Punathambekar, Aswin. "Bollywood in the Indian-American Diaspora: Mediating a Transitive Logic of Cultural Citizenship." *International Journal of Cultural Studies* 8, no. 2 (2005): 151–73.

Rand. "Cost of Spotify Premium for Different Countries in Relation to USD." *The Spotify Community*, August 25, 2012. http://community.spotify.com.

Rashy. "The Arab Gamer Episode 3—The Wrath of Region Codes." YouTube video, 11:47. April 14, 2012. http://www.youtube.com/watch?v=NHMlGnZqo8g.

"RCE Fails to Halt Play." *Video Business*, November 27, 2000.

"Readers' Comments: The Best Movies of 2003 List." *Film Comment*. www.filmcomment.com.

Reda, Julia. "'I Hate Geoblocking!' Says EU Commission VP Ansip." YouTube video, 0:52. March 25, 2015. http://www.youtube.com/watch?v=JCRG6BV0AYI.

"Region-Free DVD Deck Sales Crop Up in London." *Video Week*, April 6, 1998.

"Region-Free Xbox 360 Games." *Encyclopedia Gamia: The Gaming Wiki*. http://gaming.wikia.com.

"Regional Code Circumvention More Prevalent in Europe." *Audio Week*, July 20, 1998.

Resnikoff, Paul. "Europeans Have No Idea What a Pandora Is . . ." *Digital Music News*, December 17, 2013. www.digitalmusicnews.com.

Rivero, Enrique. "Lee's Tiger on the Loose." *Video Business*, March 19, 2001.

Rockstar Games. "Grand Theft Auto V: Supported Languages and Region-Lock Information." *Rockstar Games*, October 31, 2013. http://support.rockstargames.com.

Roettgers, Janko. "Spotify Puts the World's Music Tastes on a Map." *Variety*, July 13, 2015.

Rogers, Jim. *Death and Life of the Music Industry in the Digital Age*. London: Blooms-bury, 2013.

Rollux. Message board post. Geekzone, July 12, 2010. www.geekzone.co.nz.

Rosenbaum, Jonathan. "Global Discoveries on DVD (My 1st Column, 2003)." April 10, 2003. www.jonathanrosenbaum.net.

Rosenbaum, Jonathan, and Adrian Martin, eds. *Movie Mutations: The Changing Face of World Cinephilia*. London: British Film Institute, 2003.

Rowe, David. "Globalization, Regionalization, and Australianization in Music: Lessons from the Parallel Importing Debate." In *Culture in Australia: Policies, Publics, and Programs*, edited by Tony Bennett and David Carter, 46–65. Cambridge, UK: Cambridge University Press, 2001.

Roxborough, Scott. "Can Europe Set Up a Digital Single Market without Killing Copyrights?" *Hollywood Reporter*, May 8, 2015. www.hollywoodreporter.com.

———. "What's behind a Europe Plan That Would 'Destroy' Independent Film?" *Hollywood Reporter*, March 30, 2015. www.hollywoodreporter.com.

Rushton, Katherine. "Listing Values Loss-Making Site Pandora at £2.6bn." *Daily Telegraph*, June 16, 2011.

Saarinen, Juha. "DVDs: The Clear Picture." *New Zealand Herald*, February 20, 2004.

Said, Edward W. *Orientalism*. New York: Vintage, 1978.

Scannell, Paddy, and David Cardiff. *A Social History of British Broadcasting, Volume One, 1922–1939: Serving the Nation*. Malden, MA: Wiley-Blackwell, 1991.

Schaeffer-Grabiel, Felicity. "Planet-Love.com: Cyberbrides in the Americas and the Transnational Routes of U.S. Masculinity." *Signs* 31, no. 2 (2006): 331–56.

Schmidt, Eric. "Why Europe Needs a Digital Single Market." World Economic Forum, September 23, 2014. www.weforum.org.

Schreier, Jason. "Xbox One Needs to Connect to the Internet Every 24 Hours for Gaming." *Kotaku*, June 6, 2013. http://kotaku.com.

Science|Business. "EU Vice-President Ansip Launches the Digital Single Market Strategy." YouTube video, 2:39. May 7, 2015. http://www.youtube.com/watch?v=WlOtVgb4vhY.

Sebok, Bryan. "Convergent Hollywood, DVD, and the Transformation of the Home Entertainment Industries." PhD diss., University of Texas at Austin, 2007.

Shaw, Adrienne. "On Not Becoming Gamers: Moving beyond the Constructed Audience." *Ada: A Journal of Gender, New Media, and Technology* 2 (2013): http://adanewmedia.org.

Sheffield, Brandon. "The Brick Wall: No Close Encounters with Nintendo's Indie Exec." *Gamasutra*, April 15, 2014. www.gamasutra.com.

Sherman, Joshua. "Pandora Touts 200 Million Listeners, Continues to Curb Mobile Listening." *Digital Trends*, April 9, 2013. www.digitaltrends.com.

Silverstone, Roger. *Media and Morality: On the Rise of the Mediapolis*. London: Polity, 2006.

Smith, Steve. "Web Services Grow, but Classical Flaws Remain." *International Herald Tribune*, August 31, 2011.

"The Society for Cinema and Media Studies' Statement of Best Practices for Fair Use in Teaching for Film and Media Educators." *Cinema Journal* 47 (2008): 155–64.

Sorrel, Charlie. "BBC Launches Subscription-Based International iPlayer for iPad." *Wired*, July 28, 2011. www.wired.com.

Sporich, Brett. "'Multipath DVD Movies Contain Variable Plots." *Video Business*, August 10, 1998.

Spotify. "Musical Map: Cities of the World." OpenStreetMap. http://eliotvb.carto.com.

"Spotify Begins Rollout of Expansion to Canada." *Billboard*, August 15, 2014.

"Spotify Sets Sights on 'All the World's Music.'" *The Independent*, July 24, 2011.

SpotifyVideoChannel. "Spotify: Music for Everyone." YouTube video, 1:07. March 17, 2014. http://www.youtube.com/watch?v=nd457kHoIRQ.

Sprenger, Florian. "The Network Is Not the Territory: On Capturing Mobile Media." *New Media and Society*, July 2018. http://doi.org/10.1177/1461444818787351.

Stalter, Katherine. "Sony, WB Set DVD Date." *Variety*, January 13–19, 1997.

Stalter, Katherine, and Steve Homer. "DVD—Decision vs. Delay: Studios Tired of Waiting for Industry to Cut Regional Red Tape." *Variety*, September 30–October 6, 1996.

Starosielski, Nicole. "Things and Movies: DVD Store Culture in Fiji." *Media Fields* 5 (2011): www.mediafieldsjournal.org.

———. *The Undersea Network.* Durham, NC: Duke University Press, 2015.

Steemers, Jeanette. *Selling Television: British Television in the Global Marketplace.* London: British Film Institute, 2004.

Steimle, Joshua. "Spotify Plans to Own the Online Music Market in Asia." *Forbes*, March 18, 2014. www.forbes.com.

Sterne, Jonathan. *MP3: The Meaning of a Format.* Durham, NC: Duke University Press, 2012.

———. "The MP3 as Cultural Artifact." *New Media and Society* 8, no. 5 (2006): 825–42.

Stevens, Josh. "Stop Region Blocking: Make the 3DS and Wii U Region Free." Change.org, www.change.org.

Stewart, Mark. "The Myth of Televisual Ubiquity." *Television and New Media* 17, no. 8 (2016): 691–705.

Stone, Rob. "Notes from Region 2." *Journal of Contemporary European Studies* 15 (2007): 5–14.

Straubhaar, Joseph D. *World Television: From Global to Local.* Los Angeles: Sage, 2007.

Streeter, Thomas. *Selling the Air: A Critique of the Policy of Commercial Broadcasting in the United States.* Chicago: University of Chicago Press, 1996.

Stuart, Keith. "Xbox One DRM Restrictions Dropped After Gamer Outcry." *The Guardian*, June 19, 2013.

———. "Xbox One Region Lock and More Reactions and Details." *The Guardian*, May 28, 2013.

Sweeting, Paul. "Big Blue Kicks Codes." *Video Business*, December 8, 2003.

———. "Digital Boom Shatters Distrib Windows." *Variety*, August 9–15.

———. "Exemption Contempt." *Video Business*, November 3, 2003.

———. "French Fried." *Video Business*, March 13, 2006.

———. "Nations Search for a Hidden Code." *Video Business*, June 4, 2001.

———. "A Price to Be Paid." *Video Business*, July 2, 2001.

Taylor, Greg. *Artists in the Audience: Cults, Camp, and American Film Criticism*. Princeton, NJ: Princeton University Press, 1999.

Taylor, Jim. "DVD Frequently Asked Questions (and Answers)." *DVD Demystified: Home of the DVD FAQ*, June 27, 2013. www.dvddemystified.com/dvdfaq.html.

Taylor, Jim, Mark R. Johnson, and Charles G. Crawford. *DVD Demystified*. 3rd ed. New York: McGraw-Hill, 2006.

Thornton, Sarah. *Club Cultures: Music, Media, and Subcultural Capital*. Middletown, CT: Wesleyan University Press, 1996.

Thrift, Nigel. *Spatial Formations*. London: Sage, 1996.

Thussu, Daya Kishan. "Mapping Global Media Flow and Contra-Flow." In *Media on the Move: Global Flow and Contra-Flow*, edited by Daya Kishan Thussu, 10–29. London: Routledge, 2007.

Tomlinson, John. *Globalization and Culture*. Chicago: University of Chicago Press, 1999.

"Top Posts in Miiverse Community. Looks Like the Region Free Campaign Is Gaining Steam." Reddit, June 21, 2013. www.reddit.com.

Trimble, Marketa. "Geoblocking, Technical Standards, and the Law." In *Geoblocking and Global Video Culture*, edited by Ramon Lobato and James Meese, 54–63. Amsterdam: Institute of Network Cultures, 2016.

Tryon, Chuck. *On-Demand Culture: Digital Delivery and the Future of Movies*. New Brunswick, NJ: Rutgers University Press, 2013.

———. *Reinventing Cinema: Movies in the Age of Media Convergence*. New Brunswick, NJ: Rutgers University Press, 2009.

Tsing, Anna. *Friction: An Ethnography of Global Connection*. Princeton, NJ: Princeton University Press, 2004.

———. "The Global Situation." *Cultural Anthropology* 15, no. 3 (2000): 327–60.

Turner, Adam. "Content Unlimited." *Sydney Morning Herald*, July 14, 2013.

———. "Understanding Geo-Blocking: Watch Whatever You Want, When You Want." *PC & Tech Authority*, May 28, 2013. www.pcauthority.com.au.

Ulin, Jeff. *The Business of Media Distribution: Monetizing Film, TV, and Video Content*. Burlington, MA: Focal Press, 2000.

Uricchio, William. "We Europeans? Media, Representations, Identities." In *We Europeans: Media, Representations, Identities*, edited by William Uricchio, 11–22. Bristol, UK: Intellect, 2009.

"U.S. 'the Enemy' Says Dotcom Judge." *New Zealand Herald*, July 16, 2012.

"Use of Spanish DVD Tracks on US Releases Is Waning." *Audio Week*, February 8, 1999.

Vaidhyanathan, Siva. *Copyrights and Copywrongs: The Rise of Intellectual Property and How It Threatens Creativity*. New York: New York University Press, 2003.

Van Buskirk, Eliot. "Serendipity Visualizes Simultaneous Listening Worldwide." Spotify—News, August 21, 2014. http://news.spotify.com.

Venegas, Cristina. "Thinking Regionally: Singular in Diversity and Diverse in Unity." In *Media Industries: History, Theory, and Method*, edited by Jennifer Holt and Alisa Perren, 120–31. Malden, MA: Wiley-Blackwell, 2009.

Verhoeven, Deb. "Film, Video, DVD, and Online Delivery." In *The Media and Communications in Australia*, edited by Stuart Cunningham and Graeme Turner, 133–54. Crows Nest, NSW: Allen and Unwin, 2010.

"Veteran Laserdisc Distributor Forms International DVD Label." *Video Store*, October 12, 1997.

Vonderau, Patrick. "Beyond Piracy: Understanding Digital Markets." In *Connected Viewing: Selling, Streaming, and Sharing Media in the Digital Era*, edited by Jennifer Holt and Kevin Sanson, 99–123. New York: Routledge, 2013.

———. "The Spotify Effect: Digital Distribution and Financial Growth." *Television & New Media* 16, no. 1 (2017): 1–17.

Wagman, Ira, and Urquhart, Peter. "'This Content Is Not Available in Your Region': Geoblocking Culture in Canada." In *Dynamic Fair Dealing: Creating Canadian Culture Online*, edited by Rosemary J. Coombe, Darren Wershler, and Martin Zeilinger, 124–32. Toronto: University of Toronto Press, 2014.

Walker, Rob. "The Song Decoders." *New York Times*, October 14, 2009.

Walker, Tim. "Brown Is Frustrated by 'Psycho' in No. 10." *Daily Telegraph*, March 19, 2009.

Wang, Shujen. *Framing Piracy: Globalization and Film Distribution in Greater China*. Oxford, UK: Rowman and Littlefield, 2003.

Wang, Shujen, and Jonathan J. H. Zhu. "Mapping Film Piracy in China." *Theory, Culture, and Society* 20, no. 4 (2003): 97–125.

Warner, Gregory. "Is Netflix Chill? Kenyan Authorities Threaten to Ban the Streaming Site." *NPR*, January 21, 2016. www.npr.org.

Wasko, Janet. *How Hollywood Works*. London: Sage, 2003.

Wasser, Frederick. "Ancillary Markets—Video and DVD: Hollywood Retools." In *The Contemporary Hollywood Film Industry*, edited by Paul McDonald and Janet Wasko, 120–31. Malden, MA: Blackwell, 2008.

———. *Veni, Vidi, Video: The Hollywood Empire and the VCR*. Austin: University of Texas Press, 2001.

Weatherall, Kimberlee. "Locked In: Australia Gets a Bad Intellectual Property Deal." *Intellectual Property Research Institute of Australia* 4 (2004): 18–24.

"What Now? Future Issues for the Music Industry." *Irish Times*, May 11, 2009.

White, Mimi. "Gender Territories: House Hunting on American Real Estate TV." *Television and New Media* 14, no. 3 (2012): 228–43.

Whitehead, Thomas. "Talking Point: It's Time for Nintendo to Drop Region Locking." *Nintendo Life*, June 25, 2013. www.nintendolife.com.

Williams, Raymond. *Marxism and Literature*. Oxford, UK: Oxford University Press 1977.

Wilson, Rob. "A New Cosmopolitanism Is in the Air: Some Dialectical Twists and Turns." In *Cosmopolitics: Thinking and Feeling beyond the Nation*, edited by Pheng

Cheah and Bruce Robbins, 351–61. Minneapolis: University of Minnesota Press, 1998.

Wollen, Peter. "The Auteur Theory: Michael Curtiz and *Casablanca*." In *Authorship and Film*, edited by David A. Gerstner and Janet Staiger, 61–76. New York: Routledge, 2003.

Yoshida, Shuhei (@yosp). "And yes, PS4 is region free :D." Twitter, June 11, 2013, 12:37 a.m. http://twitter.com/yosp/status/344357778288152576.

Yu, Peter K. "Region Codes and the Territorial Mess." *Cardozo Arts & Entertainment Law Journal* 30 (2012): 187–264.

Zackariasson, Peter, and Timothy L. Wilson. "Introduction." In *The Video Game Industry: Formation, Present State, and Future*, edited by Peter Zackariasson and Timothy L. Wilson, 1–15. New York: Routledge, 2012.

Zittrain, Jonathan. *The Future of the Internet and How to Stop It*. New Haven, CT: Yale University Press, 2009.

Zuckerman, Ethan. *Digital Cosmopolitans: Why We Think the Internet Connects Us, Why It Doesn't, and How to Rewire It*. New York: Norton, 2013.

———. "Homophily, Serendipity, Xenophilia.". . . *My Heart's in Accra*, April 25, 2008. www.ethanzuckerman.com.

INDEX

Note: Page numbers in *italics* indicate photographs and illustrations.

ABOUT THE AUTHOR

Evan Elkins is Assistant Professor of Media and Visual Culture in the Department of Communication Studies at Colorado State University. He researches the globalization of digital entertainment.